THE INSTRUCTIONAL PROCESS

THE INSTRUCTIONAL PROCESS

BRYCE B. HUDGINS

Washington University

RAND McNALLY & COMPANY • Chicago

RAND McNALLY EDUCATION SERIES

B. Othanel Smith, *Advisory Editor*

This book is dedicated to
my Mother and Father

PREFACE

I have written this book for people who are preparing to teach, and for those who are engaged in the practice of teaching. In it I have tried to synthesize and integrate some of our current knowledge about teaching into a systematic form. For years it has seemed to me that significant improvement in instruction on a broad scale would occur only as we begin to organize and reflect on base-line data about classrooms and teaching. This book represents one small step in that direction, although it is clearly an imperfect one.

We stand today on the brink of discovery of new knowledge about teaching and about classroom learning that will, in my opinion, revolutionize teaching. That revolution will be partly, but only partly, technological in nature. To date, the technologists have not considered the role or the values of human teachers as they formulated and developed their machinery and the software to accompany it. That lack of consideration has led to a rejection of the technological movement in education.

In this book I have tried to demonstrate that through the systematic analysis of concepts and empirical knowledge, the teacher can gain an increased breadth of understanding about the nature of teaching and the variables that govern it. There is every reason for teachers to perceive technology as a means of extending their own professional domain and expertness.

The central view of teaching that I have presented is one of interaction between teachers and students. It is still true that the student's basic and meaningful contacts within educational institutions are those with other people in the institution, chiefly teachers. Recent innovations in teaching, such as programmed instruction, team teaching, and others, share a common function; they intensify the interaction of teachers with individual students. Most of what is truly professional in the teaching role occurs in the interactive encounter of teacher and student. Although our knowledge of the relationship between teaching and learning is fragmentary at best, I have tried in Chapters 4 through 8 to systematize much of what is known about the effect of various kinds of teacher behavior.

The author of a book can never acknowledge all the debts, intellectual and otherwise, that he incurs in the course of his work. I would like to acknowledge a few of the most obvious ones. Prof. B. O. Smith of the University of Illinois provided an example in his own work of the kinds of contributions needed in the study of teaching. I am also grateful for his editorial recommendations. I owe a singular debt to Prof. D. Bob Gowin of Cornell University and Prof. Roger E. Wilk of the University of Minnesota for their continuous intellectual stimulation during the year 1967–68, when all of us were postdoctoral research training fellows at Stanford University. To Dean W. Deane Wiley of Southern Illinois University at Edwardsville I am grateful for the resources provided during 1969–70 to complete the book. I wish also to recognize the contributions of Mrs. Mildred Becherer, Mrs. Patricia Carpenter, and Mrs. Jean Kessler for their expert preparation of the manuscript.

Finally, of course, my deepest debt is to my wife and children without whose encouragement I would never have finished this work.

Bryce B. Hudgins
St. Louis
August, 1970

CONTENTS

SECTION 1

BASIC CONCEPTS: TEACHING LEARNING PLANNING

CHAPTER 1
TEACHING

This book has been written for those who teach or who are preparing to teach, and for individuals who play consultative or supervisory roles in relation to teachers. The effort is to provide a general and, to some extent, a conceptual analysis of issues and practices in teaching. We have tried to illustrate our points with real, or at least realistic, examples from classroom events, but this is not a book exclusively for teachers of elementary or secondary students. It is no more directed to teachers who are principally interested in reading instruction than it is to those whose special competence is in the fine arts.

The intention and the hope of the book is to provide teachers and others who are concerned with instruction in schools with some general guidelines for thinking about instructional practices. For example, in the first two chapters, several major ideas are developed, namely, that "teaching" constitutes but a fraction of the activities engaged in by teachers, that the idea of teaching requires careful separation from those related activities, and that the concept of learning is of much greater magnitude than that of teaching, and not necessarily coordinate with it. Much confusion in education has arisen as a result of the assumption that is frequently made that teaching results in learning, that without learning there is no teaching, and without teaching there can be no learning.

Throughout the book, the concepts we present and the analyses we make of them do not dictate what the classroom practices of teachers ought to be. There are reasons for this. In the first place, the particulars of teaching situations can vary through such a wide range that it seems ill-advised to attempt to prescribe practices as though they could be universally and uncritically used. Further, part of the teacher's task is to exercise her skill and apply her specialized knowledge to construct the specifics of her teaching practice. That construction requires the modification of general principles about teaching in light of the context in which teaching is to occur. *Context,* in this sense, would include, at a minimum, the developmental characteristics of pupils and the materials that are available to the teacher for instructional purposes.

WHAT IS TEACHING?

We begin this section with the major question of the chapter: What is teaching? A teacher performs many activities in the course of a day. Can we say that all of them are teaching? Some of those activities occur in the absence of her pupils and represent what Jackson (1968) calls "preactive teaching," as contrasted with interactive teaching, the face-to-face classroom encounter of teacher and pupils. Will it be profitable for us to agree with Jackson that the label *teaching* ought to be applied to both sets of activities, or perhaps only to one? Another possibility is that some preparatory activities and some face-to-face interactions are better thought of as teaching, while others of each kind cannot be said to represent teaching.

An important criterion for deciding whether an activity of the teacher is or is not teaching is the purpose or intent of the teacher. We have not said that it is the sole criterion. In general, however, *when the teacher introduces or undertakes an activity with the intention that pupils will learn something as a consequence,* that activity represents an example of teaching. This condition seems to help clarify some activities as teaching and others as not teaching, but it leaves some important borderline cases. Let us consider some examples so that we can understand how the condition of teaching just stipulated begins to delimit the concept of teaching.

Teaching clearly occurs when

   —the teacher interacts directly with one or more pupils with the intention that the pupils learn from the encounter;
   —the teacher directs pupils to do certain things with the intention that pupils learn from those activities.

To be a bit more concrete, we would say that teaching occurs when, for example, the teacher explains and demonstrates to the pupils a scientific phenomenon, a procedure for solving an arithmetic problem, or a technique for memorizing poetry, and anticipates that pupils will learn the phenomenon, procedure, or technique from this activity.

Similarly, teaching occurs when the teacher prescribes tasks (reading, writing, computing, etc.) for pupils to engage in for the purpose of learning. It is obvious that the same phenomenon, procedure, or technique might be learned either directly from the teacher or from the book, film, instructional program, etc. that she prescribes. In either case, teaching occurs.

Teaching clearly does not occur when

—the teacher prescribes activity for pupils without the intention that they learn from the activity;

—the teacher engages in activities designed to manage a group of pupils, not as a means to enhance their learning.

We will now introduce two more terms that we need for discussing the complex of activities that occur in classrooms: *instruction* and *management*. Instruction is the broader term, subsuming teaching and management, which are coordinate with each other. As we proceed, we shall have a good deal to say about management in particular. At this point, suffice it to say that management functions are performed by teachers principally because they are confronted with pupils in rather sizable groups instead of in ones or twos. Secondly, management and teaching have seldom been clearly differentiated, a task that we intend to perform in the ensuing pages.

Again, in an effort to be as concrete and as clear as possible, we shall describe some illustrative classroom events. A fifth-grade teacher, for example, decides to have eighteen pupils practice arithmetic skills during the thirty minutes that she teaches reading to the remaining ten pupils in her class. That decision is based, not upon an intention that the eighteen learn arithmetic, but that they remain reasonably occupied and thus not disturb the concentration of the ten in the reading group. That is not an instance of teaching, although some or all of the eighteen children involved may learn some arithmetic as a consequence of the teacher's management directive.

At lunchtime, the teacher has her pupils clear away the work of the morning and form lines to leave the classroom. These activities are not teaching. They are not designed to foster learning, and they are clearly management activities. Let us emphasize the potential seriousness of confusing skill in management with skill in teaching. Although the two are intertwined in practice, they are conceptually different from each other. There is evidence, to be presented later, that student teachers and supervisors of teachers almost categorically tend to mistake management for teaching.

TEACHING AND LEARNING

We have suggested that misconceptions about the relationship between teaching and learning account for confusion among teachers about the nature of teaching. One such misconception derives from the belief that the occurrence of teaching can be inferred from the occurrence of learning. If there is no evidence of learning on the part of the pupil, so this argument asserts, it can be concluded that there has been no teaching. There are several consequences that flow from this contention, if it is accepted. One is that tests of teaching are empirical; therefore, teaching can only be judged in terms of its consequences. Another is to be found in the widely held belief that the quality of teaching in affluent schools is superior to that in slum schools because pupils in the former learn more than pupils in inner-city schools. Closely related to both of these is the assumption that learning is accounted for by teaching. It can be demonstrated that pupils completing elementary school in upper middle-class neighborhoods have learned more than, say, pupils in a working-class neighborhood school have learned at the same stage in their academic careers. However, learning in an educational context is affected by several variables, only one of which is teaching.

Philosophers of education have analyzed the relationship between teaching and learning. Their conclusions tend to conflict with the argument just presented. For example, Smith (1960) compared "teaching and learning" with "selling and buying." He argued that teaching and selling are coordinate concepts, but learning and buying are not; "pupiling" might be coordinate to buying if one wished to invent the idea. Thus, one cannot sell unless someone else is buying. Similarly, one cannot teach unless someone is "pupiling," that is, receiving instruction. But it is unnecessary to conclude that the pupil must learn in order to say that the teacher taught.

Scheffler (1960) builds a similar but broader case for the conceptual separation of teaching from learning. He distinguishes between the "intentional" and "success" usages of the concept of teaching. Thus, as we have already indicated, it would be meaningless to talk about teaching unless there is an intention for learning to occur. However, whether learning does in fact ensue depends upon many factors. As Scheffler puts it, "the universe must cooperate." In this connection

Scheffler introduces the notions of sets of rules that might govern the activities of teachers. There are two general sets, *exhaustive rules* and *inexhaustive rules*. Exhaustive rules are those that prescribe activities or steps to be taken and which, if taken in the sequence prescribed, guarantee success. Rules for guiding a child to spell a simple word or rules to write a computer program are of this sort.

Rules to guide teaching, however, must be of a different sort. Inexhaustive rules are characterized by the strategies people develop to win games. They do not guarantee success, although they may heighten its likelihood. It is in this sense that the universe must cooperate for the "success" meaning of teaching to be achieved. Again, we can put the issue in more concrete form. Smith (1960) illustrates with the case of a teacher on TV who is talking to an unseen audience. Who would be willing to say that he is not teaching? Even if, unknown to the teacher, a technical failure prohibited his voice and image from being received by his students, would we not still agree that his activity is teaching?

TYPES OF TEACHING

We are also indebted to Scheffler (1960) for the distinctions he has identified among "teaching that," "teaching to," and "teaching how to." These distinctions should be of use to teachers didactically as they undertake teaching for different purposes. To "teach someone that . . ." is either to teach a fact ("Sacramento is the capital of California") or a norm-statement ("children ought always to tell their teachers the truth"). Teaching consists of presenting one or another statement to the pupil in ways designed to make it likely that he will learn the statement. When the intention is to "teach that . . . ," the probable tactics are to organize the task so that it will be memorized, comprehended, or understood, depending on the teaching result being sought. When our purpose is to teach facts, such tactics are appropriate. If, however, the intention of teaching a norm-statement (e.g., "children should always tell the truth") is to influence the truth-telling behavior of children, "teaching that . . ." tactics are questionable. One would need to amass evidence to show that norm-statements learned in the manner of factual statements do have the intended impact upon behavior.

To "teach someone to . . . ," on the other hand, carries the intention implied above with respect to norm statements. Thus, to teach children always to tell the truth is a very different matter from teaching them to understand what it means to tell the truth or even to value truth-telling.

Finally, to "teach someone how to . . ." contains implications for teaching technical or skill elements. An individual could know that he ought to behave in given ways on social occasions and could desire to behave accordingly, but that does not imply that he "knows how to. . . ."

We said that these distinctions of Scheffler should have didactic value for the teacher as he plans his strategy and tactics for engaging in teaching of various kinds. Smith refers to didactics as the "art or science of teaching" to differentiate it from the "concept of teaching." One becomes concerned with didactics as one begins to think of the teaching of a given body of knowledge, attitudes, or skills to children of a given age, level of intelligence, and motivation, for example. Presumably also a teacher's preactive and interactive teaching will be different when his intention is to "teach that . . ." than when it is to "teach how. . . ." Similarly, one's choice of teaching procedures should be influenced by the characteristics of the pupils for whom the teaching is planned.

DIDACTICS

The art of teaching is practiced either as the teacher prepares for or assesses teaching encounters, or as he actually engages in such encounters. In our discussion of didactics, we focus upon the interactive phase of teaching. It is in the confrontation between teacher, pupil, and subject matter that the teacher's artistry comes into play. No matter how clearly the teacher understands the purposes and functions of teaching or the logic and the content of the subject matter he intends to teach, his success *as a teacher* lies in the quality of the performance that he is able to achieve during the teaching encounter. Such descriptives as "good" and "poor" were irrelevant to our previous discussion of the conceptual nature of teaching. There it was sufficient to distinguish teaching from learning, and one kind of teaching from another. But obviously teaching, like any other practical art, may be performed dexterously or awkwardly, professionally or amateurishly, competently or ineffectively, intelligently or stupidly, and it is not a matter of indifference which member of each pair better describes the quality of a given teaching performance.

Smith (1956) contends that the order of events that occurs in teaching encounters is beyond the control of the teacher and is, rather, characteristic of the enterprise of teaching. Thus, the teacher at the beginning of the lesson takes steps to induce the pupils to attend to him. He then presents what is to be learned. The teacher may do this in many ways, such as giving directions, explanations, or involving the pupils in planning with him. Smith also differentiates between the process of teaching as described here and phenomena that are not teaching but are so close as often to be mistaken for it. Among these he includes *skill,* that is, how well the teacher performs the arts of teaching, and *style,*

> . . . the characteristic demeanor in which the teaching acts are performed. . . . [A] teacher may be habitually dramatic, or he may show little or no feeling at all as he teaches. Unlike skill, teaching style is personal and somewhat unique for each individual. The failure to distinguish between style of teaching and teaching itself is one of the primary sources of the mistaken notion that teachers are born and not made (Smith, 1956, p. 340).

Smith (1960) also gives us a paradigm for the process of teaching. It shows the essentially interactive nature of teaching. There are two subunits, the *act of teaching* and the *act of taking instruction* which, in combination with each other, describe the *teaching cycle.* Thus, in the teaching encounter, the teacher perceives something about the state of the pupil (Pt), he diagnoses the pupil's feeling or degree of interest, comprehension, etc. (Dt), and he makes a response to it (Rt). That is the act of teaching. The act of taking instruction is reciprocal to it. The pupil perceives the teacher's behavior (Pp), diagnoses it (Dp) and, in his turn, reacts (Rp). When these acts occur repeatedly under appropriate conditions, achievement results. Schematically, the acts and teaching cycle as developed by Smith (1960, p. 235) are shown below.

$$||Pt \longrightarrow Dt \longrightarrow Rt| \longrightarrow Pp \longrightarrow Dp \longrightarrow Rp|| \longrightarrow Pt \longrightarrow Dt \longrightarrow$$
$$Rt| \longrightarrow Pp \longrightarrow Dp \longrightarrow Rp|| \longrightarrow Pt \longrightarrow Dt \longrightarrow Rt| \longrightarrow Pp$$
$$\longrightarrow Dp \longrightarrow Rp||. \ldots \longrightarrow achievement.$$

The single vertical lines separate acts of teaching from acts of taking instruction. The double vertical lines demarcate teaching cycles. Theoretically such cycles lead to achievement.

Again, we note that Smith's paradigm says nothing about how well these cycles are performed, although the skill with which the teacher acts his role will clearly influence the achievement variable. For example, the teacher first perceives something about the state of the pupils in his classroom. These states are to be diagnosed, and the teacher's action or response to pupils is based upon the diagnosis. We may suppose that one difference between a skillful teacher and an unskillful one lies in what each perceives about the pupils. Kounin, Friesen, and Norton (1966), for example, have found that elementary teachers who are highly skilled at controlling their classes (in the management sense) "see" what is going on that requires correcting, and they correct it immediately. Similarly, the teacher's skill resides in part in how well he can interpret or diagnose the behavior of pupils. One may see all the postural and gestural behavior of pupils, and take note of what the pupils say, but be at a loss to understand that these pupil reactions signal failing interest, confusion, and imminent disaster for the teaching encounter. Smith aptly describes the situation:

> Like one who must find out the contents of a sealed box by inference from its external features, the teacher can know the inner facts about his students only by influence from visible signs. From a student's facial expression, he infers that the student does or does not want to do something. The tone of the student's voice and the expression in his eyes tell the teacher whether or not the student is angry, happy, or apprehensive. And the light in his mind shows up in the light on his face.
>
> The fact that the deeper reactions and feelings of the student are hidden and that they are present to the teacher only by implication has been little noticed. Yet it may well be that the success of the teacher depends in large measure upon his accurate perception and understanding of such natural signs as posture, tone of voice, and facial expression. From practical experience it would seem that there is wide variation among teachers with respect to sensitivity to these cues. Some teachers of outstanding intellectual ability appear to be insensitive to what is going on around them, oblivious to the inner life of the student if not to the classroom itself until something happens to jolt them to their senses. Then it is often too late to redeem their status as teachers. Others seem to see all sorts of cues, but knowing not what they mean, become rattled by them and thus lose control of the teaching process. Still other teachers appear to be keenly aware of every change in these natural signs and to understand their significance. They, therefore, direct their moment-to-moment behavior as teachers in terms of information coming to them by implication from the multiplicity of natural signs around them (Smith, 1956, p. 341).

Our discussion has centered around the *expressive* behavior of pupils, but behavior may also be either *linguistic* or *performative* (Smith, 1960). To be sure, all three dimensions may go on simultaneously, and we would ordinarily expect them to be highly correlated. Obviously the linguistic dimension of pupil and teacher behavior plays a prominent role in the classroom.[1] The paradigm presented previously is equally useful for talking about the teaching cycle with any or all of the three dimensions of behavior cited by Smith. That is, the act of teaching calls upon the teacher to perceive (hear or read) the voiced or written reactions of pupils (their questions, answers to the teacher's questions, etc.), to diagnose the state of comprehension or confusion implicit in the content of the pupil's response, and to respond himself in an effort to increase the pupil's existing skill, reduce his confusion, suggest alternative modes of responding, etc.

This may be an appropriate juncture at which to foreshadow briefly one of the problems with which we deal in a subsequent chapter. The analysis we are making of teaching (a la Smith) seems to suggest quite strongly that teaching in operation is a vigorous interactive process, one in which the pupil is a partner with the teacher. We have seen that the teacher requires great skill in perceiving and diagnosing states of pupils, which in turn must necessitate a continuous and high rate of feedback from pupils to the teacher. If the language of pupils is as significant as we have argued in its ability to reflect their level of knowledge and understanding, we might well anticipate that teachers would devote a large share of their teaching behavior to checking upon the conceptual adequacy of pupils' understanding. That this is not the case comes as something of a surprise in light of the foregoing analysis. Actually studies of ongoing classes made by different investigators at quite different periods of time (between about 1909 and 1966) tend to show with considerable regularity that the teacher talks about twice as much as all his pupils combined.

IMPORTANCE OF REACTION FLEXIBILITY

However adequately the teacher may perform her diagnostic chores, little is achieved unless her reaction is appropriate. Appropriateness in this sense, when fully elaborated, has an extensive battery

---

[1] Indeed, many investigators assume that language is so dominant in classrooms and also so highly correlated with other behavior dimensions that they are content to measure only the language aspects, assuming that little or no significant information about teaching is lost as a consequence.

of characteristics. Among these are the timing of the reaction so that the critical question or item of information occurs when it will be of maximum use to the pupil, and the level of complexity of the reaction. A brief cue may be all that is needed for one pupil who is on the verge of solving a problem or understanding an argument; for another child, an extended but altered reexamination of the original issue may be necessary before he experiences any detectable enlightenment. Together these characteristics suggest that skillful teachers are capable of flexibility in their reactions to pupils. In general, the teacher who is flexible in reacting will be sensitive to the elements of a lesson that are likely to present more than an average number of difficulties to pupils, and will be prepared to help surmount those difficulties by having available alternative ways to respond. For example, he may have a number of illustrations of the point to offer for purposes of clarification, or several different ways of presenting the concept in question so that the pupil who does not grasp the idea at once has a second or a third chance, if needed, to learn it under somewhat altered circumstances.

There are two rather important points about flexibility of reaction that we wish to make. The first is to call attention to an analogous use of the term by psychologists involved in studies of creativity. One factor in creativity has been identified as "spontaneous flexibility" (Guilford, 1959). An individual with good spontaneous flexibility can produce multiple synonyms in response to a stimulus word such as *chair* or *tree*. Or he may be able to cite a much larger than average number of different uses for a common object such as a brick or a paper clip. It is in precisely this sense, but modified to deal with the responses of a teacher to a pupil, that we speak of flexibility in reacting. (This is not to suggest that the two kinds of flexibility are necessarily related.) If the factors share some psychological commonality, it seems likely that some teachers will perform with skill "naturally," as it were, while others will have to pay careful and systematic attention to building flexibility into their response repertoires.

The second point is an extension of the first—to emphasize the part that experience and analyses and systematic planning can play in helping the teacher to build skill in this aspect of his performance. What one lacks by way of natural ability or aptitude can sometimes, in part at least, be compensated for by the way one goes about his daily activities. One of the roles that experience ought to play in the life of a teacher is to provide opportunities to recognize and to correct his own mistakes the next time around. The conscientious teacher constantly questions himself: Did the science experiment go awry today? Why? Were my directions inadequate? How could they be amended? Three pupils never understood that they have to invert the divisor and multiply in order to divide one fraction by another. How can I make this process more meaningful to them?

Clearly all teachers run into rough spots occasionally in their teaching. It is the skillful teacher who first minimizes the frequency of those encounters by anticipating and planning for them and, when they do occur, handles them by behaving flexibly, suiting explanation, illustration, or other reaction to the problem as the pupil or the class perceives it.

CONTINGENCIES IN INTERACTIVE TEACHING

Jackson (1968) describes the course of events in teaching as being more like the flight of a butterfly than the trajectory of a bullet. It is an interesting metaphor. Perhaps one ought not to dissect a metaphor too completely in seeking parallels to practical human affairs, but this one contains some helpful guides to thought about teaching. Unlike a bullet that speeds predictably to its target, the butterfly's course is choppy; it contains diversions, wide swinging changes in direction; and it may vary somewhat in how rapidly it proceeds, but speed is never its major characteristic.

So it is with teaching. The teacher, when he engages in interaction with pupils, may have a general conception of the goal of his teaching. That conception, however, will be much clearer for some purposes than it is for others. But in any event, we are conceiving of teaching as an interactive process, an engagement or an encounter between the teacher and his pupils. If the teacher further defines success at his task as the arrival of himself and his pupils at approximately the same understanding of an idea and not just as his own fastest and most direct foray through the content of the lesson, the metaphor of the butterfly instead of the bullet is apt.

Children come to each day's lessons with some background of knowledge and level of comprehension of their own. Furthermore, this is different for every child in the class. A fourth grader's understanding, for example, of why rain falls may be primitive, full of inconsistencies and contradictions, partly scientific and partly superstitious and, in general, may represent a phenomenon about which he has thought very little and for which he is simply incapable of giving a coherent account. A sound, carefully planned scientific explanation presented by the teacher will surely be of immense help to many of the pupils in clarifying and furthering their understanding of the phenomenon. Admittedly we have stipulated soundness and care in planning without examining meanings, but we intend only to say that the presentation should be factually and conceptually accurate and reasonably complete, that its sequence be logically organized, and that its delivery be aurally and visually comprehensible.

Still, this cannot be the entire story of teaching. Children have questions about various elements of the explanation. A term is unfamiliar to some children, known in a different context by other children, suggestive of an entirely different subject to yet another child, and so on. By contingencies in teaching we mean the questions that children ask, the repetitions required, the diversions and digressions that external events impose as the teacher negotiates his way through the interactive encounter.

Student teachers do not appear to be very skillful initially in handling such encounters. Iannaccone (1963), who studied a group of elementary school student teachers, reports that one of the first major learnings they have to grapple with is tailoring the lesson to fit the available time. We would suggest that beginning student teachers are guided more by their concern for the details of subject matter than by the complexities of interaction contingencies. Part of learning to be skillful in teaching is learning to handle such contingencies appropriately. This in turn is related to our broader concept of flexibility. Further indirect support for our contention is found in a report by Ryan (1966) which grew out of his clinical experiences with intern teachers in secondary schools. The beginning intern teacher, who is himself devoted to the discipline represented by his major subject, tends to overestimate the extent of his students' interest in what he is teaching them. If we follow the gist of Ryan's account, it is not until the intern learns to assess and to respond more realistically to the interests and motives of his students that this difficult problem of his initial teaching is resolved.

TEACHING DIFFERENTIATED FROM MANAGEMENT

Teachers perform many activities in the course of a day that cannot properly be construed as teaching, as we have used that word. For example, the teacher has to control the behavior of boys and girls within some fairly broad and reasonably clear limits. Safety factors are the main reasons for such control but, in addition, there are considerations relevant to the control of unruly behavior fostered by the crowded nature of most classrooms, to the process of child socialization—learning respect for the rights and preferences of others, and for the authority of the teacher—and to the maintenance of a classroom environment that is conducive to learning. This latter condition is not static. There are times when a good deal of movement and noise are going to be a natural by-product of the legitimate educational activity in which children are engaged, and there will be other occasions when something akin to absolute silence will be more appropriate.

What is an acceptable level of noise and physical movement is not entirely within the province of the teacher to judge. One's colleagues and principal usually have opinions about issues such as these. It is probably safe to assume, although our ability to document the tenability of the assumption is limited, that norms pertaining to acceptable control of pupils in the classroom and elsewhere on school grounds exist in most schools. Gordon (1957), for example, describes and illustrates the point for a suburban senior high school.

> The duty of the teacher was to maintain order both as a condition for learning and because it symbolized his competence. *Teaching competence was difficult to assess, but disorder was taken as a visible sign of incompetence by colleagues, principal, parents, and students* [italics added] (Gordon, 1957, p. 42).

In this particular high school, records showed that over a period of three consecutive school years, referrals of pupils by teachers to the principal decreased from 160 the first year to 81 the second, and 50 the third year. The explanation given for this reduction was that the principal kept a "little black book" in which he recorded pupil referrals. At contract time, as rumor had it, a teacher's salary raise was influenced by the number of referrals made during the year. Furthermore, the principal's action tended to force teachers to exercise *personalized* leadership rather than *institutionalized* leadership to the extent that he placed the burden of student control directly upon the teachers instead of allowing the mechanisms of the administration to play their normal role in helping to control students. "Here," says Gordon, "differentials in status among teachers affected their ability to exercise power and their sense of adequacy since ability to *control* was equated with the ability to *teach*" (Gordon, 1957, p. 45).

Control is an element of management, but it is not the only one. Elementary teachers in particular require skill in handling children, materials, time, and space. We alluded earlier to an example in which a fifth-grade teacher assigned arithmetic tasks to one section of her class while she taught reading to another, and we said that in this instance the teacher was engaged in managing rather than teaching. In this sense, the teacher as manager is a manipulator of elements in the classroom. Any teacher has a given amount of time and space with which to work, a given number of pupils to teach, and a given range and amount of instructional materials upon which to draw. The ability to manage all these elements in harmonious relation to one another is an important instructional skill, but it ought not to be confused with teaching. We can see that teaching may often proceed more competently when the management functions of instruction are well attended to and may be impossible to accomplish under some conditions of poor management, but we must insist upon the importance of distinguishing one from the other. It may be useful to think of management skill as a necessary condition to be met for productive teaching to occur, but it is not a guarantee of such behavior.

INSTRUCTION: TEACHING AND MANAGEMENT

Instruction, according to our analysis, subsumes the concepts of teaching and of management. Thus, when we speak of instruction as taking place, we would be uncertain whether the reference is to teaching or to management. In practice, of course, the two are frequently inextricably intertwined. A skillful teacher may control the behavior of a child with a well-timed, well-chosen question as completely as if she took direct management action to exercise such control. Similarly, skill in management is necessary to organize subgroups which in turn may be a prerequisite condition for certain kinds of teaching to occur.

Earlier we promised to elaborate upon the assertion that teachers and supervisors frequently value *management* activity in the mistaken belief that they are referring to *teaching*. This mistake certainly occurred in the high school studied by Gordon. We shall now examine some of the conditions that obtain in this confusion and ask ourselves why management skills tend to be so highly valued. Finally, we shall try to determine whether any important consequences ensue from this failure to distinguish between instruction as teaching and instruction as management.

Medley and Mitzel (1959) studied a group of elementary teachers in their first year of teaching. Three kinds of data were collected: objective, observational, and test data bearing upon (1) the pupils' growth in reading skill and group problem-solving ability, and the emotional climate of the classroom; (2) teachers' self-reports of their effectiveness as teachers of fundamentals (such as reading); and (3) supervisors' (either the principal, the assistant principal, or both, depending upon who was responsible for rating a teacher) ratings of the teachers' competence in teaching fundamentals, in teaching good citizenship and self-understanding, and in her role as a colleague to other teachers and to administrators. Of all the measures taken, the teachers' self-estimates of their skill in teaching fundamentals showed the highest relationship to pupils' growth in reading through the school year. However, this relationship was not high ($r = .39$), and growth in reading was in turn found to depend upon grade level. One ought not, therefore, to conclude that teachers are necessarily good judges of their own effectiveness. Supervisory ratings, on the other hand, were no better; these related best to a dimension of pupil-teacher rapport ($r = .39$), not to growth in pupils' reading scores. As the researchers comment, "Apparently a supervisor thinks that the teacher whose class is friendly and orderly is an effective teacher" (Medley and Mitzel, 1959, p. 244).

This study provides us with an empirical observation about supervisors' ratings and an interpretation of the finding, but unfortunately it does not help us deepen our understanding of the cause of the relationship. We may speculate that the causal nexus proceeds as follows:

1. Supervisors observe in classrooms infrequently. There are multiple reasons, ranging from intense demands upon the principal to spend his time otherwise, to his own uncertainty about what to observe, to the discomfort or even hostility that supervisory, evaluative observations tend to elicit from teachers.
2. Partly because of the infrequency of observation and partly because of the difficulty of judging teaching when observations are not continuous, supervisors find it more convenient to seize upon concrete, tangible elements of classroom activity. Qualities such as orderliness, control, noise, and movement are much easier to judge than are demonstrations, explanations, etc.
3. The principal has a responsibility for representing and interpreting the school to the community which the teacher does not have. He seems to be more sensitive to signs of activity that are likely to create concern in the community. Given the supervisor's different frame of reference for viewing classrooms, it is not surprising that he make judgments about a teacher's effectiveness in terms of her managerial skills.

Teachers—student teachers, at least—also place great emphasis upon the development of management skills. There is, of course, an immediacy about management issues that demands they be dealt with, and it is easy to understand that the beginning teacher's sense of security is threatened until a reasonable level of management skill is developed. The student teachers followed by Iannaccone (1963) spent one semester as college seniors doing practice teaching on a half-time basis. Typically the student teachers begin this clinical phase of their training as observers and, after a week or two, the favorite question to ask a classmate when the student teachers congregate on campus is, "Have you taught yet?"

> Their use of the verb *teach* gives an interesting indication of their attitude. Over coffee they frequently asked one another, "Have you taught yet?" The answer to this question was the measure of their progress. But their definition of teaching is clear in their answer, "No, I'm only working with one pupil," or "I'm working with the middle reading group." There is progress when they can say, "Yes, I had the whole class all morning." For the student teacher, remedial work with individual pupils is not teaching. Teaching means taking the class through the lesson (Iannaccone, 1963, p. 79).

The student teachers mean by teaching what we mean by instruction—the combination of teaching and managing. It is less surprising that student teachers attach that referent to the word *teaching* than it is that they reject the individual tutoring of a child as teaching. For it is in such tutorial relationships that we might expect the closest approximation to pure teaching to occur, freed from virtually all considerations of management. The formal course work of the university, to the extent that it is presumed by the student teacher to have relevance, has dealt heavily with concepts of learning, child development, and the individual. Although that training would seem pertinent for tutorial situations, student teachers identify the more complex total-group management as the problem they must learn how to solve.

The student's learning experience has features that are instructive to us here. As we noted earlier, time is a most significant factor in the life of the teacher. For student teachers its importance, if anything, is heightened. They must learn how to adapt the instructional demands of the day to the available time. What we see in Iannaccone's account is student teachers developing a series of skills which, although superficially dissimilar, have the common function of reducing the complexity of the teacher's task. In part, however, these skills are learned because perspectives have first been altered. The perspectives and skills concern *pupils* and *lessons* and the interactions between them.

For example, one student teacher named Alice laments early in the semester that her critic teacher wastes the time of first graders by making them clean up paint jars, and she is stunned by the teacher's custom of "shaking Jack" to make him behave. It is not long before Alice has learned to do both these things and to redefine them as being in the children's interests.

> Ellen (another student teacher) tells how "David finally did too much." She continues, "and I marched him out into the hall just as Mrs. Eton and Mr. Elkin [the principal] were coming up the hall. When I saw them I wished that I could have left David in the room, but it was now too late, so I went back and resumed class. This time they were quiet as mice. When Mrs. Eton came back, she said Mr. Elkin was happy to see that I was taking over with discipline, because this is where most of the student teachers are failing."
>
> The criterion that identifies children who are behavior problems is divorced from child psychology. It is the classroom organizational realm and the need to keep the show on the road that defines a problem child for Ellen (Iannaccone, 1963, p. 79).

Instructional time, a precious commodity, slips away as the student teacher asks questions not covered by the questions in the book and the pupils are unable to answer. She finds that having the children look up the answers in the book as she reads aloud the questions produces much more satisfying results.

Iannaccone has summarized what the student teachers learned into a set of three principles. These principles are supported on the pragmatic grounds that "they work." They seem adequate to describe much of what student teachers learn from initial clinical practice; however, we wish to make it clear that, despite their immediate tension-reducing properties for the student teacher, the long-term consequences of these principles for both teachers and pupils may be quite different, and possibly deleterious.

1. Eliminate disruptive behavior by increasing doses of institutional pressures and sanctions to make the child conform to the organizational pattern in the room.
2. Redefine the learning goals by operationalization of these in

terms of a few precise and predetermined types of pupil behavior to be fed back to the teacher, and classify as "irrelevant" all pupil discussion which does not move the class
toward such goals.

3. Reclassify as slow and not belonging in the room those pupils
who are not primarily discipline cases, but who do not feed
back as expected (Iannaccone, 1963, p. 80).

SKILL IN CLASSROOM MANAGEMENT

We have attempted to present a balanced picture of the contributions of teaching and management to instruction. There is no intention to derogate the role of classroom management. As long as one
understands that the functions of the two are different, although complementary, no special problem arises. It is only when supervisors or
teachers themselves fail to distinguish appropriately between the
two that we may fall into the error of regarding the stern disciplinar-
ian, the taskmaster, or the teacher who possesses great skill in organizing the classroom group, perhaps in unusual ways, as an expert
teacher on that account.

Controlling Deviant Behavior

Kounin et al. (1966) have given us a picture of some attributes of
the teacher who is skilled in classroom management. Kounin video-
taped half-day sessions of thirty elementary classes, grades one
through five. His special interest was in the management of emotionally disturbed children, but since he found that teachers who
were effective with emotionally disturbed youngsters tended also to
be successful in managing undisturbed pupils, we shall disregard the
distinction throughout our discussion.

Earlier we presented a paradigm for the process of teaching originally developed by Smith (1960). It showed that the teacher must perceive classroom events, diagnose their meaning accurately, and react
appropriately. Skill in teaching is essentially a matter of how adequately each of these elements is performed. Some of Kounin's findings with respect to teacher management bear a strong familial re-
semblance to the above.

Kounin develops the concepts of "overlappingness" and "with-it-
ness" to analyze elementary teachers' success in controlling children's deviant behavior. These seem quite close to the concepts of
perceiving and diagnosing, on the one hand, and to reacting, on the
other. A teacher demonstrates overlapping when he is aware of a

deviant act but continues with his activity, such as conducting a reading group. A teacher manifests with-it-ness by intervening early enough to prevent the deviancy from spreading to other children and by selecting a major target for his initial intervention. Thus, a with-it teacher would intercede between two boys beginning a paper throwing contest before he would stop a child going to the pencil sharpener at an unauthorized time. Overlapping indicates that the teacher has correctly perceived and diagnosed events; with-it-ness has the added feature that the teacher *communicates (reacts,* in Smith's terms) to the pupils that he knows what is going on. It is this communication, the aptness of the reaction, what makes all the difference in causing a cessation of the deviant behavior. "[T]he higher a teacher's degree of with-it-ness, the higher the work involvement of the children and the lower their deviancy rate" (Kounin et al., 1966, p. 7). Overlappingness, on the other hand, is not related to controlling pupils' behavior, but it does correlate modestly ($r = .50$) with with-it-ness. Why that should be so, says Kounin, is a matter for some speculation.

> Our current interpretation is that Overlappingness *enables* a teacher to receive information about what is going on, but that the children do not perceive or categorize this teacher dimension, or even notice it. What they do see and react to, however, is what the teacher *does* and communicates—she stops deviancy in time or she makes mistakes in picking deviancy targets. When she is perceived by the children as knowing what is going on regarding their behavior, she has more surface managerial success, that is, induces worklike behavior and restrains deviancy. *Receiving or having knowledge is not sufficient unless the fact that this occurs is communicated to children* [italics added] (Kounin et al., 1966, p. 8).

Handling Transitions

Transition points, demarcated by the termination of one academic activity and the beginning of another, test the teacher's management skill. In a number of settings, teachers' techniques for resolving transitions were found to be correlated with deviancy rates of pupils. When viewed from a negative position, it is possible to characterize several antiresolution properties, that is, techniques used by teachers that tend to interfere with rather than promote a smooth transition from, say, the arithmetic lesson to a spelling period. These antiresolution properties include the following:

1. *Providing contrary props*—for example, telling pupils to begin work on arithmetic, then passing out corrected spelling tests.
2. *Returning to old activity*—starting arithmetic, then inquiring how many pupils spelled all their words correctly.
3. *Dangling*—starting a new activity, then abandoning it without further directions to the pupils.
4. *Thrusting*—ending one activity or beginning a new one without reference to the state of readiness of the participants. Kounin likens this to the behavior of a person who interrupts the conversation of others without waiting to pick up the thread of the remarks, or signalling the intention to participate by standing with the others, etc.
5. *Giving conflicting, confusing, or complicated orders*—giving children more directions than they can follow, or issuing contradictory instructions, for example.

Programming Learning Activities

Kounin's group of investigators also studied the procedures used by the thirty teachers to program learning activities and reported on the relationship between programming and the work-oriented behavior of the children. A first and somewhat obvious relationship studied was the average length of time allotted to an activity such as reading or science. There was no significant relationship between length of activity and either pupil deviancy or work involvement. Kounin does not report the actual time used by the various teachers, and thus his analysis does not rule out the possibility that either very brief or very long times would be related to the response of children.

Also, surprisingly, no consistent relationship was discovered between the amount of change between activities and the relevant behavior of pupils. However, when activities were redefined to include only learning-related activities, significant relationships did occur for first and second grades only, and then only in the special case of subgroup recitations (such as teacher-led reading groups). Thus, it does appear that in primary grades, when children are organized into subgroups working with the teacher, planning that varies the activity markedly from one period to the next (along dimensions such as content, the presentation pattern used by the teacher, the kinds of props employed, and the type of response the pupil is to make) does reduce the frequency of deviant behavior and increases the amount of work involvement.

When children are doing seatwork not directly supervised by the teacher, the amount of variety change[2] in seatwork is related to pupil behavior. The relationship, however, is different at different grade levels, being positive for the children in first and second grades and negative for children in the three higher grades. Over all grades, the average variety-change index was fifteen minutes. Kounin feels that alternative interpretations are required of this result. He suggests that for the younger children, experienced variety may be the consequential factor, whereas a feeling of progress toward learning is more salient for the middle graders who, in turn, find a 15-minute interval too brief to provide such experienced progress.

In conclusion, Kounin's work sketches some explicit relationships between teachers' management activities and the deviant and work-related behavior of children. We see that not all these relationships are easily derived from common sense views of classroom behavior. Thus, *attention span* turns out to be useless as a means of predicting children's reactions to activities, but the more complicated concept of variety-change index reveals relatively good predictive power, although for a limited range of settings. Continued investigation of issues in the strategy and tactics of classroom management will inevitably result in a more integrated and more easily understandable set of findings about these relationships. In the meantime, several of the concepts and techniques elucidated by Kounin and his coworkers demonstrate skills that teachers can develop which in turn help them to control the classroom behavior of pupils. We have also suggested that Smith's paradigm for the study of teaching may be broad enough to incorporate the analysis of management behavior as well.

SUMMARY

The chapter has been devoted to a first analysis of the two basic concepts of *teaching* and *management,* which together constitute *instruction.* Although the functions of teaching and of management are both necessary for instruction, and the two are complementary in practice, they are conceptually distinct from each other. It is easy to mistake management for teaching, and judgments about the competence of teachers are often erroneously based only upon their

---

[2] *Variety change* is a technical concept used by Kounin to measure the total change in activities at transition points. Thus, it would take account not only of the fact that "spelling drill" is a change from "vocabulary drill," but that "creative writing" involves greater variety than change from one drill to another.

skills as managers. Teaching occurs when one person communicates something to another with the intention that the something be learned. Scheffler's differentiation between the *intent* and *success* meanings of teaching was cited. Teaching can occur without the precondition that learning must take place. Also from Scheffler we found that it is important to distinguish among *teaching that . . .* , *teaching to . . .* , and *teaching how to. . . .* Strategies of teaching can be better conceptualized when one is clear about the type of teaching to be done.

Smith's paradigm for the analysis of teaching was presented. According to that formulation, teaching is an interactive process between teacher and pupil, involving each of them in perceiving classroom events, diagnosing them, and reacting to them. Although skill is distinct from the concept of teaching, performance can be assumed to improve as the teacher improves his skills in perceiving relevant classroom events, assessing their meaning, and reacting appropriately to them. The factor of flexibility is a critical feature of reacting and can be fostered through training and experience.

Skill in management is as necessary as skill in teaching. Kounin's empirical investigation of successful classroom-management techniques suggests some potentially useful skills and practices for controlling pupil behavior in certain ways. Furthermore, Smith's paradigm for teaching may serve equally well as a model to focus upon the required elements of skill in classroom management.

The tasks of instruction confront the classroom teacher with some weighty ethical issues. It is our intention neither to catalogue these issues nor to expound upon them. We wish simply to draw them to the attention of teachers and prospective teachers as matters that are fundamental to the conduct of transactions between adult and child, matters which deserve to be considered as the teacher goes about his daily round of classroom activities. The state requires children to attend school and, as a consequence, we may easily overlook the interventional features of our work as teachers. We seldom think about alternative ways in which children might spend their hours, since they are legally bound to sit in our classrooms. That requirement should, if anything, demand that we provide the best educative experiences within the powers of our knowledge and skill, precisely because children and their families have so little choice in the matter of childhood occupation.

REFERENCES

Chapter 1

Gordon, C. W. *The social system of the high school.* Glencoe, Ill.: Free Press, 1957.

Guilford, J. P. *Personality.* New York: McGraw-Hill, 1959.

Innaccone, L. Student teaching: a transitional stage in the making of a teacher. *Theory into Practice,* 1963, *2,* 73–80.

Jackson, P. W. *Life in classrooms.* New York: Holt, Rinehart & Winston, 1968.

Kounin, J. S., Friesen, W. V., & Norton, A. Evangeline. Managing emotionally disturbed children in regular classrooms. *Journal of Educational Psychology,* 1966, *57,* 1–13.

Medley, D. M., & Mitzel, H. E. Some behavioral correlates of teacher effectiveness. *Journal of Educational Psychology,* 1959, *50,* 239–246.

Ryan, K. The teaching intern: a sociological stranger. *Journal of Teacher Education,* 1966, *17,* 185–191.

Scheffler, I. *The language of education.* Springfield, Ill.: Charles C Thomas, 1960.

Smith, B. O. On the anatomy of teaching. *Journal of Teacher Education,* 1956, *7,* 339–346.

Smith, B. O. A concept of teaching. *Teachers College Record,* 1960, *61,* 229–241.

CHAPTER 2
CLASSROOM LEARNING

We asserted in the previous chapter that learning is a more encompassing concept than teaching. It is time now to consider the conditions under which learning transpires in the classroom and the variables that govern it. As we proceed, the reader will note that the theories and concepts to which we appeal are not the usual ones found in discussion of the psychology of learning. There are reasons for this departure, which can be explained briefly.

First, the learning theorist is usually interested in explaining in detail and at a high level of generality how organisms behave. Our concern is with learning at a grosser level, at a level of generality that can be seen in classroom settings. Second, the psychologist's theories about learning are efforts to *describe* how the animal or human being comes to cognize or respond to the environment, and thus to cope with it. Our intention is to emphasize conditions under which the environment can be altered to heighten the likelihood that desired academic learning will occur. Stated succinctly, our interest lies in intervening in the learner's environment with the intention of bringing about improvements in the level of his school learning. The language we use to discuss these issues is not antagonistic to the concepts and theories of psychology, or at least it ought not to be, but it is different, largely because of the differences in purpose.

At first glance it would appear that little question could be raised about the improvement of learning as the principal and proper function of teaching. Our analysis of teaching in chapter 1 is clearly in accord with such an assumption. As a matter of fact, there are serious students of education who doubt that the purpose of teaching is to promote learning, or indeed that teachers can very significantly influence pupils' learning. We need to examine the nature of such an argument with respect to the assumptions it makes both about learning and about teaching.

One point of view holds that the child's rate of growth, and not the efforts of the teacher to instruct him, plays the most important part in determining what the child learns. This theory of learning as a function of growth was stated rather explicitly by Courtis (1949) some years ago. His general argument is both simple and appealing. The child's entire development is controlled by the rate and stage of his growth. Curricular tasks, and the extent to which mastery of them is demanded, are to be geared to the child's development. Thus, according to Courtis, excessive energy of teacher and child is invested in trying to get the student to learn fully, say, the multiplication tables before the stage of growth that permits easy acquisition of such a task. The child will learn more completely and with less stress for him (and, obviously, for his teacher) if the task is postponed until a later and more appropriate stage of growth has been achieved.

Something more is involved in this position, however, than a traditional view of the role of learning readiness. Even when the appropriate growth stage has been reached, teaching has little to contribute to the child's learning. Courtis cites an interesting example to bolster his argument. The word *sincerely* appeared on the prescribed spelling list in the eighth grade of a school; *customary* was never taught directly. The percentage of children who could spell *sincerely* increased sharply immediately after teaching; a year later, the percentage had diminished to the level that, according to Courtis, growth curves would predict. Also, by the twelfth grade, about 90 per cent of the students involved were able to spell both words accurately. Courtis chastises teachers in the following words:

> Teachers try to change the rates at which children learn; teachers try to change the extent of their developments in knowledge and skill, all matters which are chiefly determined by the heredity of the child. Their efforts thus are wasted. They fail to inspire, to interpret. These are matters in which their efforts may produce very large results.

If the teacher exerts himself to keep the children happy, having

a good time, doing school work in their own way, he is doing
most for the children under his care. If the teacher is 'human,'
and establishes friendly relationships with each child, he is doing
the best he can for them. If the teacher doesn't 'teach' any more
than a farmer 'grows' his corn, the benefits to himself, the children, and the public are so great as to be almost miraculous
(Courtis, 1949, p. 323).

Although we do not altogether accept this view of school learning,
nor the very ephemeral role to which it relegates teaching, Courtis'
argument boldly dramatizes the differences in magnitude of the concepts of learning and of teaching. Courtis seems to be emphasizing
the obvious fact that children do learn in school, notwithstanding the
contribution of teaching. But, of course, in or out of school, we all
learn a great deal that we are not taught.

If for the moment at least we disregard the implications of Courtis'
concept of teaching, it is instructive to analyze the conditions under
which learning occurs. First, and of greatest importance, is growth.
This is a physical factor, principally hereditary and minimally controlled by environmental influences. From the school's point of view,
it represents a situational given. Second is an amorphous set of school
variables, which must include a physical location for learning, and a
host of stimuli which are subsumable under the general rubric of instructional or curricular materials. Thus, it would be only the rarest
child who would learn to read in the absence of books designed for
that purpose. (Whether such books and other materials can also
properly be construed as "teachers" seems to be a question worth
serious attention.) Third is a group of individual or personal variables,
including motivation, learning styles, and individual personality
needs. It is apparently to optimize these variables that the teacher
"exerts himself to keep the children happy, having a good time, doing
school work in their own way. . . ."

Carroll (1963, 1965) has suggested that several variables influence
school learning. Among them is a set of individual variables, including
aptitude, the rate at which an individual learns material of a given
kind; *perseverance,* a specific motivational variable that reflects the
willingness of the individual to attend to a learning task; and *ability
to comprehend instruction.* Carroll conceives of this last variable as
more general than the aptitude variable and apparently the equivalent
of verbal intelligence. Two other variables in Carroll's model are
school variables. One is *opportunity to learn,* a measure of time to
which the learner has access to the learning task, and the other is

quality of instruction. Translations from one set of terms to another are loaded with imprecision, but these last two variables would seem to come closest to the interpretation we placed upon teaching in the first chapter.

The model that Carroll has developed has not been thoroughly tested. It seems self-evident that the variables he has specified are related to academic-learning outcomes. The interactions among those variables are doubtless complex, and our understanding of how classroom learning occurs will be enhanced as new research efforts focus upon those variables, particularly over long periods of time such as the years of elementary school or even the entire sweep of school years from kindergarten through the senior high school.

From the sources we have thus far reviewed, it seems apparent that the *time which a student spends in commerce with the learning task* is a central variable in school learning. Although that fact seems terribly obvious, it has recently been specified as the result of an international study of the learning of mathematics. Foshay (1967), one of the educators who was involved in the analysis of data taken from thousands of students and schools around the world, summarizes the outcomes of the study:

> One of the principal findings of the study is that in spite of the fact that 45 independent variables (i.e., school variables, family variables, and student variables) were included, most of the variance in mathematics achievement could not be explained. Everything we know with any precision about why students achieve well in mathematics still fails to explain why they achieve well.
>
> Within the variance that we can explain, the greatest educator appears to be the family. That is, the educational and occupational status of the father makes more difference than everything we do in school put together. In school, the biggest contributors to the variance appear to be the opportunity to learn subject matter (under any circumstances), and the students' attitudes toward the subject matter (Foshay, 1967, p. 222).

Three operating rules for teachers now seem to be worth stating.

1. Schools and teachers are given certain pupils with whom to work who possess given talents and abilities and who also have limitations which may be meaningful in a school setting. Courtis' attention to growth factors emphasizes the develop-

mental aspects of growth, but there are wide ranges of inter-individual differences in growth as well as intraindividual variations. Foshay's reference to the family as the most effective educator points up the limitations imposed by environment as well as by the forces of heredity. Learning is governed extensively but not totally by factors that represent "givens" for the school.

2. Opportunity to learn, which operationally may be defined as the time the pupil actually devotes to learning, looms as the most important school variable in the learning process. In that form, it is a gross variable in need of more careful specification in a number of areas. For example, it calls our attention to the significance of curricular debates and their implications for the relative amounts of time and emphasis to be committed to various subject areas. Motivational variables and incentive conditions are stressed for the teacher, since these tend to control the effectiveness with which available time for learning will be used by pupils.

3. Finally, a variable like Carroll's *quality of instruction* probably affects the rate at which learning can occur once the variables alluded to in rules 1 and 2 have been taken into account. Although this may seem a trivial variable in comparison with others which seem to control pupils' learning, it represents the major impact that teachers exercise directly upon pupil learning.

TWO VIEWS OF CLASSROOM LEARNING

We now turn to two viewpoints about classroom learning that are subsumable under the general rubric of instructional quality. They are *reception learning* and *discovery learning*. Each seems sufficiently well-established in the vocabulary of the teaching profession, if not on a firm evidential basis, to merit presentation among the basic concepts of the classroom. Each has a contribution to make to the classroom teacher who desires to analyze the quality of instruction he is capable of providing. However, they differ from each other not only in the strategies they recommend for promoting learning but also in the goals toward which they are directed.

Reception learning emphasizes the organizational properties of learning tasks such as reading assignments, lectures, or educational TV programs, and seeks to reveal the conditions under which masses of educational information are optimally processed by pupils and retained in usable form. Discovery learning is oriented toward providing pupils with experiences of inquiring, of going through processes similar to those which scientists and scholars employ in their quest for new knowledge, but more structured and directed to improve the chances of the pupil's enjoying an educative experience rather than meandering at random through previously explored intellectual fields.

Central to the differences between the two systems are the assumptions made by each about the purposes of education, the nature of classroom learning, and the learning abilities of children and adolescents. Before we examine the viewpoints in detail, and the evidence that undergirds them, let us compare and contrast the assumptions upon which they rest. Among other things, it should become apparent that the advocates of reception learning and discovery learning are mutually antagonistic, but the antagonism is not necessarily intrinsic to the theories themselves. They describe, and attempt to account for, somewhat different kinds of classroom phenomena; the conflict seems to arise over the breadth and generality of the phenomena which each can account for rather than the legitimacy of either position per se.

The theory of reception learning, associated with David P. Ausubel (1963, 1968), attempts to isolate the variables that control the acquisition, retention, and transfer of large bodies of potentially meaningful, connected discourse of the kind that is typically presented to students in classrooms. For Ausubel, the chief function of the teacher and the school is to transmit subject-matter knowledge to students through such vehicles as texts and other books, lecture and discussion, films, educational television, etc. For such instruction to be effective, it must be approached as a meaningful task, and ways must be found for subject matter to become incorporated into the cognitive structures of students. In short, when potentially meaningful material such as that found in most textbooks is treated as though it were meaningless, it tends to be learned by rote, and the laws that govern the forgetting of rote material are applicable, with their attendant early and extensive losses in retention. The principal task of the teacher, according to Ausubel, is to respect the potential meaningfulness of subject matter, relating it to preexisting elements of cognitive structure and trying to insure that obliterative subsumption is halted, or at least inhibited.

Ausubel pays relatively little attention to the development of students' thinking skills. His theory explicitly deals with those elements of classroom learning that are best described as the learning of information, concepts, and generalizations rather than with the ability of students to generate (discover) such cognitive outcomes. Although the latter kinds of learning are beyond the purview of Ausubel's theory, it is also quite clear that he is pessimistic about the ability of all students to become competent critical and creative thinkers or problem-solvers; consequently, he is skeptical about the appropriateness of the school's assigning a dominant role to such outcomes.

Given Ausubel's reservations about the nature of students' intellectual abilities and his assumption that the principal responsibility of the school is to transmit large bodies of organized subject matter, we would expect him to be dubious about the values of discovery (inductive) learning in the classroom. He points out that discovery techniques demand a great deal of time and that they are not efficient for teaching those large bodies of subject matter which, for him, constitute the burden of the legitimate business of the teacher.

It is worth noting that the weight of available evidence about classroom teaching tends to support Ausubel's assumptions and contentions about the dominance of verbal activity in teaching-learning situations. Among the best-documented findings of educational research are those which establish the essentially verbal nature of the classroom, the fact that teachers tend to talk about twice as much as all their students combined (Bellack & Davitz, 1963; Flanders, 1960; Stevens, 1912), and that classroom interaction is dominated by question and answer dialogue (Bellack & Davitz, 1963; Dale & Raths, 1945; Hudgins & Ahlbrand, 1967). Ausubel apparently presupposes that an effective theory of classroom learning must be geared to the teaching-learning process as it is commonly and currently found to operate. This is not at all an unreasonable presupposition, particularly since we have good reason for believing that these fundamental characteristics of teaching are enduring ones which have been influenced mildly, if at all, by the many innovations in educational practice that have entered the scene at various times since the early twentieth century.

Proponents of discovery learning assume that active participation by the student is an indispensable condition for learning. This, too, as we have indicated, is a well-demonstrated generalization about learning. In contrast to Ausubel's position, the use of discovery techniques is seen as a way of minimizing the verbal nature of the classroom and of changing the teacher's role from that of an authoritative source of information to that of a mediator between the learner and the phenomena about which he is to learn. In a discovery situation, the learner may be presented with a series of stimuli, from which he is ultimately to induce a generalization. For example, he may be asked to find the sums of digits such as 1, 3, 5, 7; 1, 3, 5, 7, 9; and 1, 3, 5, 7, 9, 11; and to search for a generalization that will enable him to provide the sum of any such series without actually performing the computation. In this particular case, the rule is that the sum of any sequence (n) of odd numbers beginning with one is equal to n^2.

Two criticisms directed toward discovery learning are implicit in the example just given. In the first place, the structure of the stimuli, or the number of cues given to the learner, must receive careful advance consideration by the teacher or the experimenter. Thus, whether it is really appropriate to speak of a child's having "discovered" the odd-number rule after repeated exposure to series of the kind just iterated, does seem to be legitimately open to question. Second, the "discoveries" of the classroom are characteristically only discoveries as far as the learner is concerned. For example, the odd-number rule, as is true with other generalizations presented in discovery form, is itself well-known; the task for teaching is one of arranging conditions in such a way as to make it likely that the student will induce the generalization without having it told to him explicitly. The assumption is made that generalizations learned in a discovery setting are better retained and more transferable than if they were communicated intact to the student, as in reception learning.

Controversy between advocates of the two theories about classroom learning centers about issues of the meaningfulness, organization, and coverage of material, and the role of student activity in the process of learning. On the one hand, proponents of reception learning point out the limitations of discovery methods for teaching substantial bodies of subject matter; and they also note the potential danger that discovery methods can become highly stereotyped and meaningless. The former charge seems a reasonable and legitimate one that teachers will do well to bear in mind as they plan classroom learning activities. The latter appears to be true to the same extent that it would be true for any classroom procedure, whether predicated upon reception or discovery strategies. Reception learning, on the other hand, is characterized by its critics as imposing a passive role upon the learner, limiting the range of use of his intellectual abilities and teaching him that secondary sources (such as books and teachers) rather than the natural environment in which he lives are the authorities from which knowledge is derived.

In the following sections we shall present the basic tenets of each position in more detailed form and examine the evidence that tends to support or to refute the theories. Finally, we shall try to select a set of basic concepts about classroom learning, drawn from each system, that seems important for the analysis of learning in instructional situations.

RECEPTION LEARNING

Reception learning, as the name implies, is the kind of learning that occurs when the student is confronted with bodies of new information. It represents a psychological theory of learning that has been developed specifically for explaining and controlling learning in classroom situations rather than in animal or human experimental laboratories. Consequently, although it shares some concepts with more orthodox psychological theories, it is at odds with such theories on a number of critical issues.

At the heart of the theory of reception learning is the concept of cognitive structure. *Cognitive structure* refers to the organization of ideas about a subject matter or subtopic of a subject matter that the learner already possesses at the time new information is to be presented to him. Cognitive structure is posited to be hierarchically organized, with more specific items of information subordinated to and organized around more general and higher order concepts, laws, or generalizations of a field. The accuracy and comprehensiveness of an individual's cognitive structure play major roles in facilitating the acquisition and retention of new subject-matter information. It is the novice in any area of learning who encounters the greatest difficulty in grappling with a mass of new and specific factual information. Figuratively, at least, the novice has no cognitive hooks on which to hang the information. He cannot discriminate the more important from that which is of less consequence.

A learner with a viable cognitive structure in a given area has developed appropriate and relevant *subsumers,* as Ausubel calls them. These subsumers are the more general propositions about the field of knowledge. They enable the more experienced student to deal efficiently with the same welter of information that is likely to be so confusing and frustrating to the beginner.

Many university departments today insist upon assigning the responsibility for teaching introductory courses to senior members of the faculty instead of to graduate students, as was often done in the past. There may be many reasons for such a practice but one obvious and important one is that the mature scholar in a field is more likely to see the total structure of the subject, to comprehend the relationships among its various areas and, presumably, to reflect that mature understanding in his teaching in such a way as to provide a firm foundation of knowledge for the beginning student.

Possibly the most important definition in the system of reception learning is that of learning itself. For Ausubel, *learning* refers to the process of "acquiring meanings" from the potential meanings presented in the learning material, and of "making them more available" (Ausubel, 1963, p. 51). The learner's task in dealing with potentially meaningful learning material is fundamentally different in at least one respect from typical laboratory learning tasks in which lists of words or nonsense syllables are to be learned in a given order. Psychologists sometimes distinguish between rote learning and substance learning. For the moment, it is sufficient to indicate that ordinarily in reception learning the student is not attempting to duplicate the language and word order of the teacher or textbook but to master the basic ideas or concepts that are being introduced.

When new substantive information is introduced to the learner, it typically takes the form of specific facts, information, illustrative data, or some similar form, rather than that of an overreaching or superordinate proposition or generalization of the kind that is foundational to most subject matters. This information is stored by the learner with differential success, depending upon existing conditions (prior learning) and conditions of presentation and practice of the newly acquired learning material.

In general, even substantive passages learned in isolation from the more general concepts and principles of their field are less likely to be well remembered than are passages carefully articulated with those broader tenets of the discipline. To the extent that such concepts and principles are already available to the learner, his ability to incorporate new learning is enhanced. These broader principles function as subsumers for the new learning material and represent, as it were, a place in the cognitive structure of the learner where the new learning material fits appropriately, i.e., is not to be regarded as isolated.

However, under certain conditions, the new material loses its distinctive characteristics and can no longer be explicitly recalled as an entity separate from the higher-order concept or generalization under which it was originally learned. This can happen, of course, if the subsuming concept or proposition itself is for some reason unclear to the learner. With respect to retention of newly acquired information, however, at least two conditions must apparently be met in order to forestall obliterative subsumption:

1. It must initially be carefully learned, i.e., the potential meaningfulness of the learning passage must be realized.

2. The characteristics of the new material that differentiate it from the subsumer must be emphasized and understood by the learner.

Although these two statements seem almost to be self-evident, their implementation and elaboration provide challenging and productive avenues for the teacher along which to plan and organize instructional materials and strategies.

DISCOVERY LEARNING

The reader is cautioned at the outset that the label "discovery learning" is misleading and to some extent a misrepresentation of what the term in fact refers to. We continue to identify this body of facts and arguments as discovery learning simply to avoid further muddying the waters, which are already well stirred, by tossing in a new phrase.

A great deal of nonsense has been written in the past ten years about discovery learning and methods of teaching by discovery. Even its more convincing proponents, in describing it, are not talking about allowing children to engage in "pure discovery" of the sort that would demand the pupil to rediscover the wheel as it were, that is, to start at the beginning of an idea and develop it independently in a fashion similar to the way it was originally developed or discovered by a single or perhaps by generations of earlier scholars or scientists.

To put it as simply as possible, the basic educational goals for discovery learning seem to resolve into two points:

1. Discovery learning is a vehicle for encouraging students to learn subject matter in meaningful and therefore subsequently usable and useful ways.
2. It is a means for teaching heuristics for thinking.

Proponents of learning by discovery are convinced of the merits of active pupil participation in the process of learning and of thinking. These processes are fostered not by providing all of the task to be learned but by leaving gaps here and there, gaps which the student can close meaningfully through extrapolation or interpolation (or by means of other cognitive skills), aided by his substantive knowledge of the problem or topic that confronts him. Much confusion about the nature of discovery learning has occurred on precisely this point, and we wish to clarify it as carefully as possible.

When as eloquent a spokesman as Jerome S. Bruner discusses his conception of the discovery process for classroom learning, he makes it abundantly clear that the opportunities for discovery are embedded in the context of what has already been learned or can be derived from or checked against a model of such learning. We believe that these excerpts from a statement by Bruner (1966) will help to crystallize the position we have expressed.

> . . . we had better be cautious in talking about the method of discovery, or discovery as the principal vehicle of education. Simply from a biological point of view, it does not seem to be the case at all. We ought to be extremely careful, therefore, to think about the range of possible techniques used for guaranteeing that we produce competent adults within a society that the educational process supports. Thus, in order to train these adults, education must program their development of skills, and provide them with models, if you will, of the environment. All of these things must be taken into account, rather than just taking it for granted that discovery is a principal way in which the individual finds out about his environment.
>
> You make no mistake if you take the phenomena of language-learning as a paradigm. Language-learning is very close to invention and has very little in common with what we normally speak of as discovery. There are several things about language-learning that strike me as being of particular interest. For example, in language-learning, the child finds himself in a linguistic environment in which he comes forth with utterances. Take the first syntactic utterances. They usually have the form of a pivotal class and an open class, like "All gone, Mommy," "All gone, Daddy," and "All gone this; all done that." The child exposed linguistically to an adult world comes forth not with a discovery but with an invention that makes you believe somewhat in innate ideas, in a linguistic form that simply is not present in the adult repertoire. Such language-learning consists of invention or coming forth with grammar, possibly innately, that then becomes modified in contact with the world. The parent takes the child's utterances which do not conform to adult grammar. He then idealizes and expands them, not permitting the child to discover haphazardly but rather providing a model which is there all the time. . . .
>
> Thus, *within the culture the earliest form of learning essential to the person becoming human is not so much discovery as it is having a model* [italics added]. The constant provision of a model, the constant response to the individual's response after

response, back and forth between two people, constitute discovery learning guided by an accessible model.

If you want to talk about invention, perhaps the most primitive form of uniquely human learning is the invention of certain patterns that probably come out of deep-grooved characteristics of the human nervous system, with a lot of shaping taking place on the part of an adult. Consequently, wherever you look, you cannot really come away with a strong general consensus that discovery is a principal means of educating the young. Yet, the one thing that is apparent is that there seems to be a necessary component in human learning that is like discovery, namely, the opportunity to go about exploring a situation.

It seems to be imperative for the child to develop an approach to further learning that is more effective in nature—an approach to learning that allows the child not only to learn the material that is presented in a school setting, but to learn it in such a way that he can use the information in problem-solving. To me, this is the critical thing: How do you teach something to a child? . . . arrange a child's environment, if you will, in such a way that he can learn something with some assurance that he will use the material that he has learned appropriately in a variety of situations. This problem of learning by discovery is the kind that guarantees a child will use what he has learned effectively.

We know perfectly well that there are the good rote techniques whereby you can get the child to come back with a long list of information. This list is no good, however, because the child will use it in a single situation and possibly not even effectively then. There must be some other way of teaching so that the child will have a high likelihood of transfer (Bruner, 1966, pp. 101–103).

We remind the reader of the earlier reference to a similar concern expressed by Ausubel about the meaningfulness to the learner of what he is intended to learn. For Ausubel, as for Bruner, there must be an alternative to rote learning. But beyond this point of agreement, their positions depart from each other. Bruner's protests against rote learning are directed toward the level of instructional practice. He contends that material which is learned by rote lacks relatedness to other concepts, builds toward no meaningful set of relationships in the subject matter, and is, as a result, effectively useless to the learner. According to Bruner, rote learning is useless in the sense that, although it may be retained and recalled upon demand, this constitutes the limits of its intellectual utility. Such information learned by rote cannot be applied to the solution of new problems. Bruner is apparently saying that, by definition, subject matter (information) that is learned mechanically is not transferable to situations beyond that in which the information was learned.

Ausubel, it will be recalled, shares Bruner's discontent with rote learning, but his position departs from Bruner's on at least two highly significant points:

1. His distress is directed less toward the teacher who attempts to apply principles of learning by rote to educational tasks in the classroom than it is toward psychologists who have uncritically suggested that such principles, largely developed in laboratory situations under conditions not very similar to the classroom, are appropriate guides for a psychology of classroom learning.

2. Ausubel argues vigorously that the kind of substantive information to which students are subjected under conditions of ordinary reception learning is *potentially meaningful,* a term that Ausubel employs to distinguish such materials and learning tasks that are avowedly meaningless or nonsensical (and which must, perforce, be learned by rote) from connected discourse, as found in lectures or textbooks, and *meaningful* material, which for Ausubel signifies material that has already been learned.

Bruner discriminates only between discovery learning (as he defines it) and rote learning. Ausubel, on the other hand, asserts that the subject matter typically encountered in lectures, textbooks, films, and related guides is potentially meaningful and capable of being incorporated into the learner's cognitive structure. This, in turn, has implications for retention and transfer.

The foregoing analysis should not be interpreted as indicating that whatever theoretical disputes obtain between the advocates of reception learning and those of discovery learning can be totally resolved. There are fundamental differences between the two positions on some very basic issues, such as the proper goals of instruction and the nature of the learner, including his capabilities for intellectual activity at levels higher than those associated with the acquisition and utilization of knowledge.

Each of these theoretical positions, though presented as the outline of an instructional system, would seem to gain strength from some form of combination with the other. Ausubel, for example, states explicitly that he is not dealing with the role of discovery or higher order intellectual processes.

> The aim of this book is to present a comprehensive theory of how human beings learn and retain large bodies of subject matter in classroom and similar learning environments. Its scope is limited to the 'reception' learning and retention of meaningful material. 'Reception' learning refers to the situation where the content of the learning task (what is to be learned) is presented to rather than independently discovered by the learner. That is, the learner is newly required to comprehend the material meaningfully and to incorporate it or make it available or functionally reproducible for future use.
>
> It is true, of course, that the school is also concerned with developing the student's ability to use acquired knowledge in solving particular problems, that is, his ability to think systematically, independently, and critically in particular fields of inquiry. This latter function of the school, although inseparable in practice from its transmission-of-knowledge function, is less central in terms of the amount of time that can be reasonably allotted to it, the objectives of education in a democratic society, and what can be realistically expected from most students (Ausubel, 1963, p. 1).

Ausubel says, in effect, that the major substantive job that our society requires of teachers is to impart subject matter information to their students.

Children have to be taught the basic skills of reading, writing, and arithmetic. There is a wealth of knowledge about the history and geography of their own state and nation, and the rest of the world, that children have to comprehend if the enlightened citizenry of our aspiration is to be approximated. Science, mathematics, and technology have grown and are growing so rapidly that curriculum builders and teachers are hard pressed to find means of communicating such knowledge effectively and meaningfully to students.

There is a balance to be maintained between reception learning and other activities which may approximate discovery learning. This balance is weighted heavily in favor of reception learning.

The argument we are making with respect to classroom learning, the position at which we wish finally to arrive, is that both reception

learning and discovery learning occupy legitimate places in the conduct of classroom activities. We might agree with Ausubel that reception learning will play the major role in the classroom for some of
the reasons described previously. The teacher would seem to have an
obligation to be able to conduct such learning activities meaningfully with students.

One problem that needs to be confronted and dispelled once and
for all is the apparent insistence of proponents of each system to play
the role of critic by comparing their systems with the worst abuses of
the others. Poor teaching is doomed to produce poor learning, no
matter what the theoretical devotion of the teacher. Dull, stupid,
unimaginative tasks are unlikely to lead to intellectual excitement,
whether labelled discovery or reception learning. Thus, Ausubel describes part of the development of discovery techniques as follows:

> . . . two strands of the Progressive Education Movement—em-
> phasis on the child's direct experience and spontaneous in-
> terests, and insistence on autonomously achieved insight free of
> all directive manipulation of the learning environment—set the
> stage for the subsequent deification of problem-solving labora-
> tory work and naive emulation of the scientific method. Many
> mathematics and science teachers were rendered self-conscious
> about systematically presenting and explaining to their students
> the basic concepts and principles of their fields, because it was
> held that this procedure would promote glib verbalism and rote
> memorization. It was felt that if students worked enough prob-
> lems, and were kept busy pouring reagents into a sufficient num-
> ber of test tubes, they would somehow spontaneously discover
> in a meaningful way all of the important concepts and generali-
> zations they needed to know in the fields they were studying.
>
> Of course, one had to take pains to discourage students from
> rotely memorizing formulas, and then mechanically substituting
> for the general terms in these formulas the particular values of
> specified variables to given problems. This would naturally be no
> less rote than didactic exposition. Hence, in accordance with the
> new emphasis on *meaningful* problem-solving, students ceased
> memorizing formulas, memorizing instead type problems. They
> learned how to work exemplars of all of the kinds of problems
> they were responsible for, and then rotely memorized both the
> form of each type and its solution. Thus equipped, it was com-
> paratively easy to sort the problems with which they were con-

fronted into their respective categories, and "spontaneously proceed to discover meaningful solutions"—provided, of course,
that the teacher played fair and presented recognizable ex-
emplars of the various types (Ausubel, 1963, pp. 140–141).

Although Ausubel makes no effort to document his assertions,
there is little question that the kinds of abuses he charges have and do
occur, making a mockery of the legitimate purposes and uses of
problem solving, laboratory procedures, and inductive reasoning. It is
ironic that Ausubel, who so decries inappropriate attacks against expository verbal learning, should respond in kind. By the same token,
Bruner describes an "experiment" in which a class of children is
taught by reception methods. Despite the outcomes of the "experiment" (with which we are never acquainted), Bruner artfully deni-
grates the merits of reception teaching procedures. Again, note the
language in which this is accomplished.

> One experiment which I can report provides encouragement.
> It was devised and carried out by the research group with which
> I am associated at Harvard in collaboration with teachers in the
> fifth grade of a good public school. It is on the unpromising topic
> of the geography of the North Central States and is currently in
> progress [this was in 1959] so that I cannot give all of the results.
> We hit upon the happy idea of presenting this chunk of geogra-
> phy not as a set of knowns, but as a set of unknowns. One class
> was presented blank maps, containing only tracings of the rivers
> and lakes of the area as well as the natural resources. They were
> asked as a first exercise to indicate where the principal cities
> would be located, where the railroads, and where the main high-
> ways. Books and maps were not permitted and "looking up the
> facts" was cast in a sinful light. Upon completing the exercise, a
> class discussion was begun in which the children attempted to
> justify why the major city would be here, a large city there, a
> railroad on this line, etc.
>   The discussion was a hot one. After an hour, and much plead-
> ing, permission was given to consult the rolled up wall map. I
> will never forget one young student, as he pointed his finger at
> the foot of Lake Michigan, shouting, "Yippee, *Chicago* is at the
> end of the pointing down lake." And another replying, "Well, OK!
> but Chicago's no good for the rivers and it should be where there
> is a big city" (St. Louis). These children were thinking, and learn-
> ing was an instrument for checking and improving the process.

To at least a half dozen children in the class it is not a matter of indifference that no big city is to be found at the junction of Lake Huron, Lake Michigan, and Lake Ontario. They were slightly shaken up transportation theorists when the facts were in.

The children in another class taught conventionally got their facts all right, sitting down, benchbound. And that was that. We will see in six months which group remembers more. But whichever does, one thing I will predict. One group learned geography as a set of rational acts of induction—that cities spring up where there is water, where there are things to be processed and shipped, where there are natural resources. The other group learned passively that there were arbitrary cities at arbitrary places by arbitrary bodies of water and arbitrary sources of supply. One learned geography as a form of activity. The other stored some names and positions as a passive form of registration (Bruner, 1959, pp. 187–188).

There are some obvious points of contention in these comments. Clearly, at least as presented by Bruner, the children in the discovery class enjoyed a much more exciting and stimulating hour than did the control-class members. The two groups also were evidently involved in learning different things, hardly a basis for making odious comparisons between two methods of instruction. Again, one wonders if all the children involved would have been better served by some combination of the two treatments. We experience some concern for the boy who, despite his joy at having made an accurate prediction, still knows Lake Michigan only as "the pointing down lake." And what of the half dozen "slightly shaken up transportation theorists"?

PROPOSITIONS ABOUT LEARNING IN CLASSROOM SETTINGS

By way of a conclusion and summary, we offer the following set of statements about the conditions that are salient in controlling learning in the classroom. These statements are no more than a partial and tentative list of the relevant variables that influence classroom learning. Our knowledge in this domain is far from complete, although in recent years educators have once again begun to recognize the importance of learning more about academic learning. We may expect to see significant increments in our level of knowledge about this topic in the next few years. At the present time, however, it seems important to summarize for teachers some of what we do know about classroom learning in order to focus attention upon certain variables which are likely to be significant. Again, when statements are put into words, they have a tendency to take on an aura of finality; we emphasize the tentative nature of what we are here calling "propositions" about classroom learning.

Growth makes a difference. The concept of growth, with its implications for readiness and maturity of the organism, covers a multitude of conditions under which learning occurs. Although we reject Courtis' contention that the teacher's role is simply one of a facilitator or nurturing agent, it does seem quite important to recognize that children learn a great deal that cannot be accounted for by analyses of formal instruction or curriculum content. This is consistent with our earlier assertion that learning is a much broader concept than teaching. Year by year children improve their scores on academic achievement tests yet it would be most difficult to sketch clear relationships between such academic growth and the amount or quality of teaching that has been provided by the school. We make this statement not to denigrate the role of teaching in the analysis of learning but to clarify that role and to help focus upon those variables in the school setting—which are, presumably, under the control of the school to some extent—that do affect what pupils learn.

Within the delimited concept of classroom learning, as we have described it, the variables that Carroll has identified as opportunity to learn and quality of teaching are central to our understanding of classroom learning. Opportunity to learn concerns the kind of content that the student studies and includes such important variables as the level and duration of his attention to learning tasks, the motivational and incentive conditions that affect attention, and so forth. The quality of teaching, the chief variable with which this chapter has been concerned, is influenced by the learning experience. In this regard we have identified two kinds of learning or, more accurately, two different points of view about classroom learning. Our argument now is that classroom learning is significantly affected by the quality of reception learning and of discovery learning that teachers and schools afford to pupils.

Reception learning and discovery learning are considered as separate entities in the general domain of classroom learning. Although at various points it seems that the proponents of each approach see the other as antagonistic and in conflict, we tend to take a more moderate position. There appear to be excellent reasons for believing that sometimes one, sometimes the other kind of learning is better suited to the needs of learners. Some of the apparent conflict is probably associated with differences in assumptions about the developmental stage of learners. According to Ausubel, elementary school children require frequent exposure to concrete props and direct experience for reception learning to be meaningful for them. One of the characteristics of discovery learning is its insistence upon direct experience, often formalized through laboratory procedures and activities.

Finally, there seems to be consensus that classroom learning is facilitated when students are confronted with meaningful school tasks. The concept of meaningfulness suffers from vagueness, but we can specify at least two dimensions along which it is relevant to classroom learning. One of these involves the sense in which we have used the term repeatedly; that is, to differentiate it from tasks that possess no internal structure from which the learner can abstract meaning, or that are presented to the learner in such a way that he must approach the tasks as though they were meaningless. There is, however, a second usage of the term that is equally important.

Wertheimer (1959) related his experience with a little girl whose parents had been informed that she was not bright enough to remain in school but should be placed in a home for the feebleminded. The recommendation had been made in part because of the child's inability to solve abstract arithmetic problems. Wertheimer, who had known the girl all her young life, described a practical problem to her in which a mother wished to bathe her baby but lacked the required containers and other implements. The child's interest was intense and, says Wertheimer, she rather easily solved problems even more difficult than those she had previously been unable to answer. "This child was not able to deal with problems the sense of which she did not see. On the other hand, if a problem grew out of the situation, if the solution was required by the situation, she encountered no unusual difficulty, frequently showing excellent sense" (Wertheimer, 1959, pp. 273–274).

Naturally, we use the Wertheimer episode only to illustrate the point, not to suggest that all problems or all learning tasks must be of such a concrete or practical bent. Nonetheless, we view it as a basic proposition of classroom learning that when students understand why certain tasks are to be mastered, and can see a relationship between those tasks and improved knowledge of a field of inquiry, learning is likely to be enhanced. The same relationship would hold for the acquisition of practical or immediately useful knowledge or techniques, but we wish to avoid the interpretation that immediacy and utility of learning are the only, or the most important, criteria for the selection of learning tasks.

REFERENCES

Chapter 2

Ausubel, D. P. *Psychology of meaningful verbal learning.* New York: Grune & Stratton, 1963.

Ausubel, D. P. *Educational psychology: a cognitive view.* New York: Holt, Rinehart & Winston, 1968.

Bellack, A. A., & Davitz, J. R. *Language of the classroom: meanings communicated in high school teaching.* New York: Teachers College, Columbia University, Institute of Psychological Research, 1963.

Bruner, J. S. Some elements of discovery. In L. S. Shulman & E. R. Keislar (Eds.), *Learning by discovery: a critical appraisal.* Chicago: Rand McNally, 1966. Pp. 101–113.

Bruner, J. S. Learning and thinking. *Harvard Educational Review,* 1959, *29,* 184–192.

Carroll, J. B. A model of school learning. *Teachers College Record,* 1963, *64,* 723–733.

Carroll, J. B. School learning over the long haul. In J. D. Krumboltz (Ed.), *Learning and the educational process.* Chicago: Rand McNally, 1965. Pp. 249–269.

Courtis, S. A. Rate of growth makes a difference. *Phi Delta Kappan,* 1949, *30,* 316–323.

Dale, E., & Raths, L. E. Discussion in the secondary school. *Educational Research Bulletin,* 1945, *24,* 1–6.

Flanders, N. A. *Teacher influence, pupil attitudes, and achievement.* U.S. Office of Education Cooperative Research Project No. 397. Minneapolis: University of Minnesota, 1960. (Mimeographed)

Foshay, A. W. Professional education: the discipline of the act. *Theory into Practice,* 1967, *6,* 220–226.

Hudgins, B. B., & Ahlbrand, W. P. *A study of classroom interaction and thinking.* St. Louis: Central Midwestern Regional Educational Laboratory, 1967.

Stevens, Romiette. The question as a measure of efficiency in instruction: a critical study of classroom practice. *Teachers College Contributions to Education,* 1912, No. 48.

Wertheimer, M. *Productive thinking.* (Enl. ed.) New York: Harper & Brothers, 1959.

CHAPTER 3
PLANNING

Teachers plan in many different ways what they and their students will do in the classroom. Some teachers contend that they do not plan for teaching, but this seems unlikely. Most of us prepare some kind of plan for our daily lives, although it may be informal and impromptu. For example, I am writing these introductory paragraphs at a quiet desk in the library at midmorning of a glorious September day. At noon I have a committee meeting to attend, followed by a faculty meeting. That in turn will be followed by a session with a student who will be working with me during the coming year. In addition, I have planned to leave my office earlier than usual this evening because I want to stop at the nursery to buy grass seed and fertilizer for my lawn. One can describe this recital as my plan for the day. It is unelaborated; it does not provide a detailed outline of my minute-to-minute activities. Even sketchier are my plans for, say, the balance of this week and, at a more remote level, plans for the academic year.

For example, in the former case, I plan to spend several mornings this week developing the chapter that you are now reading. The afternoons are to be devoted to preparations for the upcoming school year. A business trip to another city will occupy the latter days of the week. The weekend will be busy with yardwork, a long-standing social commitment, and the hope of catching up with editorial responsibilities.

At the level of the academic year which is just beginning, plans are much more general than they are for either today or this week. It is possible for me to set aside time (plan) for teaching, office hours, and writing. A limited degree of specificity is possible even now because of several constraints on the freedom of planning. Since a university must operate on a predetermined and not altogether flexible schedule or face continual chaos, the academic calendar determines beginning and ending dates for courses, tells me when and where I will be in a classroom, when examinations are to be given, and so forth. As the weeks go by, events that are now merely part of a vague long-range plan for the year will be more carefully planned as I move closer to them in time.

CONCEPTUAL ROLE OF PLANNING

A few years ago, the progressive teacher was characterized, unkindly and unfairly in many cases, as one who started each school day by asking her small charges, "What would you like to do today?" The attitude with which the remark is made is one of contempt and mild amusement. Our purpose is not to evaluate the validity of such an image of the teacher but to comment upon the expectations that are held for how teachers are to behave. The illustration conveys a belief that what children *want* to do is unlikely to be educative; also, and more importantly, that the teacher as an adult with special competencies and knowledge *ought* to know what the children are to do and to have made preparations for their doing it. Just how or what the teacher ought to do by way of planning for teaching may be open to debate and deliberation, but whether she should or should not define planning as an integral part of her role as a teacher is not debatable.

The question of definition of a plan arises. To begin the discussion let us borrow the definition developed earlier by Miller, Galanter, and Pribram (1960, p. 16). "A plan is any hierarchical process in the organism that can control the order in which a sequence of operations is to be performed." If we have a plan, then, it enables us to choose among alternative events or behavior that might occur; it helps us establish priorities for events, both with respect to the sequence in which they occur and whether or not they occur.

A plan may be little or nothing more than a shorthand signal to ourselves of what we intend to do or to have happen. In the first paragraphs of this chapter, I described my plans for the day. They might have been listed in my appointment calendar like this:

> 9:00–Write in library
> 12:00–Committee lunch
> 1:30–Faculty meeting
> 3:00–See Steve F.
> 3:30–Correspondence
> 5:00–Stop at nursery

Although the specifics of the content are obviously quite different, the plans that teachers submit are often highly similar in format, simplicity, and intention. For example, we walk into Miss Jones's fourth-grade class and find that a child has placed the following schedule on the chalkboard:

> 8:45–Music
> 9:00–Reading
> 10:00–Gym
> 10:45–Arithmetic
> 11:30–Lunch
> 12:30–Science
> 1:30–Art
> 2:30–Social Studies

That outline of a schedule (the teacher's plan) would mean very little to one unfamiliar with how teachers and classes of children tend to work together. Indeed, it would not be of great assistance to, say, a substitute teacher who is not conversant with the particular topics the class is studying, their normal operating procedures, and so forth. Clearly, the schedule meets the criteria for a plan as defined in that it controls the sequence of events, but it is equally clear that this conception of planning is inadequate for our discussion of the part that planning plays in teaching. What else must be included in our concept of planning?

Let us use a part of Miss Jones's schedule to examine the issue. Her class studies reading for an hour, beginning at nine o'clock. She has divided her twenty-nine fourth grade pupils into three reading groups, based upon estimates of their general intelligence and their reading ability. The best readers are assigned to Group I, the poorest to Group III, and those in between to Group II. Miss Jones works directly with each group for a brief period each day. The other two groups work independently with reading materials.

With her top ability group, Miss Jones is currently working upon two broad reading skills: comprehension of what is read and silent reading speed. She devotes the first twenty minutes of the reading hour to that group. From 9:00 to 9:30 A.M., the pupils read a story about King Midas presented on the reading pacer. This is a machine that projects the printed words onto a movie screen; a simple lever controls the rate at which the words are presented. After the story has been read silently, each child writes answers to a series of questions about the story. The answers are then checked, the teacher records the grades of the pupils, notes the speed at which the story was read, and assigns material for the balance of the hour that is designed for practicing comprehension in reading skills.

The kit that the school purchased to accompany the reading pacer contains sixty stories on film. For each story, there is a set of comprehension questions and a form for recording scores and reading speeds. If Miss Jones chooses to do so, she can plan a portion of each day's reading lesson for each group in turn with the simple designation, "plan *pacer*." That plan is all the preparation Miss Jones need make to insure the occurrence, in a specified sequence, of a series of events having to do with her reading group. Each morning a new filmstrip is placed in the machine, a reading speed is established, and the lesson goes forward. Activities such as those just described, which govern some portion of a day or period but which do not specify in detail the chain of behaviors to occur within the time period, are referred to as a *teaching routine*. There are many examples of teaching routines, one of which has been provided by Miss Jones's use of the pacer.

Another teaching routine is used with the social studies class in the afternoon. Miss Jones's pupils work in small committees of two, three, or four members each. The class is studying Europe in the Middle Ages, and each committee is responsible for learning about one or more specific topics. Later they will share their learning with other members of the class and, finally, typewritten reports from all the groups will be bound together into a class book. When the clock hands reach 2:30 in the afternoon, the plan calls for social studies. The teacher and pupils implement a teaching routine which places the children in collaborative work relationships and alters the teacher's role to one of consultant, materials procurer, reference librarian, and observer.

Routines in Teaching

The concept of routine in teaching is one worthy of development. Routines, in the sense in which we are using the term, are relatively brief or short segments of teaching behavior that constitute a portion of a lesson or of a transition between lessons. Routines may be linked together to form the totality or a larger part of a lesson, or they may deal with different elements of classroom behavior which, in effect, overlay one another.

For example, we may observe that Miss Jones opens the school day in her fourth grade classroom with a sequence of activities that vary little from one day to the next. The class is greeted, windows and shades are adjusted as desired, the flag is saluted, and classroom monitors perform their daily tasks of putting out chalk and erasers, writing assignments on the board, distributing paper, collecting money, and various other kinds of minor administrative chores that occupy elementary teachers and children. The point is that the activities themselves are largely routinized. Also, the particular children who participate change from day to day or week to week, but the procedure for determining who does what is already established or routinized. Thus these two kinds of routines occur in the classroom simultaneously and, in effect, define the activities of the group, including the teacher, for those ten or fifteen minutes each morning. To the extent that routines are developed and implemented, the need for the teacher to plan in detail is obviated. Moreover, to the extent that such routines are developed and implemented, the intellectual demands upon the teacher in the interactive setting for teaching would seem to be sharply reduced.

The operation of routines is probably best seen in the context of daily lessons. For example, the language arts curriculum with which our fourth-grade teacher, Miss Jones, works calls for, among other things, the introduction each week of twenty new spelling words to her class. That activity is accomplished in essentially identical fashion from one Monday to the next. Miss Jones calls off each of the new words, illustrates its meaning by using it in a sentence, and asks the children to write it on a sheet of paper, perhaps several times. As the week progresses, at the specified time each day the teacher and pupils share other routines, all designed to lead progressively to the mastery of the correct spelling of those twenty words (or at least the identification of the incorrectly spelled ones) by the end of the week. We have used the spelling lesson illustratively because it is perhaps the most easily and most completely routinized area of the school curriculum; in principle, however, what is applicable to the spelling lessons seems also applicable to other fields of study.

Texts, workbooks and laboratory manuals, films—in fact, all instructional materials—can become incorporated into teaching routines. Teachers' manuals which accompany virtually all such materials have as a chief property the inclusion of questions and answers that cover the subject matter carved out for a particular lesson, film, and so on. Hypothetically at least, the teacher, in planning her work for a given day, need only decide upon the sequence of general activities (lessons by subject matter), the content to be covered in each (typically indicated in the textbook, the teacher's manual, or related teaching aids), a strategy for content development (again, the ubiquitous text and manual come into play), and routines for classroom management, including the control of disruptive or deviant behavior.

At various points in this book we have asserted that teaching is a complex set of activities and that the teacher who is able to behave flexibly will, in the long run, be more effective in achieving educational goals. The gist of our discussion of routines in teaching is that such routines, by definition, reduce the flexibility with which the teacher behaves; at the same time, they tend to reduce the complexity of the task of teaching. We would guess, and unfortunately we do not have evidence to support the hunch, that the establishment of routines is one of the major and early skills that teachers learn in their apprenticeship and in the early weeks and months of teaching practice.

Categories of routines. Clearly, routines in teaching may be of several different sorts. There are routines that pertain to substantive, subject matter considerations. For example, the teacher may routinely conduct class by (1) assigning a block of reading in a textbook or collateral instructional material, (2) leading a discussion about the reading assignment, (3) evaluating and (4) summarizing the major points of the reading, and/or (5) discussion. Obviously, this is simply one illustrative collection of routines to cover a subject matter presentation. Teachers undoubtedly use many specific combinations of routines in the actual process of teaching.

A second type of routine concerns procedures the teacher employs for managing subject matter routines. For example, there may be routines for conducting class discussions. The teacher may choose to have very open discussions in which the limits of ideas or topics introduced and the means by which pupils participate in the discussion are broad and essentially unrestricted. On the other hand, those limits may be highly proscribed with respect both to the content admissible and the procedures for entering the verbal arena. We have, for example, observed teachers who rigidly control the entry of pupils into any classroom discussion or recitation by calling on pupils in alphabetical order, or by rows. Other teachers usually alternate between boys and girls. We do not intend to judge these routines in the present discussion; we wish simply to indicate that the variety of routines is marked, and they seem to be very much a part of the daily warp and woof of classroom life.

Teachers may also use routines to maintain classroom control or discipline. Its use in this domain is not distinctly differentiated from those uses discussed previously for, to an extent, the success of other types of routines may help to reduce the frequency or the severity of disruptive behavior of pupils. It seems only common sense that students who become psychologically involved in the prescribed, sanctioned activities of classes will create fewer overt behavior problems than students who find their classroom chores tedious, meaningless, or otherwise unproductive or unrewarding.

Textbook-teaching as a general routine. Previously we indicated that the use of routines tends to reduce the complexity of the teacher's tasks. Perhaps this can best be seen in the use of the textbook in teaching. *Textbook-teaching* refers to the common practice of many teachers to rely heavily for content and method on the textbook itself or on related kinds of instructional materials. One can easily see that the plans to be made by, say, an intermediate grade elementary teacher need not be very elaborate if each of the day's major lessons is generated by the textbook and suggestions from the teacher's manual.

Coupled with some tested routines about classroom management and control of the kind we described earlier, routinized teaching à la textbook can virtually eliminate the planning or preactive phase of teaching. The teacher's work is then accomplished totally, or almost totally, during the interactive phase, that is, during the hours of the day that the teacher and his pupils are in direct, face-to-face contact with one another.

Some consequences of textbook-teaching routines. An interesting illustration of teaching from the text as a general routine is offered by Smith and Geoffrey (1968). Geoffrey was the teacher of a sixth- and seventh-grade class in a slum school. Smith spent an autumn semester as an observer in Geoffrey's classroom trying to learn about the operations of the teacher and the children together, without altering the circumstances under which their daily educational encounters occurred. For the most part, Geoffrey was a textbook teacher, in much the tradition that we have already described.

Smith and Geoffrey point out that textbook teaching as a modus operandi reduces the planning burden for the teacher. They elaborate this by indicating that it frees the teacher's time and energy for other professional considerations, although that point is not documented. They also make the interesting observation that this method helps pupils to clarify what sequence activities will follow and what tasks they are to be engaged in. To the extent that the method does clarify expectations for pupils, it should tend to reduce their confusion and frustration, thereby lessening the teacher's problems with classroom control. However, a routine of textbook assignments may also engender disinterest or boredom on the part of the pupils, with the consequence of heightened pupil frustration resulting in greater control problems for the teacher.

We can further summarize the position taken by Smith and Geoffrey and extend it as well with the following analysis of the consequences of textbook teaching as a general routine.

First, the teacher's role becomes essentially one of a processor of information contained in the instructional materials themselves. It seems unlikely that such a role will contain opportunities for creative behavior on the part of the teacher, or result in significant innovations in traditional approaches to problems of teaching and learning. This routine can almost be characterized as offering the teacher a kind of security at a low level of conceptualization in exchange for forays into more enterprising assaults upon the teaching act. In the final section of this chapter we shall return to a discussion of routines in teaching. In that section, our effort is to make some recommendations about appropriate ways of planning for teaching. The establishment of routines can play a constructive role in the teacher's planning activities.

Second, textbook routines tend to result in day-by-day perspectives on the goals of instruction. To the extent that there are significant educational objectives that require systematic and long-range planning, one would hypothesize that the kind of day-by-day instruction that is characteristic of textbook routines would not contribute effectively to these more complex, sequentially organized educational objectives.

Smith and Geoffrey do caution against the conclusion that "a textbook is a textbook is a textbook." For example, the system in which Geoffrey taught made two social studies textbooks available to teachers at his grade level. From time to time, Geoffrey and his pupils would come to grips with the questions embedded in the texts at the close of a chapter or unit of material. The kinds of questions posed by the two books were very different from each other, not just in the historical content but also in terms of the demands that they made upon pupils to reorganize the substance of their learning. In one text, the questions emphasized simple recall of the factual material presented in the body of the lesson. The other book, however, asked questions that called upon the learners to provide explanations for various historical events.

The essential difference between the two kinds of questions can be simply illustrated. In one, the textbook authors asked questions such as, "When did the Boston Tea Party occur?" In the other, a question on the same topic would more likely be phrased as, "Why did the colonists organize the Boston Tea Party?" or "What were the American colonists communicating to the King of England through their actions at the Boston Tea Party?" Even though both kinds of questions occur in textbooks, it seems probable that the kinds of discussions they would provoke and the cognitive operations they would involve would be quite different.

Third, probably the most general characteristic of textbook teaching, and one that tends to subsume the other elements in our analysis, is that it subordinates the autonomy, initiative, and judgment of the teacher to that of the authors of the instructional materials. The basic intention of instructional materials is that they are to be used to the extent and in ways that contribute to the educational objectives held by the teacher (or as these are mutually shaped by the teacher and his pupils).

For the most part, textbooks and their accompanying manuals are written for nationwide audiences of students. They cannot be addressed to the specific needs of regions, to say nothing of locales. In addition, heavy reliance upon printed text materials is a tacit relinquishing by the teacher of his role as a manager of the learning process; it is a concession to the efficacy of whatever set of learning concepts governed the construction of the textbook. In general, we would obviously recommend a more reflective and intellectually aggressive role for the teacher in planning educative experiences for pupils than would ordinarily be built into what we have described as the textbook routine. In a later chapter we deal in a more systematic way with the role of instructional materials in the classroom learning process. We shall return to a fuller consideration at that time of some of the issues introduced in this discussion.

PLANS AND OBJECTIVES

People ordinarily make plans in order to achieve certain goals or objectives. It is reasonable to assume that if I have an objective I wish to reach, I am more likely to achieve it, or at least move toward it, if I make some kind of plan or blueprint detailing how the objective is to be reached. The roadmap constitutes an easy analogy. If I wish to go from New York to San Francisco, the time spent in working out routes, checking on the completion and driving condition of highways and the nature of the terrain en route will be well repaid in time saved on the trip. Of course, an altogether different level of decision is required if my objective is to make the trip as cheaply as possible. It makes a difference, too, whether I need transport only myself or whether my entire family is involved. Planning of the kind we have described here can be done quite accurately in terms of time and dollars. It becomes a bit more complicated if we begin to ask whether we are willing to sacrifice some speed or economy for scenery or a little added comfort now and then. Such value issues, even these simple ones, are not easily quantified nor do they always succumb easily to precise definition.

We used the illustration of the trip and the map because it points out the general usefulness of planning in working toward objectives. Unfortunately, perhaps, educational objectives are often not as clear-cut as travel destinations. In an effort to clarify the seemingly obscure nature of many educational objectives, numerous writers have, over the past generation, argued that such objectives must be stated, to the extent possible, in behavioral terms, and that these terms should apply to the behavior of the student.

Conceptually, such action will lead toward providing the teacher, in advance of teaching, with a cognitive map of what his pupils will be able to do, that is, how they will be able to behave when instruction has been successfully accomplished. This emphasis has the effect of making us aware of the vagaries of many typical teacher objectives. Wanting pupils "to learn arithmetic" is so broad and general an objective as to be practically meaningless, but it is possible to redefine the objective into a number of fairly precise and specific smaller objectives that can be stated in reasonably behavioral terms. Thus, "the child should be able to multiply an improper fraction and a mixed number" represents a highly behavioral statement of one arithmetic skill that the child is to possess. This skill does not, in itself, constitute the totality of "learning arithmetic" but must be fitted into some larger master conception of that objective. Proponents of behavioral statements of objectives argue that more vague, global statements have the built-in possibility of failing to define an area of knowledge that the learner is to master.

Opponents of behavioral objectives, of whom there are many, claim that the practice reduces education and teaching to a matter of mechanization. Teacher and child proceed from one small item of learning to another, with neither having much to say about it or being able to invest their own talent and imagination into the teaching or the learning process. Furthermore, these critics contend, there are important experiences in education that are not easily reducible to behavioral outcomes; indeed, they may even defy such analysis. Finally, there are things that teachers want to do and ought to do in educating children that do not comply with any concept of objectives at all. Thus, to insist upon such behavioral statements for all teaching acts and learning outcomes is both to miss the point of education and to diminish its stature.

Eisner (1967a; 1967b) has been critical of what he regards as an overemphasis upon behaviorally stated objectives for teaching.

> "Educational objectives should be stated in behavioral terms" has been elevated—or lowered—to almost slogan status in curriculum circles. Yet, despite these efforts, teachers seem not to take educational objectives seriously—at least as they are prescribed from above. If educational objectives were really useful tools, teachers, I submit, would use them. If they do not, perhaps it is not because there is something wrong with the teachers but because there might be something wrong with the theory (Eisner, 1967a, p. 253).

According to Eisner, there are three major limitations to the theory that educational objectives should be specified in behavioral terms. These are (1) that educational outcomes are not highly predictable, (2) that different subject matters impose their own constraints upon the statement of objectives, and (3) that there are modes of achievement that cannot be measured. We would like to examine the first of his objections—that outcomes are less predictable than some proponents assume—with particular care, for it is related to our subsequent discussion of flexibility in teaching and of incorporating objectives into the behavior of teaching itself.

> The amount, type, and quality of learning that occurs in a classroom, especially when there is interaction among students, are only in small part predictable. The changes in pace, tempo, and

goals that experienced teachers employ when necessary and appropriate for maintaining classroom organization are dynamic rather than mechanistic in character. Elementary school teachers, for example, are often sensitive to the changing interests of the children they teach, and frequently attempt to capitalize on these interests, "milking them" as it were for what is educationally valuable. The teacher uses the moment in a situation that is better described as kaleidoscopic than stable. In the very process of teaching and discussing, unexpected opportunities emerge for making a valuable point, for demonstrating an interesting idea, and for teaching a significant concept (Eisner, 1967a, p. 254).

Classroom discussion has various properties of informal conversation and, to an extent, it does ebb and flow. To what degree the teacher should hold firmly to some preconceived objective of where a lesson should go and when he should submit to, or even initiate, digressions of the kind intimated by Eisener is not an easy matter to prescribe. Certainly the teacher needs to draw upon his or her own mature professional judgment in deciding when to persevere and when to cut and move to another, potentially more profitable, point. We would agree with Eisner that educational outcomes are somewhat uncertain, particularly if they are judged solely on the basis of individual interactive teaching encounters. However, to do justice to those who recommended stating objectives in behavioral terms, it seems unlikely that they really intend that one or more specific objectives must be reached as the result of each classroom encounter.

Another important criticism of behavioral objectives is raised by Eisner (1967b). It concerns the sheer number of objectives teachers would be involved in specifying and working toward were they to try to state objectives for all of their teaching activities. Furthermore, it would introduce a change into the nature of the teacher-pupil relationship which, to Eisner at least, is distasteful.

> Now what in fact would this [such specification of objectives] mean in the classroom? If we follow the prescription strictly the teacher would have to formulate behaviorally defined objectives for each unit of content for each educational program for which she was responsible and in the elementary school she usually teaches fourteen subject areas. Let's assume that a teacher has one unit of content to be learned by a group of 30 children for each of seven subject areas per day. Let's assume further that she has her group of students divided in thirds in order to differ-

entiate content for students with differing abilities. This would mean that the teacher would have to formulate objectives for seven units of content, times five days per week, times three groups of students, times four weeks per month, times ten months per school year. She would have to have therefore 4,200 behaviorally defined objectives for a school year. A six-year school embracing such a curriculum rationale would have to have 25,200 behaviorally defined educational objectives.

Aside from the question of the sheer feasibility of such a scheme—of a teacher having for a class of 30 children 4,200 behaviorally defined objectives—what those who object to such an approach are, I think, concerned with is that even if it could be implemented it would alter the type of relationship between the teacher and the student that they value. If a teacher is focused primarily upon the attainment of clearly specified objectives she is likely to be unfocused on other aspects of the educational encounter, for although objectives when specified clearly provide windows, they also create walls (Eisner, 1967b, pp. 18–19).

Does it necessarily follow that the teacher must have a specific and different behavioral objective for each lesson that she teaches? There seems to be no inescapable reason for concluding that he must. In the same way, it does not seem to be unalterably the case that the teacher cannot concentrate upon the essentially human qualities of her interaction with children simply because she is attempting to lead them toward achieving certain subject-matter outcomes. Eisner is calling our attention to a potential trap that we want to avoid. The quest for certainty in teaching, for reducing it to a matter of checklists and production lines and units, can obviously be overindulged. Excessive concern with precise specification of each educational outcome may lead us toward broad outcomes that we do not desire. But excesses in any dimension of life usually lead us to undesirable outcomes.

Eisner's argument is more than a blunt disagreement with statements of behavioral objectives, however. He suggests that they might be better labelled "instructional objectives." Such objectives are useful in specifying the outcomes for those subject areas, or parts of subject areas, in which it is possible to indicate in advance what the outcomes are to be, such as arithmetic skills, mastery of science concepts, the achievement of a foreign-language vocabulary, and so forth. He contrasts instructional objectives with what he terms "expressive objectives"—objectives which describe the kind of experience that the learner is to have but not what the outcome is to be. For example,

> Statements of expressive objectives might read:
> 1) To interpret the meaning of *Paradise Lost,*
> 2) To examine and appraise the significance of *The Old Man and the Sea,*
> 3) To develop a three-dimensional form through the use of wire and wood,
> 4) To visit the zoo and discuss what was of interest there.
> What should be noted about such objectives is that they do not specify what the student is to be able to do after having engaged in an educational activity; rather they identify the type of encounter he is to have. From this encounter both teacher and student acquire data useful for evaluation. In this context the mode of evaluation is similar to aesthetic criticism; that is, the critic appraises a product, examines its qualities and import but does not direct the artist toward the painting of a specific type of picture. The critic's subject-matter is the work done—he does not prescribe the blueprint for its construction (Eisner, 1967b, p. 23).

Eisner goes on to say that instructional objectives are not applicable to teaching and learning situations in which one's inventive or creative talents are to come into play, inasmuch as we cannot specify in advance of the teaching encounter what will emerge from it, although we can set a direction and evaluate outcomes after they have occurred. Eisner suspects that most teachers use "expressive objectives" with much greater frequency than they do "instructional objectives." This may be so, but we lack concrete proof. More to the point, perhaps, is the observation by Eisner and others that teachers seem unimpressed with arguments about the role that instructional objectives can play in improving their teaching and in the learning of their students.

We have tried to present a balanced argument for the use of educational objectives in planning for teaching and in implementing these plans. Moreover, we have tried to state a fair case for those who propose that objectives be specified in behavioral terms and for those who are skeptical or in disagreement with such a goal. Eisner's position reflects that opposition. We suspect that the disagreements between the two seemingly independent positions are more apparent than real and stem in part from the concern of each group should the worst excesses of the other group prevail. In the chapter summary, we shall indicate the role objectives might play in the planning activities of classroom teachers. In so doing, we shall capitalize upon the central and best reasoned elements of both positions.

Critics point to the paucity of data supporting the use of instructional objectives in teaching. There is, however, one interesting study reported by McNeil (1967) in which behavioral objectives are assessed in terms of teacher effectiveness. In this study, two groups of elementary student teachers were assigned the task of teaching punctuation skills to children who were demonstrably deficient in such skills. Performance was evaluated in terms of either the method of teaching or the results of teaching, that is, the achievement scores of pupils following a period of instruction. Teachers in the first group were told, "In a major way, you will be judged by your ability to follow the course of study and use appropriately the materials authorized for your class (i.e., textbook). Specifically, we will want a description (evaluation) of *how* you taught punctuation during the period January 3–14" (McNeil, 1967, p. 70). The second group was told, "In a major way, you will be judged by your ability to get results. Specifically, we will want evidence of changes in pupil ability to use punctuation as a result of your activities during the period January 3–14" (p. 70). Findings showed that the pupils of the second group of teachers demonstrated significantly more improvement on each of the five punctuation skills identified than did the pupils of the first group.

Questionnaire information supplied by both groups of student teachers suggested that they spent the same amount of time on the punctuation lessons. In other words, whatever the impact on teaching behavior that led to differential improvement, it was not basically a matter of one group devoting large additional amounts of time to achieving the punctuation objectives. Similarly, there was no evidence of undesirable outcomes of any sort. None of the student teachers in the second group reported feeling unduly pressured. Moreover, there was some suggestion that their pupils improved more than the others not only on the specified skills of punctuation but also on some related ones.

RECOMMENDATIONS FOR PLANNING

The educational literature has relatively little to say about the effect of planning upon teaching and learning. This is most unfortunate because it might seem to suggest what almost certainly cannot be true, namely, that unplanned teaching may be as adequate for pupils as teaching based on effective planning. However, despite the absence of an established body of research evidence, we shall try by way of a summary to state some recommendations to teachers about planning for instruction.

First, at the broadest, most general level, planning for teaching is preferable to not planning. In the absence of planning, teaching can become confused, disorganized, and chaotic, resulting in negative consequences both for the learning of pupils and for their attitudes toward the teacher and school. The teacher who can consistently provide meaningful educative experiences without giving careful prior consideration to his goals and the means for achieving them is rare or, more likely, nonexistent.

Second, plans should be made not only for the subject-matter components of instruction but also for the social structure aspects of the class—the relations among pupils and between teacher and pupils. The concern expressed by Eisner, for example, about the dehumanization of teacher and pupil relationships can be largely mitigated if such relationships themselves become part of the focus of the teacher's planning.

Third, goals and plans should be made for the long range as well as the short range. Estimable educational objectives, such as developing students who think critically, are not well achieved when goal-setting and planning are done on a day-to-day basis. For a student to become an effective critical thinker, he must master numerous intellectual skills and develop special attitudes or ways of viewing events in his world. When teachers plan over the course of the school year, for example, it is possible to think developmentally about such intellectual skills and appropriate attitudes. If evaluating arguments is one of the component skills of critical thinking, then long-range planning allows teachers the opportunity over relatively long periods of time to build in activities and exercises that provide the pupil with practice in making such evaluations.

It is not easy for the teacher to see or to assess the development of such complex abilities as critical thinking from one day to the next. More systematic, extended planning for teaching also provides the chance to build in long-range means to observe the development of these complex objectives. If the planning has been done carefully, the teacher can obtain at least a rough-and-ready estimate of his pupils' intellectual growth—in their "ability to interpret data" or "to draw inferences," for instance—between, say, September and February of the school year.

Of course, when we talk about long-range planning, it should be clear that such planning is done at a very general level. If the teacher who is planning for the entire year wishes to work toward improved critical thinking on the part of his pupils, he may do little more in August or September than sketch out the kinds of skills and abilities necessary to achieve the general objective, and a notation that his teaching will be directed toward that broad goal. From week to week, and day by day, his planning will be more specific, but it will be consistent with the overall objective or set of objectives toward which he hopes to move.

Fourth, routines should be developed to carry the major burdens of planning and implementing teaching plans. Classroom teaching is, at its best, an intensely consuming activity for the teacher—physically, emotionally, and intellectually. The novice is more or less in the position of being forced to treat each new classroom event as a novel occurrence for, of course, to him it is. However, part of the benefit of experience in teaching is that the teacher learns to cope with repetitive events, thus conserving some of his energy to think and act creatively in response to new events that are truly novel, or to construct teaching situations of high quality. Routines in teaching play an extremely useful role and contribute to the effective performance of the teacher as long as the teacher retains control, that is, uses routines to accomplish specified ends rather than allowing the routine to dictate classroom activities.

Well-developed routines can be represented symbolically by simple signal or stimulus words or phrases: "reading groups," "small-group work," "teacher-pupil planning," and many others are sufficient for the experienced teacher to note by way of making plans for specific lessons or procedures to follow. Once the appropriate technique has been decided upon, the routine will unfold during the interactive phase of teaching.

Fifth, preactive teaching should take into consideration what will occur in the classroom during the interactive phase of teaching. Although this point is obviously related to the routinizing of certain approaches and procedures, there is much that goes on in teaching encounters that cannot and ought not to be institutionalized into teaching routines. (The concept of immediacy of classroom events, which we discuss in subsequent paragraphs, is as applicable to planning as it is to teachers' objectives.)

Sixth, teachers should have objectives relevant to pupil learning and to the major outcomes of their teaching efforts, and their planning should be undertaken with those objectives in mind. Not all objectives need to be generated by that teacher, although he will undoubtedly develop some that are uniquely his. Teachers can derive objectives from various sources. Notable among these are statements of the school district, or even of the individual school where the teacher is employed. However, the point we wish to make is not that the teacher has objectives of education imposed upon him about which he has no choice; ordinarily school objectives are cooperatively arrived at by the staff or at least by some representatives of that staff. Rather our point is that the teacher is not a professional curriculum worker, nor a professional developer of instructional materials, including the development of instructional objectives and means of assessing them. We would agree with Eisner's observation that teachers do not seem to take behavioral objectives seriously. However, such objectives can provide a focus and a direction for the teacher's efforts.

We have already suggested the tremendously involving nature of classroom teaching. Jackson (1968) speaks of the immediacy of classroom events and the fact that teachers pay little attention to so-called instructional objectives, and still less to tests or other formal measures of assessing pupil progress. Jackson's study was based on interviews with a group of teachers who had been identified by administrators as outstanding. We have no way of knowing precisely what referents the administrators employed in making their nominations, nor to what extent the comments of these teachers would be representative of teachers in general; nonetheless, their reactions to Jackson's questions make fascinating reading.

When events move as rapidly as they do in most schoolrooms, it is difficult for teachers to maintain the focus of those events within the area of previously specified instructional objectives. In part, this is Eisner's point in pleading for expressive objectives, objectives that set the arena for learning and inquiry but which do not attempt to specify what must emerge from it. However, Jackson makes another point about the perceptions of teachers concerning objectives and planning. His discussion revolves around the concept of professional autonomy for the teacher. Teachers in his interview sample reacted quite negatively to the idea of planning, and particularly of feeling that they must plan in advance.

The objections voiced by Jackson's teachers would undoubtedly be expressed by many other teachers as well. They might also mistakenly be construed as refutations of the general position elaborated in this chapter. We say *mistakenly* construed for several reasons. In the first place, all the teachers interviewed by Jackson were designated by their administrative officers as outstanding teachers. Few novices would be so classified, and the teachers in Jackson's sample tended to be highly experienced teachers with many years of classroom teaching behind them. We would anticipate that these teachers had long since developed effective routines for carrying much of the ordinary planning of classroom events. Second, teachers identified as "outstanding" are likely to be those whose classrooms bubble with activities and with excited and involved students. Although we cannot document the fact, it seems likely that these teachers would tend to express views antithetical to those associated with careful and systematic planning of learning experiences; in fact, however, they may be highly planful.

To avoid potential confusion it is important to separate these teachers' antipathy to control over their actions and plans from the intended consequences of planning as we are recommending. One teacher complained of having to prepare lesson plans nine weeks in advance and that these plans must be "checked through." We would agree that such demands strongly suggest that those teachers are not planning in meaningful ways for their own teaching but are simply bowing to some administrative mandates to perform irrelevant exercises.

We wished to clarify this distinction for an important reason. Certainly teachers will resent, and properly so, the need to devote important time and energy to activities solely for the satisfaction of administrative requirements that do not pertain to what the teachers are going to do in their classrooms. We would agree with the teacher who said that writing lesson plans nine weeks in advance is absurd, if by "lesson plans" she means a detailed specification of what the teacher and pupils are going to be doing on the day that the plan is to be executed. As much as we may agree with the reservations and objections expressed by this sample of teachers, we wish to sustain the distinction between what it is they reject and what it is that we recommend in this chapter. The identification of general objectives of instruction, and the gradual working through of the means for their achievement, is essentially a matter for the individual teacher, or a small group of colleagues, to determine with their own educational program and their pupils in mind.

Seventh, plans should never be so rigid or encompassing that the teacher is unable to be flexible, or feels guilty about behaving in a way that is flexible. As one of Jackson's teachers explained, when a butterfly enters the classroom, she and the children study butterflies.

We cite this instance, of course, illustratively rather than definitively. The general recommendation we make is that teachers should always be flexible enough in their attitudes and in their behavior to depart from a preconceived plan when a worthwhile educative opportunity presents itself. Those inadvertences may be less frequent than the above illustration implies. Do we always interrupt the reading class, as was reported in one instance, to sing an earlier learned song? Do we stop to study butterflies on the second intrusion? the third? Do we always digress from the arithmetic lesson to pursue a child's question?

Obviously a fair degree of mature professional judgment is required to make good decisions about these matters. Any teacher is bound to make some mistakes, not only by pursuing spontaneous episodes that turn out to be pointless, but also by unknowingly failing to pursue those that would have had value for the class. While our basic belief is that children will receive the most valuable set of educative experiences from the teacher who tends to be thoughtful in planning for teaching, we would rather see teachers chase an occasional will-o'-the-wisp than let a rare or unique learning experience go unheeded in favor of a planned activity, especially if the planned lesson can be studied at another time.

Eighth, Eisner's distinction between instructional and expressive objectives is an important one for teachers to keep in mind as they plan their teaching activities. To paraphrase John Dewey, plans should serve as a light to the teacher's eye, and a lamp to guide his feet, not as a set of inflexible prescriptions by which his every move is bound.

REFERENCES

Chapter 3

Eisner, E. W. Educational objectives: help or hindrance? *School Review*, 1967a, *75*, 250–266.

Eisner, E. W. Instructional and expressive educational objectives: their formulation and use in curriculum. Unpublished manuscript, Stanford University, 1967b. (Mimeographed)

Jackson, P. W. *Life in classrooms*. New York: Holt, Rinehart & Winston, 1968.

McNeil, J. O. Concomitants of using behavioral objectives in the assessment of teacher effectiveness. *Journal of Experimental Education*, 1967, *36*, 69–79.

Miller, G. A., Galanter, E., & Pribram, K. H. *Plans and the structure of behavior*. New York: Holt, Rinehart & Winston, 1960.

Smith, L. M., & Geoffrey, W. *Complexities of an urban classroom*. New York: Holt, Rinehart & Winston, 1968.

SECTION 2

CLASSROOM INTERACTION: THE CLASSROOM AS A SOCIAL ENVIRONMENT

CHAPTER 4

THE ROLE
OF THE TEACHER
IN CLASSROOM
INTERACTION

Classrooms are inevitably social. Although curricular tasks outline and define in broad terms the activities in which the teacher and students are to be engaged, the processes by which these activities are carried out are largely social. Teachers give directions to children about what they are to do, students and teacher become involved in discussions about planning the work for a day, or the solution to a problem. With the pupils watching, the teacher demonstrates a science principle, or he verbally imparts some body of subject matter information. The children enter into the communication patterns of the classroom in various ways—often by answering questions, but also by asking questions of their own, volunteering information, and chatting with other students or the teacher.

We have analyzed some of the major concepts of concern to teachers: teaching, learning, and planning, and the various subconcepts derived from each. We now begin to look seriously at classroom events. Even here, however, our purpose is to describe systematically and analytically a single dimension of classroom events, namely, the interaction between teachers and pupils. A central theme of this book is that teachers must understand how classrooms function if they are to operate effectively and comfortably in them, and that such understanding is a prerequisite to the design and implementation of reasoned and viable educational change. This section contributes to that purpose by dealing with three broad questions: What is the role of the teacher in classroom interaction? How do pupils participate in the interaction of the classroom, and what is the range of individual differences among them in this respect? Can these patterns of teacher-pupil interaction be altered and, if so, what are the forces that control them? Before undertaking this discussion, we need to clarify what we mean by the central concept of the section, *interaction*.

THE CONCEPT OF INTERACTION

Social scientists use the term interaction to refer to the act of communication between or among people. When people interact, a two-way process is involved. For example, in a classroom, the teacher may open a lesson by asking a question. One of the children answers it, and we say that interaction has occurred between the teacher and that child. George C. Homans, a sociologist, conceptualizes interaction in the following terms: "When we refer to the fact that some unit of activity of one man follows, or, if we like the word better, is stimulated by some unit of activity of another, aside from any question of what these units may be, then we are referring to *interaction*" (Homans, 1950, p. 36).

Interaction may be verbal or nonverbal. Although we usually think of it as a verbal process, it need not be. The loving caress a father gives his small son, and the smile he receives in exchange, are eloquent examples of what we mean by interaction, with never a word uttered. And, of course, interactions may be mixed—partly verbal, partly nonverbal. The child of whom the teacher asks the question may not have a verbal answer, but the shuffling feet and blushing face represent units of activity stimulated by the behavior of the teacher.

That the classroom is an arena in which a great amount of talking occurs is obvious. Everyone takes the mere fact of extensive verbal communication for granted, since observations of it are so much a part of the daily experience of students and teachers alike. In this chapter, however, we will attempt to state something more than this obvious fact. How verbally active are classrooms, and what is accomplished by all the talking that goes on within their walls? Furthermore, what is the role of the teacher in this busy atmosphere?

AMOUNT OF TEACHER TALK

An informal observer of classrooms could conclude very quickly that teachers talk a great deal; however, as a former student, the observer may not think to comment on this obvious fact because it is so taken for granted. Teachers, too, are aware of the preponderance of talking that they do in classrooms, if one can judge from the informal comments they sometimes make: "I talk too much," "Teachers talk all the time," etc. There has been sufficient observing and quantifying of classroom language through the years to permit us to state a fairly accurate rule of thumb about the verbal role of teachers in classrooms. According to this rule, someone is talking in classrooms about two-thirds of the time, and about two-thirds of that time it is the teacher. Thus, a rough estimate is that, on the average, the teacher will be talking almost 50 per cent of the time his classes are in session. It is not our purpose here to say whether teachers are too vocal, or whether classrooms might do well to de-emphasize talking in favor of other kinds of activities, but it is our intention to bring to the reader's attention this fundamental observation about interaction in classrooms. Although we will reserve the main discussion of student participation for the next chapter, we can note here that the verbal role of students is very much less than that of the teacher; collectively, it is only about half as large. Not only is the classroom verbally oriented, but the talking is teacher dominated.

The same general point is reflected by another set of observations about teachers' verbal behavior. If one thinks of interaction as including verbal and nonverbal contacts between teachers and students, it seems likely that during an average day a teacher may engage in somewhere between two and three thousand interactions. That is a ponderous number of interactions, particularly when we take into account the many different kinds of interactions the teacher is confronted with. They range from the virtually reflex verbal and nonverbal signals, such as the look or light touch on the shoulder which says, "Quiet, please," through assignment-making and homework-collecting routines of the day, to the ideational efforts to find ways to present a subject clearly and the clinical-professional demands of diagnosing the learning difficulty of individual children. Among the most taxing interactions teachers have to contend with are those that involve dispensations from the regular operating rules of the classroom, or that demand from the teacher seemingly simple answers but which, in fact, overlay and possibly conflict with earlier decisions, procedures, and commitments to other children. It is terribly easy to underestimate the on-the-spot information-processing demands that pupils and the exigencies of classroom life impose upon teachers.

WHAT TEACHERS TALK ABOUT

How do teachers use language to control or to direct the activities of classrooms and the behaviors of students? Teachers exert a high degree of direct influence in the classroom. By direct influence, we refer to the teacher's information-dispensing function and those having to do with giving instructions and telling pupils what, when, and how to do things in the classroom, then determining how adequately they have been done. The teacher is the judge of what tasks are to be performed, how they are to be performed, and how well they have been performed.

Throughout this discussion, we will touch on research studies of teachers' use of direct influence; however, the researchers have used different terms in talking about their work. Some studies employ *dominative behavior* or *teacher-centered behavior* to refer to behavior that conceptually is quite similar to direct influence. To make the exposition as clear and simple as possible, we shall use *direct influence* throughout in the belief that this usage will not do any harm to the presentation and discussion of the investigations being reviewed.

In the mid-forties, a series of studies was reported by Anderson and his associates (Anderson & Helen M. Brewer, 1945; Anderson & J. E. Brewer, 1945; Anderson, Brewer & Reed, 1946). These monographs dealt with the classroom behavior of kindergarten and primary-grade teachers, and they furnished us with the first systematic account of teachers' classroom behavior vis-à-vis direct influence. Several generalizations about the behavior of teachers in classroom settings emerged from this series of studies:

1. *Teachers differ widely in the extent to which their classroom behavior is direct.* As with most psychological variables, there is a broad range of individual differences. At the same time, it is conceivable that despite the observed differences, the direct-influence dimension is a relatively inconsequential one when compared with the total tapestry of classroom interaction.

2. *Teachers tend to use higher proportions of direct influence in their contacts with the total classroom than with individual pupils.* Probably management considerations of the kind introduced in the opening chapter help to inflate the directive quality of teacher interaction with the whole class. Presumably in individual conferences the teacher is freer to explore the ideas and needs of the pupil with whom he is working.

3. *The classroom behavior of teachers exhibits a high degree of stability.*
4. *The direction of influence in the classroom tends to run from teacher to pupils.* Anderson studied the behavior of two second-grade teachers in the same building. They were unlike in their treatment of children, one being highly direct, the other much less so. The pupils in the two classes were also quite different, and in ways that Anderson argued are consistent with the behavior patterns of their respective teachers.

Correlation of this sort obviously does not constitute proof of cause and effect between two sets of events. An equally acceptable argument can be made for the view that the more disruptive pupils in the one class essentially compelled the teacher to behave directively. In other words, cause and effect run from pupil behavior to teacher behavior, instead of vice versa.

The following school year it was possible for Anderson to observe the same two teachers again, working with different groups of pupils. Each of the two teachers was found to behave the second year much as she had the first. Interestingly, too, the now-third graders who had previously been in the class of the highly direct second-grade teacher no longer manifested the dominative, conflictful behavior of the year before. These findings tend to suggest the validity of our third and fourth generalizations.

Procedures to measure direct and indirect influence of teachers have been developed by several investigators, including Anderson. In the interest of brevity and clarity, we shall present only one such schedule, that developed by Flanders (1965). The reader will do well to recognize, however, that the concepts and some of the procedures for measuring classroom behavior reflected in the Flanders' interaction-analysis system owe a debt to the work of predecessors, notably Withall (1949).

Withall's analysis of the classroom verbal behavior of teachers represented in part a natural extension of the earlier studies of Anderson. Withall argued theoretically that human beings are driven toward self-actualization, and that the most effective climate for learning is one in which learning tasks are meaningful (in the sense of being perceived by the learner as relevant to his needs or as means toward the solution of his problems) and in which learning occurs in a nonthreatening situation. He assumed that social emotional climate is a group phenomenon, that the teacher is the principal agent for establishing classroom climate, and that the verbal behavior of a teacher is representative of his total classroom behavior. Withall developed a set of categories for coding the verbal statements of teachers to reflect whether the teacher was essentially supporting, accepting, and extending the ideas of students, or whether he was directing them, reprimanding their behavior, or justifying his own.

An intensive experimental study was conducted by Flanders (1951) to determine whether students felt differently about and responded differently to experimenters playing the role of teacher in either a highly direct or a highly indirect fashion. Flanders concluded from the experiment that when students are anxious, they tend to direct their efforts toward reducing their anxiety instead of confronting the academic problem that is the ostensible occasion for teacher-pupil interaction. Moreover, highly directive behavior on the part of the teacher is likely to lead to pupil behavior that is hostile, aggressive, apathetic, or withdrawn, whereas teacher behavior that is supportive of the student (that is, behavior that is acceptant, problem oriented, and evaluative) tends to elicit pupil behavior that is problem oriented and integrated, and results in reduced interpersonal anxiety.

There is an obvious relationship between Flanders' analysis of classroom interaction and the earlier work of other investigators. More recently Flanders (1965) has developed a scheme for scoring and analyzing the verbal classroom behavior of students and of teachers, concentrating more heavily upon the behavior of teachers. His basic scheme separates the behavior of teachers into seven categories which, although somewhat more elaborated, resemble the categories devised by Withall. These seven teacher categories are then classified into two segments of behavior which he identifies as *indirect influence,* and *direct influence.*

Teachers apply indirect influence when they behave in ways designed to accept, clarify, or extend the thoughts and feelings of students. Direct influence, on the other hand, is used by a teacher when he directs or otherwise controls the behavior of the student, or when he acts in ways to justify or defend his own position. Flanders uses categories 4 and 5 to record questions and lecturing (information imparting). As would be expected in actual practice, these two categories account for a great deal of teachers' classroom verbal behavior.

Flanders' system also has two categories for recording pupils' classroom verbal behavior. These categories indicate whether the pupil initiated the behavior or was directed by the teacher to participate.

The ten categories of the original system of Flanders are included in Table 4.1.

TABLE 4.1   CATEGORIES FOR INTERACTION ANALYSIS

<table>
<tr><td rowspan="7">TEACHER TALK</td><td colspan="2">INDIRECT INFLUENCE</td></tr>
<tr><td colspan="2">1. ACCEPTS FEELING: accepts and clarifies the tone of feeling of the students in an unthreatening manner. Feelings may be positive or negative. Predicting or recalling feelings are included.</td></tr>
<tr><td colspan="2">2. PRAISES OR ENCOURAGES: praises or encourages student action or behavior. Jokes that release tension, but not at the expense of another individual, nodding head or saying "um hum?" or "go on" are included.</td></tr>
<tr><td colspan="2">3. ACCEPTS OR USES IDEAS OF STUDENT: clarifying, building or developing ideas suggested by a student. As teacher brings more of his own ideas into play, shift to category 5.</td></tr>
<tr><td colspan="2">4. ASKS QUESTIONS: asking a question about content or procedure with the intent that a student answer.</td></tr>
<tr><td colspan="2">DIRECT INFLUENCE</td></tr>
<tr><td colspan="2">5. LECTURING: giving facts or opinions about content or procedure; expressing his own ideas, asking rhetorical questions.
6. GIVING DIRECTIONS: directions, commands, or orders which students are expected to comply with.
7. CRITICIZING OR JUSTIFYING AUTHORITY: statements intended to change student behavior from unacceptable to acceptable pattern; bawling someone out; stating why the teacher is doing what he is doing; extreme self-reference.</td></tr>
<tr><td rowspan="2">STUDENT TALK</td><td colspan="2">8. STUDENT TALK-RESPONSE: talk by students in response to teacher. Teacher initiates the contact or solicits student statement.</td></tr>
<tr><td colspan="2">9. STUDENT TALK-INITIATION: talk initiated by students. If "calling on" student is only to indicate who may talk next, observer must decide whether student wanted to talk.</td></tr>
<tr><td>SILENCE</td><td colspan="2">10. SILENCE OR CONFUSION: pauses, short periods of silence and periods of confusion in which communications cannot be understood by the observer.</td></tr>
</table>

Source: Flanders (1965, p. 20).

Flanders and his associates conducted field experiments in which they carefully examined the relationship between the behavior of teachers and the academic achievement of junior high school students in two curricular areas: mathematics and social studies. Two-week long instructional units were developed for each of the subject areas. Achievement tests were given to the students in a set of arithmetic and social studies classes prior to the experimental units, and again immediately after the units had been taught. The following hypotheses about teacher behavior and pupil achievement were tested in this well-known experiment.

1. Indirect teacher influence increases learning when a student's perception of the goal is confused and ambiguous.
2. Direct teacher influence increases learning when a student's perception of the goal is clear and acceptable.
3. Direct teacher influence decreases learning when a student's perception of the goal is ambiguous (Flanders, 1965, p. 16).

Hypothetically, learning will be enhanced when the teacher helps the students to clarify the goal of learning and lends his support in the endeavor of clarification. Indirect influence here implies accepting students' ideas, opinions, and emotions or feelings, and helping them to extend their ideas and become clear about purposes. In this case, the teacher is creating a classroom climate in which exploratory intellectual and emotional behavior can safely be engaged in by the student. After goals are clarified, according to the theory, teachers help to improve learning by behaving more directly, by communicating information, suggesting procedures, etc. But when goals have not yet been clarified for pupils, direct influence diminishes learning. It does so, hypothetically, by increasing the pupils' dependence upon the teacher for direction and guidance.

In the field experiments, these three hypotheses were substantiated for the teaching of both mathematics and social studies. Students that were taught by the more indirect teachers in each subject learned more from the two-week unit, as measured by gains on their achievement tests. But the positive effects of indirect teacher influence upon classroom climate and learning are associated not just with a greater frequency of indirectness by some teachers, but also with the circumstances under which the indirect teachers exercise indirectness.

An index used by Flanders to indicate the relative indirectness of a teacher is the i/d ratio. This is simply the ratio of the teacher's attempts at indirect influence in relation to his attempts at direct influence. Ratios above one indicate that the teacher is relatively more indirect than direct; ratios below one indicate the reverse. In analyzing the teachers' behavior during the two-week experimental units, classroom activities were separated into six categories (five in the case of mathematics). These categories were designated as "planning," "introducing new material," "other class discussion," "routine administration," "evaluation," and "supervision of work."

Table 4.2 indicates that indirect teachers are much more flexible in their classroom behavior than direct teachers. Whereas direct teachers have low i/d ratios throughout (with moderate exceptions

TABLE 4.2   MEDIAN I/D RATIOS IN CLASSROOM ACTIVITIES FOR ALL SOCIAL STUDIES AND MATHEMATICS TEACHERS

CATEGORIES	INDIRECT		DIRECT	
	SOCIAL STUDIES	MATH	SOCIAL STUDIES	MATH
Planning	5.14	—	1.31	—
New Material	3.25	3.64	0.23	0.72
Discussion	1.72	6.83	0.51	0.21
Work	0.84	2.24	0.03	0.15
Evaluation	0.93	2.24	0.20	0.25
Routine	0.30	0.59	0.17	0.14

Source. Flanders (1965, p. 108).

for the planning of social studies teachers and introducing new material for mathematics teachers), indirect teachers as a group are quite varied in the degree of indirectness exhibited in their behavior. These teachers are at their most indirect during activities of teacher-pupil planning, introducing new material, and class discussion; they are less indirect during work periods, evaluation sessions, and when conducting routine administrative chores. If one further accepts the argument that it is during periods of planning, introducing new material, and class discussions that goals are likely to be most obscure for pupils, the flexibility whereby the teachers become more indirect during these periods seems to be a powerful factor in improving students' achievement.

A more recent investigation of the direct and indirect influence of teachers has sought to determine whether there is a level beyond which indirectness by the teacher decreases learning, and whether the optimal level of teacher indirectness may be different for different kinds of learning tasks (school subjects). These questions were raised and investigated by Soar (1968). Using fifty-four intermediate grade classes, Soar tested the hypothesis that different levels of teacher indirectness will be optimal for pupil growth in reading, vocabulary, and creativity, and that increasingly higher levels of indirectness will be optimal for those three abilities in the order in which they are stated. Associated with that hypothesis was one that predicts that decreasing levels of teacher criticism will be optimal for the same pupil abilities, and in the same order as expressed by the first hypothesis.

The results of Soar's tests confirmed the first hypothesis, but only partially confirmed the second. Elementary classes that showed the greatest achievement gains in reading had teachers whose behavior was somewhat less indirect than the classes with optimal growth in vocabulary. Improvement in pupil creativity scores was linearly related to the indirectness of the teacher's behavior; that is, in general, the more indirect the teacher, the greater the growth of his pupils on a measure of creativity.

The results of the hypothesis concerned with teacher criticism did not fully confirm the predictions. Optimal growth in vocabulary appears to be a function of an even lower level of teacher criticism than was observed in the sample of fifty-four elementary classes. Optimal levels for reading and creativity are similar, but growth in creativity drops off sharply as teachers become more critical.

Soar is careful to observe, and we must reinforce his cautionary statement, that these findings are only suggestive of hypotheses that need to be tested with larger, independent samples. The hypotheses of his study were generated from examination of the results of test scores that had been collected for a previous investigation. The present analysis is post hoc and, to be confirmed, would require another test with a new sample of students. However, the ideas he presents can serve a purpose, if they are understood to be tentative conclusions awaiting further testing.

In summary, what can we say about the impact of indirect and direct teacher influence upon pupils? Flanders' work identified the importance of teachers' indirect behavior during periods of goal ambiguity. Once the goals of learning are clear, direct teacher behavior is more effective. Soar, on the other hand, stresses the relationships between directness-indirectness and the type of content to be learned. Thus, when content is concrete (spelling words or foreign language vocabulary, for example), the teacher does well to behave highly directly and to impose structure upon his presentation. This point is reminiscent of Grimes and Allinsmith's finding (1963) that poor achievers tended to become less anxious as more structured teaching helped them to become more academically competent.

Two observations by Soar deserve special emphasis: (1) Teachers require the ability to shift their behavior from direct to indirect, or vice versa, depending upon the immediate objectives of instruction. This recommendation is congruent with our earlier discussion of flexibility in teacher behavior. (2) The concept of permissiveness in teaching would probably be more useful if it were differentiated into two components: "warmth," which appears to be an important element in facilitating pupil learning, and "teacher control" (including direct teaching). Thus, teacher control should be direct when the content of instruction is concrete.

CONTROLLING FUNCTIONS OF TEACHERS

The extent to which the teacher's role involves him in focusing, channeling, and narrowing the range of classroom interaction can be seen from another point of view. Hughes (1959) headed a team which conducted a study of the classroom behavior of forty-one elementary teachers. Her purpose was to identify the various kinds of verbal functions that teachers perform and to try to develop what she termed "a model of good teaching" based upon ideal values of the various functions of teaching.

What is most striking about her observations in terms of our present discussion is the preponderance of controlling acts committed by teachers. By controlling functions, Hughes means the behavior by which teachers structure and regulate what will occur in the classroom. Hughes' concept of controlling functions is obviously similar to what we identified as direct influence. Teachers use controlling functions principally to tell children what it is they are to do: what questions to answer, what pages to read, what problems to solve, and so forth, as well as the sequence in which these activities are to be performed. Typically the teacher also designates the child who is to answer or perform, or the circumstances under which the entire class, or some particular fraction of it, is to carry out the assignment. The dominance of controlling acts by teachers is demonstrated by the fact that, of all the acts coded by Hughes's observers in the classrooms of the forty-one elementary teachers, slightly more than 45 per cent were controlling acts.

> The present cultural concept of the teacher's job as that of purveyor of information and checker of the facts children have acquired actively fosters classroom interaction that *places limits on the intellectual activity of children*. This is an outcome of the excessive and nondiscriminating control exercised by teachers. This control is manifest, not only in 'the what' to which children give attention and 'the who' to respond, but in the teacher's power to approve or disapprove the response of children. The teacher alone serves as judge of the correctness of the response of children. Such control is pervasive and continuous from kindergarten through the graduate school. The teacher's lesson plan and the teacher's choice of answer takes precedence over the actual intellectual exploration of the children. The teacher's plan is the one that is followed and, for the most part, no cues are picked up from the responses of the children. This fact is un-

fortunate. The responses of children disclose (for those who will hear) the information they already have and that which they are seeking; furthermore, children's responses provide continual evidence of the variety of ways their minds are working. Any appraisal of quality of the educational process must raise the question: Are the mental explorations of the children facilitated or hindered by the instructional procedures manifest in teacher interaction with children? Are the children in situations where a variety of intellectual activities are invited? (Hughes et al., 1959, pp. 95–96)

In Chapter 6 we shall consider in more detail the impact of teachers' controlling acts upon the cognitive activity of children (see pages 111–113). At this time, however, our interest is principally in demonstrating the extensiveness of such control.

In another classroom study, this one conducted among senior high school students and teachers, Bellack and associates (1966) supply additional information that supports our general portrayal of teachers as being highly direct, highly controlling in the classroom. These investigators examined a variety of language moves made by students and teachers and recorded the sequences of such moves, which they called *cycles*. (A frequently occurring cycle is one in which the teacher asks a question and the pupil answers it.) Based upon the language employed in sixty high school social studies lessons, Bellack's findings revealed that teachers initiated 85 per cent of the total number of cycles that occurred.

When we place the evidence of all these studies together in context, we are confronted with the inescapable conclusion that the teacher's role in classroom interaction is a highly dominant one. The teacher not only dominates the scene verbally but, more importantly, he also controls the verbal tasks of the students, deciding who will contribute verbally and under what circumstances, and judging what is an adequate response and what is not. Virtually all of the verbal initiation in the classroom stems from the teacher; even some that is purportedly on the initiative of students may in fact be fostered by the teacher. We would do well to reflect about the significance for teaching and for learning of this classroom role of teachers.

IMPLICATIONS OF THE TEACHER'S ROLE

Based upon observational data, and upon conceptual systems that in turn have evolved from classroom observations, it seems beyond dispute that, in general, the role of the teacher in classroom interaction is a role of controlling and of limiting pupil participation in classroom activities.

What significance can we attach to these observations about the role the teacher plays? In the first place, the role seems to be highly generalized; that is, teacher dominance is the rule in those classes sampled in the various studies we have reviewed. For whatever reasons, the role of teacher in our society is structured as a heavily dominant function. Second, there seems little likelihood that the role can be changed. Dominance is built into the fine grain of the teacher's role. Therefore, anyone considering teaching will do well to ask himself whether he can meet the expectations that others hold for the role.

A common complaint among teachers is that they have difficulty involving students in the academic activities of the class. Yet, as we have seen, it is the teacher and, unfortunately, often only the teacher who becomes deeply involved in setting goals, developing learning tasks, assessing progress, and adapting the instructional program to achieve the goals more adequately. Under these circumstances, is it really so surprising that pupils often find little in the academic program to become excited about?

Flanders' concept of direct and indirect influence on the part of the teacher leaves some question about the impact of such behavior, but it also suggests some interesting hypotheses. Apparently the teacher's ability to understand when to behave directly or indirectly is as important as his ability to shift from one kind of influence to the other. Flanders has provided good evidence that learning is enhanced when the teacher behaves indirectly during periods of planning, goal setting, and working toward the clarification of objectives. At these times the teacher should encourage questions and ideas from pupils, help them to see the implications of alternative courses of action, etc.

This strategy seems to blend well with Soar's hypothesis that indirectness in teaching is associated with improved creativity. Planning and goal setting are open, unstructured activities that require an environment in which trial behaviors can be acted out without censure or ridicule—an environment that is both supportive and, at the same time, intellectually stimulating and inviting. Apparently indirectness in teaching helps create such an environment for pupil thinking and planning, and teachers are well advised to adapt their influence accordingly.

Conversely, Flanders has suggested that once goals have been fixed, teachers' influence should become more direct. It is then that the teacher should emphasize his information-giving, content, and directive functions in order to supply the kinds of data that pupils need to achieve their academic goals. Again, Soar's hypotheses about optimal levels of indirectness and criticism help to elaborate and make more precise these formulations. Not only are there *times* when the teacher does better to behave directly than indirectly, there are also kinds of tasks or content that appear to be better learned when the teacher employs an optimal level of directness. Hypothetically, the optimal level of indirectness is lower for concrete learning tasks and higher for more abstract, unstructured tasks.

Because the teacher exercises so much power over the verbal activities of the classroom, there is always the temptation for him to believe that whatever he does or whatever he says in the classroom is right simply because it comes from him, the teacher. Bellack and his associates summarize the language roles of teacher and student in the framework of the rules for a game. One of these rules is that the teacher speaks the truth (Bellack et al., 1966, p. 247). We do not mean to imply that teachers often do not "speak the truth." We do suggest, however, that teachers must continually maintain surveillance over their own intellectual assertions to insure that their validity and accuracy are checked as throughly, and criticized as rigorously, as are the contributions of any student, or other source of information.

Our earlier contention that part of the teacher's moral obligation involves exposing his reasoning processes, his sources, and the procedures by which he reaches conclusions to examination by students can now be seen as a guarantee not only for the learner but also for the teacher. It is a vital means by which the teacher protects his intellectual integrity against the potency of his own position in the classroom.

REFERENCES

Chapter 4

Anderson, H. H., & Brewer, Helen M. Studies of teachers' classroom personalities. I. Dominative and socially integrative behavior of kindergarten teacher. *Applied Psychological Monograph,* 1945, No. 6.

Anderson, H. H., & Brewer, J. E. Studies of teachers' classroom personalities. II. Effects of teachers' dominative and integrative contacts on children's classroom behavior. *Applied Psychological Monograph,* 1946, No. 8.

Anderson, H. H., Brewer, J. E., & Reed, Mary F. Studies of teachers' classroom personalities. III. Follow-up studies of the effects of dominative and integrative contacts on children's behavior. *Applied Psychological Monograph,* 1956, No. 11.

Bellack, A. A., Kliebard, H. M., Hyman, R. T., & Smith, F. L., Jr. *The Language of the Classroom.* New York: Teachers College Press, Columbia University, 1966.

Flanders, N. A. Personal-social anxiety as a factor in experimental learning situations. *Journal of Educational Research,* 1951, *45,* 100–110.

Flanders, N. A. *Teacher influence, pupil attitudes and achievement.* Cooperative Research Monograph No. 12. Washington, D.C.: U.S. Office of Education, 1965.

Grimes, J. W., & Allinsmith, W. Compulsivity, anxiety, and school achievement. *Merrill Palmer Quarterly,* 1961, *7,* 247–271.

Homans, G. C. *The human group.* New York: Harcourt, Brace, 1950.

Hughes, Marie, et al. Development of the means for the assessment of the quality of teaching in the elementary school. Unpublished manuscript, University of Utah, 1959. (Mimeographed)

Soar, R. S. Optimum teacher-pupil interaction for pupil growth. *Educational Leadership,* 1968, *26,* 275–280.

Withall, J. The development of a technique for the measurement of social-emotional climate in classroom. *Journal of Experimental Education,* 1949, *17,* 347–362.

CHAPTER 5

THE ROLE
OF THE PUPIL
IN INTERACTION
WITH THE TEACHER

Much can be said about the participation of students in the verbal activity of the classroom. Some of this knowledge is derived from sociologic and sociopsychologic studies of small groups, which allows us to argue an analogy to classroom settings. However, a great deal of the evidence concerning student participation comes directly from observational records made in a wide range of educational settings: kindergartens, elementary and secondary classrooms, and sometimes college classes. The body of this evidence, accumulated over the years, is large enough and consistent enough for us to formulate with some confidence several generalizations relevant to pupil participation. We will follow these statements with an account of the evidence upon which each rests. The reader may evaluate for himself the extent to which the evidence cited supports the generalization, as well as the applicability of the generalization to classroom teaching.

1. Students participate unequally in the interaction of the classroom.
2. The inequality of participation varies with the size of the classroom group.
3. Structured discussions lead to less inequality than free or open discussions.

4. Frequency of participation is modestly related to students' knowledge and ability.
5. The sex of the pupil is also related to interaction between teacher and pupil.

GENERALIZATIONS ABOUT THE PUPIL'S ROLE

Several other aspects of classroom participation by students have been examined, and we shall present that evidence also, but only the five propositions listed appear to be sufficiently well established at this time to be presented as empirical generalizations.

1. Students participate unequally in the interaction of the classroom. Formality and inequality of participation are a necessary consequence of grouping together twenty-five or thirty (or more) young people and one (or several) adult leaders for purposes of conducting educational tasks. It is evident that individual members of a classroom group behave quite differently with respect to the formal verbal or non-verbal interactions in which they become involved.

This phenomenon has been cataloged repeatedly over the years by educational researchers, and it is a phenomenon that is particularly easy to observe. Nevertheless, classroom teachers appear to have great difficulty accepting the fact that inequality of participation is the rule rather than the exception in their classes (Ahlbrand, 1968).

Perhaps the first person to deal with the explicit question of individual classroom participation was Horn (1914). He found, as several subsequent investigators have also found, that inequality characterizes the participation of individuals in the verbal interaction of the classroom. Horn collected data from 229 classrooms at all educational levels from kindergarten through college, although most of the classes studied were in elementary or secondary schools. For each classroom, Horn arranged the students into quartiles based upon their frequency of interaction. The values of the various quartiles are shown in Table 5.1. In describing the average performance of classes, Horn summarized his finding this way: "The first quartile does about four times as much reciting as does the fourth quartile" (Horn, 1914, p. 18).

When data about classroom participation are analyzed by slightly different criteria, the discrepancy between frequent and infrequent participators is even greater than Horn suggested. Jersild, Goldman, Jersild, and Loftus (1941) reported the results of an innovative pro-

TABLE 5.1 INEQUALITY OF CLASSROOM PARTICIPATION

VERBAL PARTICIPATION OF PUPILS IN CLASSROOM DISCUSSIONS (N = 229 classes)	FREQUENCY OF PARTICIPATION (%)
1st quartile	40
2nd quartile	28
3rd quartile	20
4th quartile	12

Source: Horn (1914, p. 33).

gram undertaken in several elementary schools in New York City during the late 1930s. This program was known as the "activity school" experiment, and was conducted during the years when progressive education flourished. New York City selected certain elementary schools for the sanctioned introduction of the "newer" school practices, one of the major purposes of which was to involve children more directly in goal-setting and educational planning. The school system wished to be able to tell what differences, if any, were resulting from their innovations. Consequently, research studies were conducted in a selected set of four activity schools and four control schools. Eight classes from the activity schools were compared with an equal number of control classes. The paper by Jersild and his colleagues is one in an extensive and fascinating set of careful reports upon this project.

Jersild's records discriminate between recitational contributions, which are directly under the control of the teacher, and self-initiated communications by pupils. This subdivision adds some interesting and useful information to our discussion. The contribution to discussion made by the most frequent participator must now be differentiated in terms of recitation and self-initiated behavior, and the values are considerably different.

For the sample of classes in Jersild's report, the median per cent of the total comments made by the most frequently interacting pupil is 9 per cent for recitations and 16.5 per cent for self-initiated comments. When the categories are combined, we find that of all the classroom talking done by the pupils, just over 10 per cent of it is done by the most talkative pupil in the class. The top three participators account for approximately one-fourth of all comments.

Like Horn, Jersild, too, has a summary statement about the verbally most productive quarter of the class. "It . . . appears that approximately one-fourth of the children in the various classes did approximately two-thirds of the talking. It is rather interesting to note that a commodity so abundant as hot air should be monopolized so much" (Jersild et al., 1941, p. 131).

Jersild also reports that the most frequent participator interacts as much, on the average, as the six to eight least frequent participators. This figure is quite different, however, when only pupil-initiated interactions are considered—a point to be discussed in connection with our third generalization.

The generality of the inequality phenomenon is great. Hare (1962) has found it in small groups. It appears also in recent educational studies (Ahlbrand, 1968; Hudgins & Ahlbrand, 1967; Jackson & Lahaderne, 1967). The obtained results do not seem to be simply a function of the particular samples discussed. There is sufficient variation in time, research methods, educational levels of pupils, etc. to discount such specificity. Furthermore, mathematical predictions of the percentage of verbal participation that individuals (other than formal leaders) will produce, given their rank in the group, closely approximate the observed distribution of communicative acts (Stephan & Mishler, 1952).

2. Inequality in participation varies with the size of the classroom group. Several kinds of changes in participation occur as the size of the group increases. Most notable is the fact that the gap between the member who talks the most and the next most frequent speaker expands.

At least one observational study has been made in an educational setting that demonstrates the applicability of the size-participation relationship. Dawe (1934) observed kindergarten groups that ranged in size from fourteen to forty-six pupils (although not every size in between these limits was included). She found that, with an increase in size, the mean number of contributions per child diminished, a smaller number of children made comments, and the total amount of discussion was lessened.

Although we have no very good explanation for the phenomenon, what apparently happens is that as the size of the group increases, members become more inhibited about expressing their views publicly. Boy Scouts who participated in an experiment by Hare (1952) reported that, when in large groups (twelve members), they felt that their individual opinions did not count for much, and they were consequently reluctant to communicate them.

Carter, Haythorn, Shriver, and Lanzetta (1951) studied contributions of members in groups of four and eight. In the smaller groups, each person had time and opportunity to express his ideas and to demonstrate his ability. When groups of eight participants were observed (under the same time limit), only those who were most aggressive were able to make such expressions and demonstrations.

The crucial effects of group size seem to occur when the group expands from three or five members to eight or more. It is difficult to identify a precise number at which qualitative changes in participation occur. However, it must certainly be true that for virtually all classroom groups as they are today constituted, the differences between different sized groups are relatively inconsequential compared with differences between much smaller groups (of three or four members) and typical class groups.

3. Structured discussions lead to less inequality than free or open discussions. It is difficult to judge the extent to which the data used to support our first two generalizations were collected from groups engaged in free, as opposed to structured, discussions, as we are using the terms. By a *free* or *open* discussion, we simply mean one in which no designated leader or moderator deliberately attempts to control entry into the conversation. Of course, so-called leaderless groups can use devices for controlling access of individual members, but the discussion would still be free in our sense.

The study by Dawe (1934) involved kindergartens in which the teachers presumably were in a position to control communication, whether or not they did so. Groups in Hare's (1952) study were led by other Boy Scouts, who may also have exercised control over participation.

Jersild et al. (1941), in particular, examined the consequences of free versus controlled discussions. One of the purposes of the activity program launched in New York City, and studied by Jersild and his associates, was, in fact, to free pupil problem-solving and thinking from teacher domination. The comparative data reported by Jersild speak unequivocally to the consequences. Under conditions of recitation—that is, when the teacher is asking questions and probably exerting maximum control over the participation of pupils—the most vocal student does 9 per cent of the talking done by all students. When only contributions initiated by the students are considered, this same top participator accounts for 16.5 per cent of all student contributions.

The three pupils who contribute most, on the average, collectively do between one-fifth and one-fourth of all student talking during *recitations,* and make two-fifths of the *self-initiated* comments. Looked at from still another point of view, the top participator *recites* as often as the six least verbal of his classmates; he *initiates* as often, on the average, as thirteen to sixteen of his peers.

4. Frequency of participation is modestly related to students' knowledge and ability. A commonsense approach to the issue of pupil participation would suggest that those students who tend to dominate the discussion are also likely to be the class members who have the most to say substantively, that is, those who possess the best store of knowledge and who are generally the most intellectually able. The evidence tends to support this commonsense hypothesis, but only to a limited degree.

Typically a low but positive relationship exists between such variables as rank in participation and judged knowledge of subject matter, for example. The relationship is low enough, however, to mean that we will find high participators who are average or below average in ability and able members who are low participators. In other words, one's intellectual and knowledge capacity are not sufficient to predict relative vocal contributions to the group. Strangely, little systematic knowledge seems to have been developed about the personality characteristics or traits that would improve the prediction.

Jersild et al. (1941) examined the relationship between participation and a host of academic and personality variables. In general, Jersild's high-participating students tended to be slightly superior to the others in the areas of knowledge, academic achievement, and social adjustment. In that particular sample of classes, the relationship between participation and knowledge of current events appeared to be about the most consistent finding. As with any correlation, the question of causal linkage remains open. Do students who seek out knowledge about what is going on in the world then tend to find opportunities to communicate it? Do students who are verbally dominant discover that such information is natural grist for their oral mills? Or is there some alternative explanation that better accounts for both phenomena? For example, children (and adults) with high levels of energy may be more likely than others to read (or watch) and to talk. Of course, this is clearly speculative.

Horn's (1914) study of classroom participation introduced some interesting data on this issue. At the time of the study, intelligence tests were not yet much in use, but Horn asked the 229 teachers in his study to rank their students according to ability in general, and according to special subject matter ability. He then arrayed the students for each grade (one through twelve) into quartiles according to the rank assigned by their teachers, and compared across quartiles the percentage of talking done by the various pupils. The rankings do not vary greatly across the twelve grades. In general, pupils who were judged to be in the top quartile in general ability did about 30 per cent of all student talking. Students in each of the lower three quartiles contributed somewhat less verbally in class than did those in the quartile immediately above. Pupils in the quartile judged lowest in ability made about 20 per cent of the total contributions.

Horn also arranged his data according to the kind of subject matter or content under discussion. This arrangement yielded a rough scaling of subjects ranging from those that are most concrete, and for which the most structured recitational procedures have been developed, to those that are most demanding of "appreciation" or "problematic organization" by the student [Horn's terms]. It is interesting to note that the frequency of participation by the students in the top quartile, as compared to the bottom, increases markedly as the abstractness of the subject matter increases.

5. The sex of the pupil is also related to interaction between teacher and pupil. The relationship between teachers and boys and girls has been examined frequently. Most recently Jackson and Lahaderne (1967) have shown intermediate-grade boys to be more frequent interactors with the teacher than are the girls. At least part of this superiority is accounted for by the more frequent disciplinary encounters of the boys. Some years ago DeGroat and Thompson (1949) found that sixth-grade pupils who are perceived by their classmates as being frequent recipients of teacher praise and infrequent recipients of disapproval tend to earn better scores on academic achievement and personality adjustment tests than do students for whom the reverse set of conditions is true.

Meyer and Thompson (1956) made extensive observations in three sixth-grade classrooms of the frequencies with which pupils received either approval or disapproval from their teacher. They also asked the pupils to name their classmates who received approval and disapproval from the teacher. This observational data and the estimates by pupils agreed on one major point: boys receive more disapproval from their teachers than do girls. But little sex difference was visible with regard to the teacher's distribution of approval. Although the pupils tended to report that girls receive more praise from teachers, the observations did not support their belief. In fact, there was a mild tendency for boys to be the more frequent recipients of praise.

The relative occurrence of teacher approval and disapproval has been found to differ from one study to the next, perhaps because of differences among investigators concerning what kinds of behaviors to code. As we pointed out previously, the teacher's use and distribution of praise appear to be more crucial in their effect than simply the amount of praise he administers.

It frequently has been observed that classrooms are relatively affect free. People interact in essentially emotionless terms. One of the rules of the classroom game devised by Bellack et al. (1966) is that students do not (vocally) evaluate the performance of the teacher. Evaluation of this sort is a one-way process, conducted by the teacher with regard to the child. Nonetheless, evaluation is one of the less frequently occurring classroom behaviors.

From observations of small business-conference groups, Bales (1951) has concluded that members are at least twice as likely to respond positively rather than negatively to the previous contribution of another member.

The comments by Jersild et al. (1941) about teachers' positive and negative responses to pupil behavior seem to summarize aptly the status of the issue. Their first comparison is between activity classes and the conventional or control classes. In both situations, pupils received more negative and less positive feedback from both classmates and teachers. For the activity classes, these ratios were approximately five to one and, for the control classes, about three to one. Jersild and his group feel that part of the explanation for the high ratio of negative to positive comments by teachers lies in the large class sizes. Similarly, activity classes are more freewheeling than their control counterparts, which accounts for the teachers' need to bring students to account more frequently.

> The fact that there is a preponderance of negative over positive responses from the teachers in both groups of schools is of passing interest in view of findings by Thorndike and others, that indicate that rewards tend to be more effective than punishment as incentives to learning. It is possible that efforts by the teachers to use a higher proportion of positive remarks would have a salutary effect. It may be pointed out, however, that the 'rewards' received by the pupils are not limited to words of praise or commendation such as those here classified as 'positive' responses. In a great many instances, the pupils undoubtedly receive the equivalent of a reward through the experience of success that they have when they answer correctly or contribute effectively to group work or class discussions, even though they

win no tangible rewards or expressions of praise. In some instances, no doubt, the very fact that a teacher accepts a pupil's contribution without comment or criticism may, in effect, represent a form of commendation. If effects of this sort, together with subtle forms of commendation that a teacher might communicate by means of facial expressions or other signs could have been taken into account, it is quite possible that the ratio of 'positive' to 'negative' items, as here reported, would be considerably changed (Jersild et al., 1941, p. 126).

TEACHER INFLUENCE ON STUDENT INTERACTION

A latter-day interpretation of the evaluative aspects of classroom interaction has been made by Jackson (1968). He views the child's world in the classroom as one laden with evaluations, the source of which (as in Jersild et al.) are teachers, peers, and the substance of the problems and activities upon which the child is working.

A legitimate question to ask at this point is, To what degree are teachers aware of the existence of the patterns of pupil interaction that we have just described? There is little clear-cut evidence. One would guess that a wide range of individual differences is to be found among teachers with respect both to the operation of classroom participation and to their concern for maintaining or changing it in some predetermined way.

Withall (1956) studied the interactions of an eighth grade art teacher with a class composed of twenty-six students. Over a period of several lessons, Withall kept records of the frequency with which the teacher interacted with each pupil individually. He found that, on the average, the teacher interacted with each pupil about sixteen times an hour. As we would expect, the differences in rates among the individual pupils were enormous, ranging from a low of about two interactions an hour for one pupil to a high of almost sixty-three interactions each class hour for another student.

The teacher's beliefs about teaching included a respect for the worth and dignity of each child in his charge and a genuine desire to treat children equally. He was unaware of the inequalities occurring in his contacts with students and agreed with Withall to attempt to equalize those contacts in a series of "controlled" sessions. The results of those subsequent class sessions showed that the teacher did succeed in interacting more frequently with several of the eight students whom he had identified for additional attention; however, the two students with whom the teacher had interacted most frequently continued to account for large proportions of the interactions in the controlled sessions. One of the most striking results of this teacher's efforts to achieve greater equality of contact with all students is that his rate of interacting skyrocketed from an average of about sixteen interactions per hour with each student to about twenty-six inter- actions per hour, an increase of slightly more than 50 per cent.

This simple study by Withall is not definitive, but it does suggest that teachers are probably quite oblivious to how their attention is distributed among pupils, and that even deliberate efforts to change that distribution may be less than successful. The following quotation from Withall's paper summarizes the situation as he reported it.

> It appears that we may not readily assume that even a teacher who displays a high degree of social sensitivity and who develops considerable rapport with his pupils will distribute his attention in the way which he and others on the basis of objective evidence and assessment of each pupil's needs would deem desirable and necessary. Likewise, it seems that once the teacher has been apprised of the imbalance of the distribution of his time and efforts among his charges, it is no simple task to redistribute his attention. Nonetheless, it appears likely that through the use of small, cohesive, working groups of learners who encompass among them the scholastic and social skills required for enhanc- ing both group and individual productivity, a teacher may make considerable improvement in the direction of becoming more accessible to all his charges and hence a more effective facilitator of pupil learning (Withall, 1956, p. 212).

IMPLICATIONS OF PUPILS' ROLES IN CLASSROOM INTERACTION

The most salient fact about the roles that pupils play in classroom interaction is that they are very unequal. Inequality, as we have used it in this chapter, can be conceived of as simple arithmetical inequal- ity; that is, one person speaks more frequently than another. There is no question about the goodness or badness, rightness or wrongness, of these processes. They can be regarded as simply representing the way in which people behave when certain conditions of space, time, tasks, and power are introduced into their lives. Many teachers, obvi- ously, do regard these conditions as containing value elements, and they do wish to try to alter them. Our final concern, then, is to specify the conditions under which the teacher may wish to intervene in predetermined ways, or for predetermined purposes.

1. Simple justice. The first and most obvious reason we might cite for wishing to alter the typical pattern of classroom communication is fairness. At first blush the great disparity among students in the frequency of their verbal participation in class seems to work an injustice upon some members of the class. That is, they are prohibited from their "fair share" of one dimension of classroom activities by the vocal aggressiveness of one, two, or perhaps three other members. Yet, when we reflect about it, there really seems little basis for objecting to the inequalities that we find unless they are more substantial than simply observed differences in frequency of contact between teacher and child. The simple justice notion, as we have introduced it, implies that equality of numerical contact is the value to be striven for. But is it? As long as each student achieves sufficient contact with his teacher to meet his intellectual and social needs, identical frequency of contact is probably irrelevant.

2. Individual differences in pupils' needs. Children vary widely on such personality dimensions as social ascendancy, aggressiveness, and energy level. It seems likely that children are quite different from each other in terms of how extensively they need to be involved in the verbal workings of the classroom group. Withall's study of the art class demonstrated dramatically that the two highest participators were socially active and highly socially skilled children. At one level, certainly, it can be argued that frequent interaction with the teacher was helping to meet the needs of these students. If interaction with one child tends to interfere with the teacher's ability to meet the intellectual or social needs of other members of the group (as was apparently the case in the Withall example), then we seem to have a firmer basis for recommending that the teacher intervene in ways to alter the interaction patterns.

3. Consequences for the academic learning of individual pupils. There is no good evidence to show that students learn less in school because of any failure to participate verbally in the classroom, but the question is an open one. There is at least one experiment which has tried to answer the question.

Van Wagenen & Travers (1963) undertook to teach a series of German words to groups of intermediate-grade children. In each "classroom group" of eight children, only four were repeatedly called upon to answer teachers' questions. The other four children in each group were systematically excluded from verbal participation. The groups met for one period on each of three consecutive school days, learning a different list of twenty German nouns each day. On Friday of that week, they were given a test over the entire list of sixty words. Children who did participate verbally scored an average of 54 per cent on those words about which they had interacted with the teacher. Children who were never directly involved in interaction received average scores of 44.3 per cent on the entire list. As the writers explain, however, the experiment apparently became extremely dull for the nonparticipators, who lost interest and may have paid relatively little attention on the later days of training.

Although the experiment is highly interesting and provides us with some data about this issue, we are left without a satisfactory answer to the basic question: Do children who participate less, learn less? It would seem that the answer is yes, if the teacher systematically precludes the possibility of a child's participating directly and verbally in the classroom. There are, obviously, other factors that can retain a child's interest in what is occurring intellectually in the classroom.

4. Group problem-solving and decision-making. We come now for the first time to a point which may argue for intervention by the teacher in the "natural" phenomenon of student interaction. It was indicated earlier that the correlation between amount of student participation and intellectual ability is positive, but modest, in magnitude. When a decision is to be reached to which all members of the class are to be bound, or a conclusion achieved that is to represent the thinking of the total group, there is reason to believe that those decisions or solutions will turn out, on the average, to be superior when steps are taken to insure that minority or deviant points of view are given a full hearing. We would extend this principle to include the voices of seldom-heard group members.

Indirect behavior on the part of the teacher seems to be particularly important in this connection. It is the willingness of the teacher to listen to, support, try to comprehend, interpret, and perhaps extend the thinking of students that leads to the development of better group decisions or goal statements. Also, the supportive behavior of the teacher would seem to be of especial significance with regard to the interactive contributions of infrequent participators. Asch (1960), for example, has shown how the recognition of a single ally, who might well be the teacher, helps a minority member to defend his position. Similarly, Maier and Solem (1952) reported a series of small-group experiments in which the correct solution to a problem was achieved more frequently when the group leader provided a supportive climate for minority views to be expressed and explained.

5. Development of social skills of individual children. This final point deserves some reflection. Any list of educational objectives will include attention to the development of social and communications skills of students. To achieve these skills requires participation by students in the verbal activities of small groups and of the total classroom group. Thus, limiting the domination of the classroom by either the teacher or a small group of vocal students becomes a relevant issue if such domination threatens to interfere with the opportunity of other children to develop those appropriate skills which demand practice in interaction with others. This point also raises the question of whether the teacher can legitimately excuse from such practice in participation the child who, by temperament or lack of skill, prefers not to participate.

Without being judgmental, we have tried deliberately to raise certain questions for the teacher which must be answered in terms of his own strategy for the conduct of classroom interaction and his own sense of values. The empirical data currently available is not, in most cases, sufficiently complete to compel one answer as opposed to another. That the teacher will, from time to time, feel constrained to use his power to intervene in the "free" interaction of the classroom seems assured, but at what times and over what issues remains very much a matter to be resolved by individual teachers.

REFERENCES

Chapter 5

Ahlbrand, W. P., Jr. Correlates of pupil participation during classroom questioning in selected fourth, fifth, and sixth grade social studies classes. Unpublished doctoral dissertation, Washington University, 1968.

Asch, S. E. Effects of group pressure upon the modification and distortion of judgments. In D. Cartwright & A. Zander, *Group dynamics research and theory*. (2nd ed.) Evanston, Ill.: Row Peterson, 1960. Pp. 189–200.

Bales, R. F. How people interact in conferences. In Alfred G. Smith (Ed.), *Communication and Culture*. New York: Holt, Rinehart & Winston, 1966. Pp. 94–102.

Bellack, A. A., Kliebard, H. M., Hyman, R. T., & Smith, F. L., Jr. *The language of the classroom*. New York: Teachers College Press, Columbia University, 1966.

Carter, L. F., Haythorn, W., Shriver, E., & Lanzetta, J. The behavior of leaders and other group members. *Journal of Abnormal Social Psychology*, 1951, *46*, 589–595.

Dawe, Helen C., The influence of size of kindergarten group upon performance. *Child Development*, 1934, *5*, 295–303.

DeGroat, A. F., & Thompson, G. G. A study of the distribution of teacher approval and disapproval among sixth grade pupils. *Journal of Experimental Education*, 1949, *18*, 57–75.

Hare, A. P. A study of interaction and consensus in different sized groups. *American Sociological Review*, 1952, *17*, 261–267.

Horn, E. Distribution of opportunity for participation among the various pupils in classroom recitations. *Teachers College Contributions to Education*, 1914, No. 67.

Hudgins, B. B., & Ahlbrand, W. P., Jr. *A Study of classroom interaction and thinking.* Technical Report Series No. 8. St. Ann, Mo.: Central Midwestern Regional Educational Laboratory, 1967.

Jackson, P. W. *Life in classrooms.* New York: Holt, Rinehart & Winston, 1968.

Jackson, P. W., & Lahaderne, Henriette. Scholastic success and attitude toward school in a population of sixth graders. *Journal of Educational Psychology,* 1967, *58,* 15–18.

Jersild, A. T., Goldman, B., Jersild, Catherine L., & Loftus, J. J. Studies of elementary school classes in action. II. Pupil participation and aspects of pupil-teacher relationships. *Journal of Experimental Education,* 1941, *10,* 119–137.

Maier, N. R., & Solem, A. R. The contribution of a discussion leader to the quality of group thinking: the effective use of minority opinions. *Human Relations,* 1952, *5,* 277–288.

Meyer, W. J., & Thompson, G. G. Sex differences in the distribution of teacher approval and disapproval among sixth grade children. *Journal of Educational Psychology,* 1956, *47,* 385–396.

Stephan, F. F., & Mishler, E. G. The distribution of participation in small groups: an exponential approximation. *American Sociological Review,* 1952, *17,* 598–608.

Van Wagenen, R. K., & Travers, R. M. W. Learning under conditions of direct and vicarious reinforcement. *Journal of Educational Psychology,* 1963, *54,* 356–362.

Withall, J. An objective measurement of a teacher's classroom interaction. *Journal of Educational Psychology,* 1956, *47,* 203–212.

SECTION 3

CLASSROOM INTERACTION: THE CLASSROOM AS AN ENVIRONMENT FOR PRODUCTIVE THINKING

CHAPTER 6

COGNITIVE CHARACTERISTICS OF TEACHER-PUPIL INTERACTION

We have seen that the teacher's role is the dominant one in the classroom. In the present chapter, we shall continue to discuss the teacher's classroom functions, but we are now less concerned with social domination and more interested in what we shall call the cognitive characteristics of classroom interaction between pupils and teachers. By *cognitive characteristics* we refer to the content of communications that occur in interactive teaching. Our fundamental purpose in this chapter is to review and summarize the data that has been developed from systematic studies of ongoing classes. To the extent that the data are available, we shall attempt to answer such questions as (1) How is classroom discourse distributed between substantive issues and other topics necessary to the maintenance or control of the classroom? (2) What functions are performed by teachers and by students in developing classroom discourse? (3) How can the level of intellectual demand of classroom discourse be summarized?

We should point out that the studies upon which this discussion is based are of limited generality and that the inferences we have drawn go well beyond the limits of the available data. We feel, however, that tentative answers to these questions are preferable to ignoring the important topic of the cognitive characteristics of classroom discourse.

AMOUNT OF SUBSTANTIVE DISCOURSE IN CLASSROOMS

According to the available data, classrooms are highly content oriented. At least two independent studies have differentiated between management and substantive elements in classroom discourse, and their findings have been remarkably similar. Smith and Meux (1962), who analyzed the logical behavior of teachers and secondary school students, report that 9.4 per cent of the discourse in the classrooms they studied was devoted to management considerations. Hudgins and Ahlbrand (1967) found that 12.4 per cent of all pupil communications in a sample of nine junior high school classes was attributable to either management or disciplinary matters.

If we take appropriate note of the limited samples involved, it seems reasonable to conclude tentatively that approximately 90 per cent of classroom discourse is given to substantive issues and only about 10 per cent to matters of classroom management, including discipline and control. We would suppose that in elementary schools a larger proportion of classroom language would be required to handle management considerations, but we have no basis for suggesting how much larger the percentage would be. Regardless of whether the percentage distribution we have specified is or is not reliable, the conclusion seems inescapable that classrooms are not only highly verbal, but the verbalizations are predominantly statements about the subject matter of the curriculum.

FUNCTIONS OF TEACHERS AND PUPILS IN COGNITIVE DISCOURSE

To put the basic elements as simply as possible, the chief verbal business of the teacher in the classroom is to ask questions, and the major responsibility of the pupil is to answer them. Sometimes, not always, the teacher follows a student's response with an evaluative or judgmental reaction. Bellack, Kliebard, Hyman, and Smith (1966) produced sixty typescripts based upon four lessons in each of fifteen high school social studies classes. Their intention was to study the language behavior of teachers and students, principally to make definitive statements about who speaks in the classroom under what circumstances, what they talk about and to whom. From these detailed analyses of the sixty lessons, Bellack and his associates developed a set of rules for the classroom language game, which we have paraphrased as follows:

1. The game is played with words.
2. The object is to carry on a discourse about subject matter.
3. Any number up to thirty or more can play.
4. There are only two roles: a single teacher and many pupils.
5. The teacher plays (speaks) more than all the other players combined.
6. The teacher establishes whatever modifications of the rules occur.
7. The teacher establishes the direction and duration of phases of the game.
8. The teacher controls the extent to which pupils play.
9. The teacher uses several kinds of moves to carry on his part of the game.
10. The pupil has one basic move with which to play his part.

Overall, without the teacher, the game cannot be played. If for some reason the teacher cannot attend school, another teacher must be obtained. But who ever heard of a substitute pupil?

Let us now consider in more detail how the classroom game proceeds. The gamelike quality of the classroom ought not to be carried too far. For most games there is a winner and a loser. The analogy to teaching breaks down at this point, since concepts of winning and losing are not totally appropriate to describe what happens in classrooms, principally because the final outcomes for both teacher and students must be congruent.

Moves

In the language game, a *move* is a basic unit of discourse in the classroom. Bellack's group has identified four types of moves, depending upon whether the discourse involves *structuring, soliciting, responding,* or *reacting.*

Structuring moves serve the purpose of setting the context for subsequent behavior—sometimes for the entire lesson, usually for only a portion of it. Structuring moves are extremely important inasmuch as they set the direction in which the verbal behavior of the group is going to travel. Structuring moves are not questions; they do not call for answers; but they do represent what the speaker believes should be said or taught at any given time. As we shall see, structuring is a move that is almost exclusively in the teacher's domain, except as she assigns it to students. Structuring accounts for 7.7 per cent of the moves made by the teachers. These moves are used by teachers to exercise great influence over the events of the classroom. The following examples of structuring moves are cited by Bellack et al. (1966, p. 17):

> *T/STR:*[1] Last night I was sitting out on the porch trying to cool off and also trying to ask myself how to best begin this unit on international economics, international trade, world trade, or whatever else one wants to call it. And after thinking over a number of approaches, I wrote down on paper a number of items that are connected with our story; some of them are within your experience. Some of them are found in your pamphlet.
>
> *T/STR:* Well, tomorrow, we'll continue to talk about the problem of investments. I'd like to show you tomorrow another slide through the projector so that you can perhaps understand this more fully. Also tomorrow we'll move into the realm of some of the problems that people face when trying to engage in trade abroad.
>
> *T/STR:* All right, getting down to it now. I think international trade, then, or international economic relations, whatever you want to call it, is a field of study within economics which in many cases has been unfortunately divorced from or too far divorced from domestic trade because there are great similarities, and also there are some rather distinct differences.

We noted previously that when students do engage in structuring, it is characteristically at the invitation or even the directive of the teacher. An illustration of such a case is seen in the next example. (The appended A indicates the "assigned" nature of the structuring move.) Only 1.8 per cent of the moves pupils made were structuring moves.

> *P/STR-A:* Well, I was asking my father on, well, he imports watches—that's his business. I wasn't able to interview him, but there was one thing I found out from—you know—when he just started importing. When you import watches from Switzerland, you have to have a code of letters you get from the Swiss government so that you can show that these watches aren't smuggled, and I thought that this was a very interesting thing,

---

[1] This format is used to identify the speaker: T = teacher, P = pupil; and the type of move: STR = structuring, SOL = soliciting, RES = responding, REA = reacting.

and that way the American buyer can check also as they're brought over, these are not smuggled watches, or that, that they're not fake watches (Bellack et al., 1966, pp. 17–18).

Soliciting moves occurred in the fifteen classes with great frequency, and they are the teacher's chief stock in trade so far as the conduct of the lesson is concerned (46.6 per cent of all teacher moves were solicitations). As with structuring, soliciting tends to be initiated by the teacher, not the student. Solicitations may take a variety of forms, though the interrogative is the most characteristic. Classroom solicitations call for an active response from the person addressed, usually a cognitive one, although it may call for a physical response, as we see in these examples from Bellack et al. (1966, p. 18):

T/SOL: What are the factors of production?
P/SOL: May we keep our books open?
T/SOL: Turn the lights out, Bobby!
T/SOL: Pay attention to this!

Questions demand answers, and the answers in classroom interaction are designated as responding moves by Bellack's group. Responding moves occur in relation to soliciting moves. In this sense, a response is always elicited by a solicitation. Bellack et al. (1966, p. 18) cited the following exchanges:

T/SOL: What are the factors of production?
P/RES: Land, labor, and capital.

T/SOL: Why didn't you do the assignment?
P/RES: I was absent yesterday.

T/SOL: What is exchange control?
P/RES: I don't know.

Responding is the principal verbal implement of the student. His chief verbal job in the classroom is to answer the teacher's questions. This can be seen from the fact that 65.4 per cent of all pupil moves were responses.

Reacting moves can occur after any of the other types, but they are most likely to follow responding moves. Again, it is typically the teacher who reacts, since this move involves modifying or evaluating what has just been said. Of the moves made by teachers, 39.2 per cent were reacting moves. Conversely, pupils devoted only 1.8 per cent of their moves to reacting. One student may occasionally do this vis-à-vis another, but seldom if ever would a student legitimately react to a teacher's behavior.

> *T/REA:* All right.
> *T/REA:* That's partly it.
> *P/REA:* But he left out the most important part.
> *T/REA:* Good. It limits specifically the number of items of one type or another which can come into the country. For example, we might decide that no more than one thousand of German automobiles will be imported in any one calendar year. This is a specific quota which the government checks (Bellack et al., 1966, p. 19).

Cycles

When the four kinds of classroom language moves occur together in repeated cyclical patterns, such patterns are designated as *cycles* by Bellack's group. A cycle begins either with a structuring move or with a soliciting move that is not preceded immediately by a structuring move. There is no natural ending point for a cycle; it is defined simply as the last move prior to the one that opens a new cycle. Twenty-one different cycles are possible, but far fewer actually occur with much frequency. Two very simple cycles occur most often.

The most frequently occurring cycle begins with a solicitation or question, is followed by a response, which in turn is followed by a reaction. For the total sample of classes, this cycle accounted for 26 per cent of all cyclical patterns. The cycle that begins with a solicitation and ends with a response comprised 22.3 per cent of all cycles. Most of the major cycles involve some variation upon the basic teacher-question–pupil-answer cycle. Thus, for the fifteen social studies teachers observed by Bellack's group, the basic tools of verbal instruction are the solicitation and the reaction. They use these to control entry into the classroom discourse and to determine and shape the kind and level of substantive content that will make up the discourse.

In her study of forty-one elementary teachers, Hughes and her associates (1959) identified seven different types of functions that teachers perform. These include *controlling functions* (structuring and regulating what will occur in the classroom); *imposition functions* (moralizing or informing); *facilitating functions* (demonstrating, clarifying, or checking); *content-development functions* (acting as a resource, stimulating or evaluating pupil response); *functions of response* (meeting pupil requests, interpreting problems, clarifying personal situations, acknowledging mistakes); *functions of positive affectivity* (supporting, encouraging, being solicitous); and *functions of negative affectivity* (admonishing, reprimanding, threatening, or ignoring pupil behavior).

We first mentioned the Hughes study in Chapter 4 to document the extent to which elementary teachers' classroom behavior dominates the scene. The Hughes report shows that of all the acts of teaching recorded in that extensive study, 45.8 per cent were controlling functions; of these, some 87 per cent were characterized as being structuring and regulating in nature. Where previously our concern with such behavior pertained to the consequences for interpersonal relationships between teachers and pupils, we are now more interested in its impact upon the operations of thinking and learning. The findings of Hughes et al. point up a highly significant characteristic of teacher control which is relevant to our present discussion, namely, its relentless encompassment of the variety and level of thinking done by the students.

The following series of representative examples of such control occurred during lessons conducted by the forty-one teachers observed by the Hughes group. Note that the mental processes required of the students by the questions the teachers ask are restricted almost exclusively to simple memory and recall.

> *Setting:* An intermediate grade was identifying the things in pictures that started with different letters.
> *T:* What about the H's?
> *Ch:* There are four H's.
> *T:* There are several. Let's don't repeat any and listen to what everyone else says.
> *Ch:* (Says one.)
> *T:* Yes, that's one. What's another?
> *Ch:* Honey.
> *T:* What is the honey in?
> *Ch:* A container.
> *T:* Well, that's a fancy word. I'd call it something real easy like a pail or a pan. I'd call it a pan.
> *Comment:* The unexpected response from the children is frequently non-accepted, yet the unexpected, the unusual, is more often than not an aspect of creativity. In this case the child was

using an abstraction of a relatively high order of generalization.

Setting: A primary teacher asked the children to give so-called story problems using the number eight. The teacher gave them a model, and at the same time drew a picture on the board of a house with an upstairs and a downstairs.

T: There were eight in the family—a father, mother, and six children. From this family of eight, three went to town. How many were left at home?

Ch: Five.

T: All right, could you show it on the board, _____? Eight take away three.

(Child comes up.)

T: All right, maybe you can put it on the side over here.

(Child does.)

T: My, it looks like a three. Could you make the five look more like a five?

(Child writes it over.)

T: I think if you put it just a little higher.

(Child does so.)

T: I think that is much better.

Comment: The quick response of the children to the problem was correct. The time of the entire class was consumed with one child writing the numbers in formalized manner on the board in the exact place designated by the teacher.

(Two other children followed the same kind of problem as teacher had given and had children in their story leave home. Each child had to write out his problem on the board.)

T: You don't always have to go away from home. You can make up addition and subtraction problems.

Leslie: There are six children in the family. One is outdoors raking the lawn, one is weeding the flower beds, one is picking rocks out of the border, and one is in a tree watching them. How many are in the house?

Dick: Two.

T: Two. That's right. That's a real good problem, but let's limit it to two parts. (Hands.)

T: All right. Sally. (Sally starts.)

T: Use all eight of them.

Comment: The control of the teacher was on the precise procedure the children were to follow in making this story problem. This control extended to the numbers to use. For example, children were asked to return to number eight and to keep to two numbers of the one-step problem (Hughes et al., 1959, pp. 97–100).

Control over the behavior of students is also exercised by the situations in which and the circumstances under which the teacher responds positively or negatively to the behavior of students. Hughes found that teacher responses tend to be positive somewhat more often than they are negative, positive responses accounting for about 13 per cent of all teacher acts, negative ones just 10 per cent.

Finally, Smith and Meux (1962) have argued that classroom discourse is conducted by means of two basic units: episodes, in which members (usually the teacher and one or more students) interact with one another, and monologs, or lectures, which are almost always soliloquized by the teacher. The analyses of Smith and Meux, like those of Bellack and of Hughes, are also based upon actual verbal events that occurred during a number of secondary school classes, including lessons in science, English, social studies, and mathematics.

Smith and Meux suggest that most episodes and monologs are initiated by teachers (this is consistent with Bellack's finding that teachers initiate 85 per cent of classroom moves). The initiation begins with an entry, either a statement or question that points the direction of the discussion to come. Again, this analysis is very similar to the observation of Hughes that the teacher directs and controls the substantive nature and direction of classroom thinking.

Our previous discussion of the basic characteristics of classroom language would lead us to anticipate that episodes are much more frequent than monologs. And so they are. Smith and his associates have subdivided episodes into two kinds, which they call *reciprocating patterns* and *coordinate patterns*. Episodes are introduced by a statement or question, almost invariably by the teacher, that sets the topic for the ensuing bit of discussion. This statement is called an *entry*. We have reproduced passages from the Smith and Meux monograph to illustrate the two kinds of episodes that occur in the classroom. The first illustration is of the reciprocating episode, in which each speaker responds to what was said immediately before. Entries are italicized. This illustration incorporates three episodes which are separated from each other by pairs of slashes.

Episode 1

T: Now do you know who was the first person to discover the Hawaiian Islands? Steve?

Steve: Was it Captain Cook?

T: That's right. // *Do you know about what time it was,* Steve?

Steve: 1670 something?

T. No, it's not that early. Come down about a hundred years.

Steve: 1770?

T: Yes, it was 1778, actually during the time of our American Revolution. // *And do you know what he called the islands?* They weren't Hawaii at the time. Anybody know? Oh, I think this is an easy name to remember—especially around noon. Steve?

Steve: Cook Islands.

T: No. They weren't Cook Islands. That's a good guess, but that doesn't happen to be it. The Sandwich Islands.

Steve: Oh.

T: Do you eat sandwiches at noon, too? (Smith & Meux, 1962, p. 15.)

These illustrations move through the typical three phases of the reciprocating-pattern episode: an opening, designated by the entry; a continuing phase; and a closing phase. In the coordinate pattern, several different persons may participate in the episode. It is characterized by the fact that each contribution is addressed to the entry of the episode, and not to elaborations upon it or rejoinders to it which may have occurred prior to any given part of the episode. The following excerpt from an eleventh grade English class involved in a discussion of the novel as a propaganda medium is typical of the coordinate episode.

Episode 2

T: All right, now, as Carol pointed out, Alan Paton is pleading for the alternative solution—that of brotherly love or peaceful co-existence between the races. *Now, what do you think of a novelist who tries to preach a lesson or to promote his point of view through the medium of fiction?* You think of that. Mary?

Mary: I was just going to say that I think it's the type of the novel. I mean it's the way that it is presented that moves us. He could present it in different ways if he wanted to. Not necessarily the—the novel or—oh, something that teaches you a moral lesson.

T: All right, just as we discussed, it's a short story. Some stories do have a moral lesson to preach and then they become parables rather than just generalized short stories. And others simply are entertaining. Denny?

Denny: Well, I think that more people would be interested in the fiction form of the novel than in just a pamphlet giving specific reasons why the two races should live together in brotherhood. I think it would attract more attention and would be more interesting.

Judy: Well, since it's—When people read it, it's more parallel to everyday life. You might be able to understand it a lot better in a novel and so on. Otherwise, you just see these facts and you wouldn't associate yourself and how you would feel and react to it.

T: All right. // (Smith & Meux, 1962, pp. 16–17.)

Unfortunately, Smith and Meux tell us nothing about the occurrence of one kind of episode relative to the other or to monologs, except that monologs are comparatively rare. Also, we know nothing of the classroom conditions that lead to one type of episode instead of the other. Is it a significant or a trivial datum that these two kinds of episodes occur in classroom discourse? It is impossible to judge on the information given because we have no way to observe the consequences.

We might suppose that the entries themselves heavily determine the kind of episode that will follow. Compare the entries from the two illustrative episodes. In the first one, a call for highly specific and limited information is given. If Steve correctly names the discoverer, as he does, the episode must move to a close, as it does. The entry of the coordinate pattern asks for pupil opinions, perhaps implicitly for evaluations of the author's behavior. Since there is no single correct answer, it is possible for several students to advance opinions about the question.

COGNITIVE LEVELS OF CLASSROOM DISCOURSE

If on the one hand we have been able to establish that the content of classroom discourse is predominantly substantive or subject-matter oriented, on the other hand it appears to be equally true that the cognitive level of most classroom discourse seldom rises above that of factual statements. On average, probably half or more of classroom discourse is carried on at the level of dealing with facts.

Bellack et al. (1966) developed a variety of categories for determining the meaning of classroom language as well as identifying the conditions under which it is employed. Those categories that deal with the substantive-logical meanings include *analytic processes* (defining and interpreting), *empirical processes* (fact-stating and explaining), and *evaluative processes* (opining and justifying).

Examples of each of these substantive-logical meanings are given here. The examples come from the typescripts of project lessons; they were not invented to fit the demands of the categories. On the contrary, the categories were devised to make it possible to deal with the totality of classroom language by reference to a relatively few descriptive terms.

Defining:[2]
> *T:* What are public utilities?
> *P:* Light, power, gas, water.

> *T:* Can you give an example of a machine tool, Alex?
> *P:* A press.

> *T:* Now what do we mean by quotas?
> *P:* The government sets a special amount of things that can come into the country in one year, and no more can come in.

> *T:* What are machine tools?
> *P:* Tools that make tools.

Interpreting:
> *T:* What does President Kennedy mean when he says, "We must trade or fade?"

> *T:* What does the slogan mean, "Buy American—the job you save may be your own!"

Fact-stating:
> *T:* Now in 1934 . . . in 1934 . . . who was President?
> *P:* Roosevelt.

> *T:* The United States will say that the French franc is exchanged at how many per dollar?
> *P:* Five.

---

[2] Bellack discriminates between denotative and connotative definitions. We have made no effort to retain that distinction.

Explaining:

> *T:* Why do industrialized countries trade the most?
> *P:* Because they have more . . . more to offer each other.

> *T:* What would happen if we raised the tariff on transistor radios?
> *P:* Prices would go up.
> *P:* Japan would raise its tariffs on American stuff (Bellack et al., 1966, pp. 23–25).

In the Bellack system, explaining is a rather broad, loose category. It includes not only statements that give reasons for an event or outcome and effects imposed upon one state of affairs by another, but it also includes as an explanation any explicit statement of comparing and contrasting.

Opining:

> *P:* I think the farmer is being exploited.

> *T:* Do you feel that a company who has gone into another country, has invested time, has invested money, has invested its knowledge, its skill and so on, has a right to make a profit?
> *P:* Yes.

Justifying:

> *P:* I feel that the reason why the United States should not and probably will not in a number of years join the Common Market is that because the Latin countries with which we are associated would feel that we are no longer interested in their opinion.

> *T:* Is it the government's responsibility then to train you for some other job, assuming that you couldn't get a job on your own?
> *P:* I believe that they should train them over again and give them government jobs or something because, I mean, after all if it weren't for the tariff and barriers, they'd still be in work (Bellack et al., 1966, pp. 25–26).

Justifying usually appears immediately after an opinion has been expressed or implied. Opining is the occasion for justifying, which may or may not then occur. Justifying is a matter of giving reasons in support of an opinion about a norm or value.

Many classroom-language moves have instructional components as well as substantive ones. References are sometimes made to assignments, materials of instruction, procedures to be followed, etc. These, together with the instructional-logical meanings that occur, are too numerous to specify. Instead we wish simply to indicate that Bellack's total system pays attention to all such behaviors.

We have already seen that about half the verbal moves made by secondary school teachers are solicitations. Approximately 60 per cent of the teacher's solicitations call for substantive information, usually empirical, with requests for explanation more frequent than for fact-stating. When the teacher calls for analytical meanings, definitions are required more frequently than interpretations. Evaluative meanings are rarely requested, and justifying responses are wanted less often than opinions.

When the various responses are measured by lines (that is, actual lines of typescript, based upon classroom discourse) for the entire sample of sixty lessons, 72.8 per cent of all lines fell into substantive-logical categories. Sixty per cent of the total were empirical, divided 14 per cent and 46 per cent between fact-stating and explanation, respectively. Slightly more than 5 per cent of the lines were analytic, and almost all were definitions rather than interpretation. Evaluative comments accounted for 7.5 per cent of the total, with justifying occurring almost 6 per cent of the time.

Smith and Meux's analyses of the language behavior of secondary school classrooms reveal that some twelve kinds of logical behavior occur. Teachers within and across subject areas differ in the frequency with which they enter the various logical categories. Overall, approximately 10 per cent of the entries used by the teachers fell into non-logical categories of classroom management and control. The largest proportion of behaviors, approximately 25 per cent, was devoted to descriptions. The criteria for discussing descriptions are not clear, and Smith and Meux do not include them in their final formulation of categories of logical behavior. We are left with the feeling that much classroom discourse deals in a general way with subject matter, but is too amorphous in content to be logically classified.

In order that the reader will have a clear conception of what is meant by logical behavior, the criteria for and illustrations of episodes will be presented for the two next most frequently appearing categories, *designating* and *explaining*. Of the total number of entries in the sample, about 15 per cent are designations and 13 per cent are explanations. Altogether some 60 per cent of entries were divided among control, description, designation, and explanation.

The remaining entries were distributed among defining, stating, reporting, substituting, evaluating, opining, comparing and contrasting, and conditional inferring.

Designating Episodes

Two major subcategories of designating have been labeled: *identifying* and *specifying*.[3] Identifying connotes use of the definite article, and includes selecting a given object by reference to a noun, a name, or a definite description.

> **Identifying:**
> *T: What are the different parts of the brain? Let's begin with the lowest part.*
> *S:* The medulla?
> *T:* All right.
>
> *T: Well what part of the nerve cell is the axon? What structural part?*
> *S:* It's a fiber.
> *T:* It's a fiber. All right. It carries the impulse away from the nerve cell (Smith & Meux, 1962, p. 90).

Specification differs from identification in the sense that no highly specific designation is made. Rather, although the existence of the class or category is assumed, there may be several instances or examples, only one or two of which are called for by the teacher's entry, or the entry may demand an exhaustive listing of them. The following episodes illustrate these two subcategories of specifying behavior. The first three are cases of *examples;* the last two of *listing.*

> **Specifying:**
> *T:* Now, I have all these pencils—and *give me a comparison.*
> *S:* The blue one is the largest of the four.
>
> *T:* Another one?
> *S:* Another system is the brain, the nerves, and the sense organs.
> *T:* All right.

---

[3] In the interests of brevity and clarity, the present discussion excludes several subcategories identified by Smith and Meux (1962). For a more complete and detailed treatment, the reader must consult the original monograph.

T: Now, will you give me an example of—several examples of some of our strong hydroxides and also our strong electrolytes. What about hydroxides?
S: Sodium hydroxide.
T: All right, sodium (Smith & Meux, 1962, pp. 95–96).

T: In today's work, we have the three simplest figures—to measure by square units. *What are they?*
S: The square, the rectangle, and the triangle.
T: All right.

T: Could you name them all?
S: Well—uh—they have—uh—they have a bunch of jaws. They have three jaws—this is in pairs—three jaws, I think it meant. They got maxilla—pair of maxilla—maxilla, and mandibles, two—and antennae and antennules. Then they've got a bunch of jaws and I never did get that completely straight. And claws and walking legs and swimmerettes. And then the—well I guess—the flippers.
T: Flippers. All right, that's pretty good (Smith & Meux, 1962, p. 96).

Explaining Episodes

In general, explanations are required to develop or to expand an individual's understanding of a phenomenon or event.[4] The event may be outside his realm of experience, or it may not be seen as pertinent to his experience. The assumption is made by Smith and Meux that when the logical demands of explanation are met, considering the individual's background, explanation has occurred. However, at least one psychologist, Thyne (1963), defines explanation in terms of how adequately it leads to understanding.

The reader should recognize this dispute as an instance of the more general controversy between those who conceptualize teaching as an independent entity, to be judged by its own rules, and those who evaluate teaching only in terms of its empirical relation to learning in a generic sense.

One basis for the classification of an explanation is to be found in the nature of the relationship between the subject of explanation and

---

[4] Once again, only two of the several kinds of explaining behaviors analyzed by Smith and Meux are dealt with in the present discussion.

other "actions, objects, events, or states of affairs" (Smith & Meux, 1962, p. 140). The relationship may be warranted either by empirical generalizations or by conventional rules. As a second basis for classification, Smith and Meux also used the "structure of the explanatory operation." The structure required by the entry might be deductive, temporal or spatial, or perhaps a loose judgmental one that is open to broad objections.

We have selected for discussion here only two of the types of explanation formulated by Smith and Meux, *normative* and *empirical-subsumptive* explanations.[5]

Normative explanations. When a subject of explanation can be subsumed under a more general and widely accepted rule or norm, we have an example of normative explanation. The sorts of rules appealed to include law (in the jurisprudential rather than the scientific sense) and conventions about behavior. Evidence must exist to show that the action or belief to be explained in this way is an instance of the class subsumed by the rule. This first illustration contains all the normal elements for such an explanation.

> *T:* Why do we use 'shorter'?
> *S:* Because there's only two objects being compared.
> *T:* If there are only two being compared—if there are just two involved, we use the comparative degree which ends in 'er.' Many of these adjectives do form their comparison by adding the 'er' for the comparative and 'est' for the superlative (Smith & Meux, 1962, p. 141).

In this illustration the teacher identifies the action to be explained with his question, "Why do we use 'shorter'?" Evidence that the present instance is covered by a general rule is provided by the student. Note, though, that the student's elliptical statement implies that he knows more about the issue than he actually verbalizes. The teacher closes the episode with a somewhat vague allusion to the rule. Normative explanations in the classroom do not, however, always include all the elements of the paradigm. In the following illustration, no evidence for the applicability of the rule cited is mentioned.

---

[5] The other kinds identified by Smith and Meux are judgmental, procedural, sequent, teleological, mechanical, and explanation by consequences.

> *T:* How do we know that this angle—SC—down here is 120°?
> *S:* Because the opposite angles in a parallelo—or a rhombus—
> are equal.
> *T:* The opposites are equal, and of course every two adjacent
> are—since it's a parallelogram—will be supplementary, because
> this is just another form here. That's right, and since this is a
> rhombus, it makes them equal, which makes 60 and 60, and
> therefore an equilateral triangle (Smith & Meux, 1962, p. 142).

The following quotation from Smith and Meux is an apt summarization of the criteria for normative explanation:

> The epistemic rules[6] by which normative explanations are appraised are as follows: (1) The rule must be one which is accepted or agreed upon. (2) If empirical, the evidential statements indicating the applicability of the rule must be true; if classificatory, the particular must be an instance of the class covered by the rule according to an accepted definition of the class term. (3) The action or belief being explained must not be a recognized exception to the rule. (4) The action or belief must be logically derivable from the rule in conjunction with the evidence cited (Smith & Meux, 1962, p. 144).

Empirical-subsumptive explanation. Empirical-subsumptive explanations are analogous to normative explanations. In both, an outcome exists that is to be explained, some evidence must be adduced, and it must be demonstrable that the evidence is subsumed by a broader generalization. The basic difference between empirical-subsumptive and normative explanations is to be found in the nature of the covering generalizations, empirical as contrasted with normative.

Three illustrations of empirical explanation are reproduced here. Note that the generalization appears in the explanations with varying degrees of specificity. In the first example, the student supplies evidence, but fails to cite the generalization. The teacher supplies it in turn. The second example illustrates the use of a generalization as evidence, and the existence of a further generalization is implicit. Finally,

---

[6] *Epistemic rules* are logical rules that concern the correctness of a response. In the sense in which Smith and Meux use the term, the concept of correctness is broader and more comprehensive than truth or validity (alternative classes of logical rules).

in the third example, the empirical law is alluded to rather than stated with precision.

> *T:* Why is that possible? *Why can he* (insect) *do that* (see in more than one direction at a time) *and you and I can't?*
> *S:* Cause they have more than one lens.
> *T:* They have more than one lens. All right. They have a multitude of lenses. A number of lenses makes it possible to see in many directions at one time (Smith & Meux, 1962, p. 145).

> *T:* What can you tell us about—we haven't talked about this as yet but we will, I think, in the next chapter—about cold-blooded and warm-blooded animals. *Why is it more cold-blooded animals live in the South than in the North?*
> *S:* Because the cold-blooded animals—don't they have to have the same kind of temperature as their surroundings?
> *T:* They have the same body temperature as their surroundings (Smith & Meux, 1962, p. 145).

> *T:* *What produces all of that?* Now, we're not pulling backward on the block. What produces all that?
> *S:* Friction.
> *T:* O.K. That's the frictional force (Smith & Meux, 1962, p. 146).

Hudgins and Ahlbrand (1967) studied the teacher-pupil interaction in nine junior high school English classes. Five lessons were tape-recorded in each of those classes, and the tapes later reduced to transcripts. A major purpose of the study was to examine the distribution of classroom communications of teachers and students across various cognitive levels. To do this, an analytical scheme based upon one developed by Gallagher, Aschner, and others (1965) was employed.

The cognitive components of the Aschner and Gallagher system are based upon Guilford's (1956) structure of the intellect. We modified the existing system and classified all verbal behaviors or utterances in the English classes as belonging under the heading of either substantive or management behaviors. Within the substantive categories were several subdivisions, including *cognitive memory,* involving either old classroom facts or newly introduced facts; *convergent thinking,* leading toward identifying a correct answer; *divergent thinking,* capable of going in different directions and an important ability in creativity; and *evaluative thinking*. (Some of the details of our cognitive classifications are included in Table 6.1.)

The study's most important finding is that pupils in those nine English classes operated verbally at the level of cognitive memory 80 per cent of the time. For the teachers, the frequency of fact-stating was 55 per cent, but this is chiefly attributable to the fact that the system classifies teacher-reacting statements as management behavior, related to the substance of the discussion. If a somewhat different analytical system had been used in this study, it seems probable that the frequency of fact-stating by teachers would have been much closer to the 80 per cent level found for students.

A few words need to be said about the content of Table 6.1. In this table we have tried to bring together data from several of the studies cited in this chapter that have dealt with the cognitive or logical distributions of classroom discourse. It is true, of course, that none of the investigators used the same systems of analysis. Even where some of the same terms are used they are not necessarily conceptually identical. For example, Smith and Bellack each have a category labelled Explaining, but for Smith, certain fairly rigorous logical criteria must be met in order for an entry to be classified as an explanation. For Bellack, who classifies Explaining under the broader rubric of Empirical moves, the criteria are somewhat broader. They explicitly include comparing and contrasting within explaining, for example.

The model used by Hudgins and Ahlbrand is a psychological model for classifying utterances and, in contrast to those of Smith and Bellack, undoubtedly overestimates the proportion of fact-stating behavior by comparison with the others. With systems that are so different from each other, any broad generalizations are impossible, and there is considerable risk in attempting inferences about commonalities across the studies. Nonetheless, if we remain aware of those potential risks, it is possible to see some similarities among these three studies with respect to the amount of classroom discourse that occurs at the factual level. For example, by combining the percentages of entries recorded by Smith and Meux for describing, designating, stating, opining, and reporting (which seem to demand the least intellectual operation by teachers or students), we arrive at a figure of 55 per cent of all entries. In the Bellack study, 60 per cent of all lines spoken are subsumable under Empirical meanings (a combination of fact-stating and explaining). In the Hudgins and Ahlbrand study, teachers devote 55 per cent of their utterances to fact-stating, and pupils devote 80 per cent.

TABLE 6.1   DISTRIBUTIONS OF CLASSROOM DISCOURSE ACROSS
SUBSTANTIVE CATEGORIES

INVESTIGATOR	SAMPLE	UNIT OF ANALYSIS	CATEGORIES	PER CENT	
Bellack et al. (1966)	15 secondary school social studies classes	4½ inches of lines of typescript	Analytic	5.6	
			Defining	4.9	
			Interpreting	0.7	
			Evaluative	7.5	
			Opining	1.6	
			Justifying	5.9	
			Empirical	59.5	
			Fact-stating	13.6	
			Explaining	45.9	
Smith & Meux (1962)	14 secondary school classes includes several subjects	Entry	Defining	4.1	
			Designating	14.8	
			Conditional inferring	7.3	
			Opining	5.3	
			Comparing and contrasting	3.3	
			Classifying	3.0	
			Substituting	0.3	
			Describing	25.3	
			Explaining	12.9	
			Stating	6.8	
			Evaluating	4.6	
			Reporting	2.9	
			(Classroom management)	(9.4)	
				Tchrs.	*Pupils*
Hudgins & Ahlbrand (1967)	9 junior high school English classes	Utterance	Evaluative thinking (using norms)	0.1	0.1
			Divergent thinking	0.2	0.1
			Convergent thinking	2.3	2.2
			Evaluative thinking (using own values)	0.7	0.9
			Cognitive memory		
			Old facts	25.8	41.4
			New facts	29.8	39.2
			Management Related to subject	37.5	8.1
			Unrelated to subject	3.5	1.7

Although our effort to sketch some similarities among three sets of data about classroom discourse hardly proves the point, a strong presumption exists that, on the average, students and teachers devote a large amount of their classroom discourse to subject-matter facts. Again, one must exercise appropriate intellectual restraint, but it seems reasonable to conclude—at least tentatively—that operations with facts account for about half of the verbal behavior that occurs in the typical schoolroom. There are good reasons why students, and teachers, too, should have a firm grasp of the facts about the subjects with which they are dealing. One's ability to think about a topic will be facilitated by an accurate knowledge of the major facts, laws, theories, and generalizations upon which the field is constructed.

On the other hand, intense concentration in the classroom upon factual knowledge has distinct limitations. For one thing, facts in themselves tend to be forgotten easily and soon. Unless students are learning some forms of intellectual operation that go beyond the memorization or recall of factual material, the residue of their learning is likely to be meager. In addition, one of the traditionally espoused values of education is that of teaching students to think. The studies we have reviewed provide relatively clear evidence that factual learning was emphasized in the classrooms involved. There is must less evidence that the teachers stressed such logical processes or educational skills as defining one's terms, providing clear and accurate explanations of a natural phenomenon, or developing new and original solutions to problems, whether mathematical, scientific, social, or literary.

In sum, there is reason to believe that classrooms today, on the average, are characterized by discourse that is largely related to the subject matter traditionally assigned to the course, and that such subject matter is more likely to be dealt with at the level of factual learning than through extended explorations of its possibilities as an intellectual domain. We have tried to suggest that factual learning plays an important, but limited, role in education. In the following chapter, we shall examine the results of some recent efforts to systematically raise the level of cognitive operation through the deliberate manipulation of teaching tactics and strategies.

REFERENCES

Chapter 6

Aschner, M. J., Gallagher, J. J., Perry, J., Afsar, S., Jenner, W. C., & Farr, H. *A system for classifying thought processes in the context of classroom verbal interaction.* Urbana, Ill.: Institute for Research on Exceptional Children, University of Illinois, 1965.

Bellack, A. A., Kliebard, H. M., Hyman, R. T., & Smith, F. L., Jr. *The language of the classroom.* New York: Teachers College Press, 1966.

Gallagher, J. J., & Aschner, M. J. A preliminary report on analyses of classroom interaction. *Merrill Palmer Quarterly,* 1963, *9,* 183–194.

Guilford, J. P. The structure of intellect. *Psychological Bulletin,* 1956, *53,* 267–293.

Hudgins, B. B. Attending and thinking in the classroom. *Psychology in the Schools,* 1967, *3,* 211–216.

Hudgins, B. B., and Ahlbrand, W. P., Jr. *A study of classroom interaction and thinking.* St. Louis: Central Midwestern Regional Educational Laboratory, 1967.

Hughes, M., et al. *Development of the means for the assessment of the quality of teaching in the elementary school.* Salt Lake City: University of Utah, 1959. (Mimeographed)

Smith, B. O., & Meux, M., *A study of the logic of teaching.* Urbana: Bureau of Educational Research, University of Illinois, 1962.

Thyne, J. M. *The psychology of learning and techniques of teaching.* New York: Philosophical Library, 1963.

CHAPTER 7

THE IMPROVEMENT OF PRODUCTIVE THINKING THROUGH TEACHER-PUPIL INTERACTION

We suspect that teachers most often formulate instructional goals—to the extent that they formulate them at all—to emphasize mastery by their students of such factual information as "the causes of the First World War" or "the names of the 50 United States and their capital cities." Goals that concern students' abilities to draw inferences, to evaluate arguments, or to generate alternative solutions to problems are seldom defined by teachers, or are assumed to be by-products of factual learning or a consequence of the student's increasing intellectual maturity.

One of the assumptions made continuously throughout this book is that student behavior is guided by the behavior of the teacher. We have demonstrated that the social climate of the classroom, for example, tends to be set by the demeanor of its teacher. Congruently, the teacher's role possesses the greatest latitude available in the classroom, whereas the student's role is highly proscribed. The teacher asks the questions, the student answers them, and the teacher, if he sees fit, judges the merit of the pupil's reply. It would seem, therefore, that the possibility exists for teachers to manipulate and to elevate the level of quality of thinking that most students engage in during classes.

Several conditions must be met in order to accomplish this desired outcome. First, the teacher's goals must include the development of thinking skills as an intended outcome of instruction. Second, he must have a clear conception of "productive thinking," not only the end product but also the process by which thinking skills are developed. Third, he must be skillful in the practice of teaching as it relates to the improvement of pupils' thinking skills. Fourth, the teacher must apply his skills toward the achievement of desired goals of productive thinking. This is not to suggest that these conditions can be met in a mechanical way, or that success in fulfilling each of them necessarily guarantees an automatic improvement of children's thinking skills. Here it would be well to recall Scheffler's admonition regarding the "success" uses of teaching—"the universe must cooperate."

In this chapter we shall examine various strategies of teaching, particularly as they apply to improving the quality of classroom thinking. We shall also review the evidence relating to the training of teachers to execute strategies, as well as the results of teachers' efforts to implement these strategies.

PRODUCTIVE THINKING

What do we mean by *productive thinking*? Essentially, we mean the ability of a student to identify, select, and organize concepts, information, or other data in his environment in order to answer questions that cannot be answered directly from the data available to him. That is, the student must perform one or more cognitive operations before the answer can be constructed. Productive thinking can be contrasted with reproductive thinking, in which the learner uses habitual responses to answer questions or to solve problems.

We have shown that, on the average, teachers and their students devote half or more of their total classroom discourse to facts and statements about facts. That, of course, does not mean that the other half deals with higher order intellectual skills. For example, in the Hudgins and Ahlbrand (1967) study, only about 5 per cent of the language used by teachers and pupils in those nine junior high school English classes was classified at a cognitive level higher than that of facts. However, Gallagher and Aschner (1963) classified the oral thought processes of a gifted group of junior high school social studies students for a week. Approximately 60 per cent of the expressed thoughts of these students was distributed among convergent, divergent, and evaluative thinking.

The term *thinking* is notoriously ambiguous. Thomson (1959), for example, reviews some half dozen senses in which the word is used colloquially as well as scientifically. Even in the latter sense it is possible to differentiate critical thinking, problem-solving, and creative thinking (Smith and Hudgins, 1964). Since presumably each of these kinds of thinking is more or less independent of the others, a single instructional emphasis will be inadequate for bringing about improvement in all areas simultaneously. If that assumption is tenable, then it follows that one must be as clear as possible about specifying the type of thinking in which instruction is to be offered, and setting about defining one's terms and indicating the operations that are chosen as most likely to lead to the desired end.

Taba (1950) forcefully called attention to the influence of curriculum materials and achievement tests in controlling teachers' efforts to develop critical thinking. It seems that school systems give lip service to the importance of developing critical thinking skills, but adopt or construct curriculum materials that are organized around chronological or factual schemes instead of conceptual ones that might ease the task of teaching thinking skills. Moreover, the achievement tests which are used to reflect the academic progress of pupils rarely include tests of thinking ability.

Gallagher and Aschner (1963) modified the intellectual products categories of Guilford's (1956) structure of intellect. Their system for the analysis of classroom interaction consists of categories of cognitive memory, convergent thinking, divergent thinking, evaluative thinking, and routine. The routine category is the recipient of all noncognitive aspects of classroom discourse. Gallagher and Aschner's interest was in the study of productive thinking, which they define as ". . . those divergent, convergent and evaluative operations whereby the individual draws upon available past and present acts, ideas, associations and observations in order to bring forth *new* facts, ideas, and conclusions . . . [It] includes both the creative and critical-analytic dimensions of reasoning" (Gallagher & Aschner, 1963, p. 185).

Taba's view of productive thinking was more developmental. For Taba, thinking consists of specific, describable acts which, moreover, develop in sequence; that is, simpler mental questions must first be developed to serve as a basis upon which more complex, abstract thinking is built. For example, to achieve a concept, the teaching sequence must include (1) the enunciation of specific instances of the concept, (2) grouping them together, and (3) labelling them with the appropriate name. Taba's explicit formulations of the skill of productive thinking, and instructional strategies for their achievement, led her to develop an extensive program for training teachers to improve the thinking skills of elementary school children.

STRATEGIES OF TEACHING

When Montgomery and Rommel faced each other at El Alemain, two of the greatest strategists of the Second World War were brought into direct confrontation. Success for one meant disaster for the other, implying the typically competitive nature of strategies. Strategy involves more than the skilled performance of the individual; it also takes account of his behavior in relation to that of his opponent. Thus, Montgomery argued that Rommel would anticipate flanking movements by the British and ordered instead a direct frontal assault, counting upon elements of surprise and deployment of German strength to carry the day.

Strategy need not always involve direct conflict by force. Two parties may strive to achieve a larger share of the total prize, yet at the same time recognize that their fates are intertwined. This is often the case when labor and management meet to negotiate union contracts. Each employs a strategy designed to curtail the gains of the other, but tries to avoid a strike vote, which represents a common loss.

A more recent development in the work of B. O. Smith and his associates has been the study of strategies of teaching (Smith, Meux, Coombs, & Nuthall, 1964; Smith, Meux, Coombs, Nuthall, & Precians, 1967). By strategies of teaching Smith has reference to larger maneuvers that concern control of the content of instruction. Strategies are related to instructional objectives; they provide a means for reaching goals.

As was true in the study of the logic of teaching, the first demand of this investigation was to determine a usable unit of analysis in which to seek strategies. The unit finally established is called the *venture*. The venture meets the two chief criteria for the appropriate unit: that it deal with a single topic, and that the verbal transactions occurring within the unit be relevant to an identifiable objective, such as a cause-effect relationship or a concept. As defined by Smith et al. (1964, p. 5), "A venture is a segment of discourse consisting of a set of utterances dealing with a single topic and having a single overarching content objective."

Nine types of ventures were identified. Each is characterized by its content objective. *Content objective* refers to what a reader or listener would understand as the central point or focus of the venture. The nine types of ventures are causal, conceptual, evaluative, informatory, interpretive, procedural, reason, rule, and system.

According to Smith and his associates, teaching situations differ from strategies in three ways: (1) Pupils gain from transactions in the classroom at no loss to the teacher. (2) In strategic situations, opponents are typically peers; this is virtually never true in teaching situations where the teacher's influence is always dominant. (3) Teaching activity is cooperative, and the student enters the teacher's domain of knowledge. Despite these differences, Smith regards it as feasible to use the concept of strategy to analyze teaching behavior.

Amelioration of the Controlling Functions

Hughes et al. (1959) stress the point that teachers appear to be unaware of the importance of reducing their power over the teacher-pupil relationship. She also identifies means available to them for effecting such a reduction. In essence, the tactics that she recommends involve institutionalizing certain elements of the teacher's behavior with the consequence of shifting, at least partially, the onus of control and decision making from the teacher to others—possibly to the students, or the school, or even society at large.

Specifically, three tactics are proposed to bring about the reduction of the teacher's control: neutral regulation, open structure and regulation, and public criteria.

Neutral regulation. In this tactic, management activities of the classroom are assigned on a systematic basis, one that is as well known to the students as it is to the teacher. This regulating function can relieve the teacher of an endless burden of small decisions as well as impose upon the pupils some responsibility for seeing that the system works adequately.

Open structure and regulation. We have already seen how the characteristic pattern of teacher questioning, coupled with designation by the teacher of who is to answer, leads to a limited set of intellectual demands upon students. The designation of one individual to respond to a question may be interpreted by other students as terminating their responsibility to continue to think about the answer. In contrast to this pattern, Hughes proposes that open questions be used with greater frequency. An open question is one which has no single correct answer, or at least one for which an answer other than a precise word or phrase is acceptable. Questions such as the following illustrate the concept of open structure:

"Does anyone have another idea?" "What do you think should be done?" "Why did the Utah pioneers make the first settlements where they did?" "What do you think may happen because of the St. Lawrence Seaway?" (Hughes, 1959, p. 136.)

Obviously not all questions that teachers ask in classrooms can or ought to be open. There are many occasions when the teacher must insist upon precise responses that meet rigorous criteria of the subject matter at hand. No other interpretation is appropriate. The issue, then, is not to find ways to allow sloppy thinking, but rather to encourage teachers to behave so as to expand the range of thinking done by students by providing both the opportunity and the challenge for it to occur.

Hughes has expressed the notion that a teacher's questioning procedure is characterized by its idiosyncratic structure, which often leaves students puzzling over, What is it she wants? rather than, What is demanded by the problem? Another consequence of closed structure and regulation is that the bulk of the burden of thinking is imposed upon the teacher rather than the students.

Public criteria. Essentially this amounts to informing students or somehow allowing them to recognize that many demands imposed by teachers are not idiosyncratic but are required by the situation, or by the larger society. Coupled with this is the use of *universals,* activities aimed at teaching the broader applicability, appropriateness, or utility of which the student's present endeavor is an example.

> Classroom standards and requests are often carried out with little meaning to children. The relationship of what is required of them to the larger society is seldom clarified. For example, a group of intermediate grade children were making designs with tile. The teacher spoke to them. "We want to be sure the design is here the way you want it. It's easier to erase a paper. That's the reason I have you do it this way." Here the teacher had an opportunity to indicate the universality of making of models, of drawing plans and specifications before attempting the work in the final medium. Instead, he made himself the source of requirement with "You can erase it" as a weak public criteria [sic].

> Another teacher used a generalization of universal application in the episode that follows:
> A primary teacher was helping a child who was preparing a story for tape recording.

> *T:* Maybe you're reading just a little too fast to put on the tape recorder. You read rapidly when you read to yourself but when you read to others you need to read slowly enough for others to hear.
> *Ch:* (Makes comment which indicates that she thinks all reading should be slowed down and says she will slow down all of her reading.)
> *T:* No, don't slow down when you read to yourself. When you read to yourself and see the words you can think about them much faster than when you hear them. So when you read out loud you have to read slowly but when you read silently read as fast as you can.

Rules and standards related to safety on the street, highway, school bus, and swimming pool are Universals. Behavior appropriate to public places, such as a library, a bank, a restaurant, a lecture, are sufficiently prescribed and approved to be upheld as Universals of the culture (Hughes, 1959, pp. 139–140).

Content Development

Of the major functions identified by Hughes, the functions that develop content deserve our attention at this point. These functions are basically sets of responses by the teacher to the student's efforts at grappling with the subject matter. They represent acts by the teacher that help the student to expand and extend his grasp of content and the intellectual operations he performs with or upon it.

Two of the most significant of the content-developing functions are clarifying and evaluating. We have included here examples from Hughes's classroom protocols to illustrate these functions. The first example demonstrates acts of clarification and the induction of a generalization. The setting is a discussion by an intermediate grade teacher and his students of a current winter storm occurring in the Eastern United States. The teacher is reading the account of the storm in the local [California] newspaper.

> The account in the paper contained the phrase, 'impeded traffic.'
> *T:* What do you suppose that means?
> (Several children offer ideas.)
> *Ch:* (Adds that chains are needed.)
> *T:* Yes, why do you think chains helped?
> *Ch:* (Gives idea.)

T: In these places where it snows, will they have chains on for a number of months now?

Ch: (Three children who had lived where they had snow tell of their personal experiences: car stuck, the putting on of chains, etc.)

T: Aren't we lucky to have so many people who have lived where they have snow? Bert was going to tell us about snow on the desert.

Bert: (Tells of experience going up to Mount Bruno via the desert.)

T: Yes, he would have to have chains going up to Mount Bruno. Does anyone else know what is needed for cars where they have snow?

Ch: Fog lights.

Ch: Heaters.

Ch: (Gives another idea.)

T: Yes, all those things are needed. What is needed in the car where it is cold?

Ch: (Offers guess.)

T: What might freeze?

Ch: Oil?

(Other children offer guesses.)

T: What about the water? Does water freeze?

Ch: Yes. (Explains about water.)

T: Yes, water freezes in the radiator and when it freezes it breaks the pipes so that all of the water runs out. Does anyone know what they put in to keep the water from freezing?

Ch: Oil?

Ch: I've seen some stuff like that advertized [sic] on T.V.

Ch: Oh, yeah. I remember my dad used to get some and put it in our car.

T: It's called anti-freeze.

Chn: (Comments come in rapid succession.) Oh, yeah, I remember now. Yes. I know . . . etc.

T: (Reads again from article; comes to place where the name 'Catskills' appeared again.) What did we say had happened in the Catskill Mountains that we know about?

Ch: Rip Van Winkle fell asleep and slept for twenty years.

T: That's where we heard about Rip Van Winkle. It wouldn't be very good sleeping, would it? (Teacher goes on reading about depth of snow, appearance, etc.)

T: So we were talking about the snow and what happened

when it fell. Would this mean that snow which fell on grass, trees and flowers would have them covered all winter?

Ch: (Tells of personal experience seeing the snow on the trees, shrubs, roofs—its extent, etc.)

T: Snow can be a lot of fun for people; snow can cause trouble and difficulty for people.

Comment: Again the teacher and children were working together in an exchange of experience. A great deal of data about themselves and others were woven together. With these data a generalization was made (Hughes, 1959, pp. 148–151).

Our second set of examples illustrates evaluative acts by teachers. The function of evaluation in the interactive phase of teaching is to point out to the student what he is doing that is correct and should be continued and what is incorrect and should be extinguished. Again there is the importance of giving the student reasons for the evaluation that is made.

Setting: An intermediate grade class were giving reports from their reading: After a report:

T: Betty, I'm glad you chose an easy book and I like the way you told it. There are quite a few people in our class who need to know there are easy books in our room that are also interesting. I think you gave a little too much attention to details. If someone else reads this book, they don't want all the surprises told beforehand.

Comment: The evaluation, both positive and negative, was given with discrimination; that is, the child had something specific to do to improve his report. Incidentally, note the teacher's imposition of appraisal of other children's needs in reference to easy books; also, the imposition of self in "I'm glad," "I like," "I think." A more impersonal evaluation would have kept it problem-centered; a personalized "we" which would have made it more group-centered would have been preferable to teacher-centered.

The children continue to make their reports.

T: Ken, yours was a good report. It would help if you faced your audience. You started out all right and then looked away. This takes away from your report. You should hold your pictures up higher so people can see.

Comment: The Evaluate-positive was made without discrimination. Why was it a good report? The negative evaluation was made with discrimination. The child knows what to do to improve, but not what is good to retain.

> Reporting continues; Jo Ellen finishes her report.
> *T:* Jo Ellen, your report was helped by your pictures. Your drawing was very good.
> *Another ch:* She can draw real good horses.
> *T:* Yes, Jo Ellen loves horses and it comes out in her drawing.
> *Comment:* The positive evaluation with discrimination and
the supportive response in this sequence is of interest (Hughes, 1959, pp. 151–153).

Criteria for Instructional Behavior

As we indicated earlier, the criteria by which judgments were made for developing the Model of Good Teaching are not specified. The model itself is a model only in the crudest usage of the word. Estimates are made of the range of teacher behaviors that may fall within each of the seven categories identified. Hughes insists that good teaching cannot be rigorously characterized by specific values of behavior; rather, she believes that many combinations of the various functions may lead to similarly positive outcomes. Since efforts to discover *the* method, *the* style, or *the* personality for successful teaching have been unfruitful, Hughes's assertion receives at least indirect support from research evidence.

Hughes et al. (1959, p. 223) have recorded the range of values for each function included in the Model of Good Teaching.

The percentage scale for each category:

Controlling functions	20–40 per cent
Imposition	1–3 per cent
Facilitating	5–15 per cent
Content development	20–40 per cent
Personal response	8–20 per cent
Positive affectivity	10–20 per cent
Negative affectivity	3–10 per cent

(Figure 7.1 presents the model graphically.) Notice that no effort is made to develop a calculus of the maximums and minimums of the several functions in combination with each other. Likewise, this model only identifies the distribution of teaching behaviors among the seven functional categories. The problem of sequence of be-

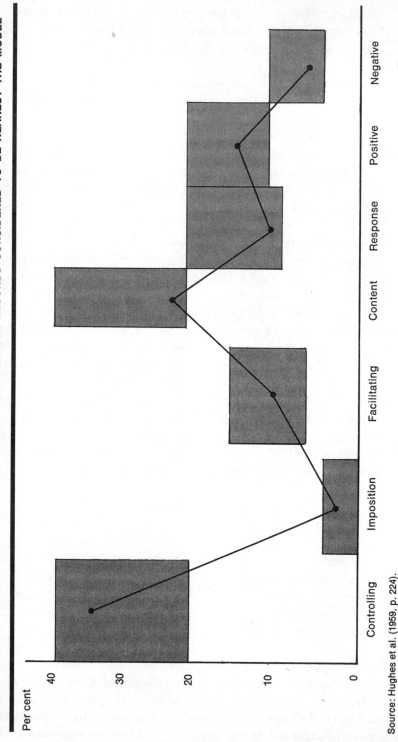

FIGURE 7.1 MODEL OF GOOD TEACHING EXPERIENCED AS PERCENTAGE RANGE FOR EACH MAJOR FUNCTION WITHIN WHICH TEACHING ACTS SHOULD FALL AND THE MEAN OF THE SIX 30-MINUTE RECORDS CONSIDERED TO BE NEAREST THE MODEL

Source: Hughes et al. (1959, p. 224).

haviors is not dealt with. Yet we might anticipate that the temporal distribution of behavior is at least as significant as the overall amount of behavior that occurs in a given category. This issue remains to be resolved. How should Hughes's model be regarded? Although it is in no formal sense a theoretical model of the teaching process, it would seem to have value as a heuristic for the teacher who desires to have a series of criteria by which to measure or to judge his own instructional behaviors.

Unfortunately, Hughes does not provide data in a form that makes it possible to see immediately what the typical performance of the forty-one teachers is. However, we can report something about the extremes of their teaching behavior. In the Hughes sample, no teacher engages in controlling less than 39 per cent of the time, nor more than 68 per cent. Imposition occurs with comparative rarity; a high of 7 per cent was recorded for one teacher, with a low of 1 per cent for several teachers. Ten per cent represents a high for facilitating behavior, and 3 per cent a low. Content-development functions range between 8 and 26 per cent; response, between 2 and 11 per cent; positive affectivity, between 7 and 21 per cent; and negative affectivity, between 3 and 20 per cent.

We might suppose that grade level and subject matter would be significant dimensions for discriminating among behaviors of teachers. Actually, some significant differences do appear, but many of the comparisons across grade level and content do not reflect differences. For purposes of grade-level comparisons, eleven first and second-grade teachers were designated primary teachers, and eleven fifth and sixth-grade teachers were designated intermediate teachers. These two groups were found to differ on a limited number of bases. The primary teachers performed more functions than the intermediate teachers and were both more controlling and more negative.

With respect to differences in teaching behavior across curricular areas, the major ones are found between the activity periods and the more academically oriented arithmetic, reading, and social studies lessons.

Concept Development

By what means are the skills of thinking to be developed? This question is intended to indicate the necessity for the teacher to make several kinds of decisions relevant to his efforts to improve thinking. First of all, how are these efforts to be incorporated into the curriculum? Should thinking be construed as a separate endeavor, constituting its own justification, so to speak, or is skill in thinking better developed within the constraints of more orthodox curricular divisions, such as mathematics, science, history, etc.? Affirmative answers have been given to both sides of this question. However, while it has been demonstrated on several occasions (Fawcett, 1938; Glaser, 1941) that thinking skills can be developed more or less independently of more traditional subject matter without impairing academic progress, that approach has not been highly successful in establishing a firm place for itself in the curriculum.

Taba's (1950) answer to this question is that each area of the curriculum has some unique contribution to make to the development of critical thinking. Evaluation of scientific evidence is not the same as evaluation of evidence in the social sciences. In the social sciences, for example, the thinker must be able to treat attitudes and emotions as part of the data with which he has to work. Consequently, Taba recommends that students should have exposure to systematic training in thinking in a wide variety of curricular fields.

The investigations of Taba (1966; Taba, Levine, & Elzey, 1964) into the development of thinking abilities of elementary school children represent the culmination of her long-time interest in this subject of thinking. Taba's goal was to examine the development of pupils' thinking skills in the classroom under optimum conditions. These optimum conditions included a curriculum that was itself developed for and geared to an emphasis upon critical thinking; teaching strategies that focused upon the development of cognitive skills as well as factual knowledge per se; and a span of time of sufficient duration to allow for some significant development of thinking skills. Virtually an entire school year elapsed while data about thinking were collected from the participating classes.

Only classes in the social studies were included in Taba's sample. This restriction was partially a function of her concern that the standard models of thought to which children are exposed are those of science and mathematics, models which are too precise for fields such as the social studies, where probabilistic forms of thinking are required. A second reason was her obvious disagreement with curriculum reformers who assume that an appropriately structured body of knowledge is both the necessary and sufficient condition for producing critical thinking.

Another issue is that of the extent to which training in thinking needs to be emphasized consciously and the extent to which the necessary cognitive training is provided simply by "penetrating the structure of content" and by following the sequences of thought dictated by that structure. Some curriculum experiments, especially those which concentrate largely on producing texts and sequences of materials, seem to take it for granted that content organizations automatically provide training in the development of necessary thought processes. Since the structure of the subject is most easily discernible in fields like mathematics and science, it is easy to be deluded into thinking that proper arrangement of content automatically provides an appropriate sequence for learning the required cognitive operation (Taba, Levine, & Elzey, 1964, p. 27).

This investigation focused upon three clusters of thought processes: grouping and classification of information, interpretation of data and making inferences, and the application of known principles and facts to explain other events or phenomena. These cognitive tasks were analyzed both for the elements and operations involved in them and the sequential steps in mastering them.

Taba's basic hypothesis was that concepts constitute the basic form of cognition from which all other cognitive processes flow. She defined concept development as having three components: *differentiating* specific properties of objects or events, *grouping* items together on the basis of specified properties, and *labeling* or *categorizing* objects after they are combined.

Major attention was paid to what each of these operations would look like in the interactive setting of the classroom. For example, at the concept-development level, differentiating could involve enumeration or the specification of items while grouping would require placing together a series of diverse items such as parks, hospitals, and schools—all of which can be grouped as community facilities. Labeling, on the other hand, involves decisions about subsumption: Is weather subordinate or superordinate to climate?

Data interpretation and drawing inferences from such interpretations is typically an inductive process of arriving at a generalization. The operations to be performed at this level involve assembling concrete information, explaining certain events, relating points of information to each other, and formulating a generalization or inference.

The application of principles to new phenomena involves first making a prediction, and then establishing parameters either empirically or logically that allow for a test of the prediction.

Taba has recognized the ubiquity of teachers' questions in the interactive process of teaching. If the goal of improving children's thinking is to be reached through the verbal activities of the classroom, teachers must give careful thought to the formulation of their questions, and what it is that they expect question asking to accomplish.

> The role of questions becomes crucial, and the way of asking questions by far the most influential single teaching act. A focus set by the teacher's questions circumscribes the mental operations which students can perform, determines which points they can explore, and which modes of thought they learn. A question such as "What are the important cities in the Balkans?" provides a poor focus in several respects. Because no criterion of importance is available, such a question develops an unproductive mode of thinking in addition to training in arbitrary judgment. Such a questions suggests, first, that one can judge the importance of cities without a criterion. For example, does one look for large cities, capitals, ancient ones, or what? Most students faced with such a question have only two alternatives: guessing what the teacher wants or trying to recollect what the book says of the topic, both cognitively not the most productive activities (Taba, Levine, & Elzey, 1964, pp. 53–54).

Questions ought not to be viewed solely as single entities entirely independent of each other. Rather, for questions to be productive, teachers should plan strategies of questioning, strategies that interlard the constraints of specific focus with those that provide a degree of latitude to the pupil in how he chooses to construct his response.

> The impact of teaching lies not alone in its single acts, but in the manner in which these acts are combined into a pattern; the particular combination of focusing, extending, and lifting; the length of time spent on a particular operation in preparation for another level, how the functions of "giving" and "seeking" are distributed; and the way in which the intake of information is alternated with processing, transforming, and synthesizing the information (Taba, Levine, & Elzey, 1964, p. 55).

EXPERIMENTAL STUDIES OF TEACHERS' ABILITY TO EXPLAIN SUBJECT MATTER

The organization of this and the following section follows Smith's analysis of teaching behavior as consisting of monologs and episodes. Monologs occur less frequently than episodes and tend to be given by teachers rather than by students. Recently an experimental program under the direction of Gage (1968) has sought to discover the variables that control effective explaining behavior. Because the form in which the experimental explanations were made is similar to the typical form of monologs or brief lectures, we shall devote this brief section to an examination of Gage's research program. In the next section, we shall review the more extensive body of literature on classroom discussions and productive thinking.

Gage (1968) contends that explaining is a central intellectual component of the teaching role, and that one is never playing the role of teacher more completely than when explaining content to students. To study the phenomenon of teacher explaining, the following general procedure is used. Teachers are given an article on some topic such as "Yugoslavia" to read and study. They are then asked to give about a fifteen-minute lecture or monolog to their students, who in turn are examined by the researcher to determine their comprehension of the teacher's explanation.

Although the research program is continuing, several variables related to the effectiveness of teachers' explanations have been specified.

1. There is some generality in the ability of teachers to explain. Pupil comprehension scores based upon two different explanations by the same teacher showed a significant relationship. At another extreme, little or no correlation was evidenced between scores of two different classes who were given explanations of different topics by the same teacher. In other words, a teacher whose explanation produced high comprehension in one lesson does not necessarily achieve it in a second lesson. The emphasis of the research program is to discover variables that determine such outcomes and, ultimately, to devise ways of training teachers as more effective "explainers."

2. The clarity of the teachers' explanations as rated by other adults correlates highly with students' comprehension scores. Unfortunately, ratings of clarity do not provide information about the variables of an explanation that render it clear. Other variables, such as the teacher's planning and organization of the lesson, also tend to be related to comprehension although not as frequently as clarity or skill of presentation. Noncognitive variables (for example, estimates of the rapport between teachers and pupils, humor, warmth, or voice quality) are not related to achievement.

3. Several kinds of teacher behaviors have been found to differentiate good from poor explainers (as inferred from achievement scores earned by their students). Some of the findings are specific to given content areas, others apply across several subject matters. Teachers whose pupils achieve higher scores tend to manipulate the content verbally, exploring concepts with pupils; to use introductions consisting of overviews or analogies; to use repetition and review; to praise students' responses; and to integrate these responses into the lesson.

Other behaviors noted are gestures and movements, the use of "rule-example-rule" patterns (that is, the teacher sandwiches an illustration between two statements of a rule or generalization), and explaining links. These links are prepositions or conjunctions that signal the teacher's giving of the cause or purpose of an event or idea.

On the other hand, vagueness in teachers' explanations has been shown to be related to lower comprehension by students. Vagueness is indicated by a high proportion of *indeterminate qualifiers* ("rather," "very," "any number of," etc.) and of *probability* words ("sometimes," "most of the time," etc.).

The conclusions we have cited here were summarized by Rosenshine (1968). The research program is moving into a phase in which teachers will be trained to increase the use of rule-example-rule teaching, and explaining links, and to diminish the vagueness of their explanations. The fact that these variables have been found to be correlated with success in post hoc analyses does not prove that they are causal. If, however, the training of teachers leads to improved student comprehension scores, Gage and his associates will have made an important contribution to the improvement of teaching and learning.

AN ANALYSIS OF PROGRAMS INTENDED TO IMPROVE CLASSROOM THINKING

There is reason to believe that skill in thinking productively is teachable. Taba contends that children can learn to think; therefore, they can be taught to think. If teachers can teach children to think, then it follows that teachers can learn strategies of instruction that make such an outcome more probable.

The Taba Project to Develop Productive Thinking

In her project, Taba provided a training program for the teachers. Twenty teachers of grades two through six were involved. They were selected principally because of their interest in participating and because of an expressed willingness to change their own teaching behavior in the interests of fostering pupil skills in thinking. The teachers represented a school district in which the social, economic, and ability levels of the pupils were above average.

It is important to note that the teachers' schools were already using curriculum materials in elementary social studies which Taba had helped to develop and which were intended to emphasize intellectual skills of pupils. Thus, there is a strong presumption that efforts by teachers to strengthen thinking abilities would be highly congruent with the demands of the existing curriculum. When the teacher and the curriculum combine to work toward common purposes, it follows that teachers are less likely to experience frustration and conflict associated with dissonance between their goals and those of the textbooks and other materials in use; moreover, common educational goals are more likely to be achieved because the teacher and the teaching materials reinforce each other rather than work at cross-purposes.

A total of ten days' training was given to the project teachers during the year of this study. One full week prior to the opening of school was devoted to an analysis of the structure and rationale of the social studies curriculum. This training incorporated considerations of the sources used to develop and select criteria for curriculum development, the objectives of the curriculum for the elementary school years and for each grade level, and explanations and clarifications of issues pertinent to the selection of social studies content, and its sequence and organization within the curriculum.

The remaining days of training were distributed among half-day training sessions conducted throughout the school year. Most of those sessions concentrated upon procedures for teaching cognitive skills. The intent of these sessions was to communicate certain knowledge, develop instructional skills, and instill or alter teacher attitudes about pupil thinking. In particular, efforts were made to help teachers to understand that not all subject matter is equally worthwhile, to learn to discriminate the important from the trivial, and to distribute instructional emphases accordingly.

Attention was called to the importance of studying the process of children's thinking, as well as the products or final outcomes, and to the significance of the sequential steps that lead to the mastery of a skill. Also emphasized was the role played by the maturity of pupils in both the process and product. The function of information in thinking was dealt with, special reference being accorded to the potential detrimental effects of too great detail at the wrong time. Finally, an effort was made to develop an understanding that the inductive development of ideas is a time-consuming process compared with more traditional expository methods of communicating subject matter.

The methods of training used with the teachers were designed to involve them actively in the process of teaching for new purposes, and to provide concrete models for them. For instance, care was taken to present in terms the teachers could easily comprehend the nature of the theory underlying teaching strategies.

Work on each of the cognitive tasks involved three steps: (1) A presentation was made of the process itself and of the progressive steps involved in securing mastery of it. These presentations were always accompanied by illustrations of the tasks and procedures. (2) A typescript of one discussion involving the task under study was scored by the teachers. Group discussion then centered around an analysis of the patterns used, and the teacher's successes and failures. (3) Each teacher was provided with a typescript of one of his own lessons and was given the task of scoring and analyzing it. Taba opined that the teachers appeared to learn most about teaching behavior from the practice of analyzing scripts, their own and those of colleagues. Despite the seeming reasonableness of this contention, evidence is needed that the anticipated outcomes do in fact occur.

Classroom discussions. Four lessons of each of the teachers were tape-recorded at intervals throughout the year. The first record was made at the initial session and dealt with grouping and classification. Interpretation of data was the focus of the second and third tapings made at different times during the middle of the school year, and the final tape was recorded at the end of the year. The purpose of the final record was to produce data about the behavior of teachers and pupils as they applied previously acquired knowledge to make predictions about consequences that will ensue from described hypothetical conditions.

There were some commonalities of approach to each lesson by all of the teachers, at least at each grade level. One or more questions called *focusing questions* were agreed upon by the teachers for each lesson. The following excerpts illustrate the range of such focusing questions employed to stimulate discussion.

> *Discussion 1:* Cognitive tasks: *grouping and classification.*
> *2nd grades:* When you go to the store, what do you buy?
> *4th grades:* What do you think California might have been like long ago?
> *6th grades:* What differences would you expect to find if you lived in Latin America? (Taba, Levine, & Elzey, 1964, p. 109.)

Maximum commonality across all classes was achieved with the second recorded lesson. A film called "African Girl" was shown to the pupils of each class. The teachers constructed a common set of questions to initiate discussion after viewing the film.

> *Discussion 2:* Cognitive task: *interpretation and inference.*
> **1.** What happens in this picture? (Let the class mention items on any level to make sure that there is sufficient basis in concrete descriptive information for the second question.)
> **2.** Which of these things stood out especially for you . . . and why?
> 2.1 What did you notice about home life?
> 2.2 What did you see about the market place?
> 2.3 What did you notice about food? (Taba, Levine, & Elzey, 1964, pp. 109–110.)

Prior to the third discussion, each class had pursued a topic to the point of having accumulated data that now required interpretation, integration, and generalization.

> *Discussion 3:* Cognitive task: *interpretation and inference.*
> *2nd grades:* What kinds of services are available in the local community?
> *3rd grades:* What changes are occurring in Africa?
> *5th grades:* What changes have been made in America by other people coming here?

> *Discussion 4:* Cognitive task: *Applying known information and principles to explain new phenomena or to predict consequences of described conditions.*

2nd grades: What would happen if all of a sudden the farmers in (name of local town) did not have irrigation water?
3rd grades: Suppose all the deserts were irrigated with water. How would this change the nomad's way of life?
5th grades: Suppose that Americans suddenly discovered a large, beautiful island out in the Pacific Ocean right close to California, inhabited by uncivilized people who were farmers. Gold was discovered on this island. What would happen? (Taba, Levine, & Elzey, 1964, pp. 110–111.)

As in the Bellack and Smith studies, Taba had to develop a unit for the analyses of classroom language. She settled upon the *thought unit* which she ". . . defined as a remark or series of remarks which express a more or less complete idea, serves a specified function, and can be classified by a level of thought" (Taba, Levine, & Elzey, 1964, p. 115). Thus the length of a thought unit is controlled conceptually rather than by time or length of passage. A single thought unit may be one word or a paragraph.

Because the total analytical scheme is quite complex and no purpose would be served by presenting it in its entirety, we have tried to select for discussion only those few elements which have most direct relevance for teachers. Taba identified four groups of function codings that are of particular importance in describing the relationship of teaching strategy to thought levels. These are focusing (F), extending thought on the same level (X), lifting thought to a higher level (L), and controlling thought (C).

Focusing centers the topic for discussion. The following question, "If the desert had all the water it needed, what would happen?" designates the content to be discussed, and the level (kind) of cognitive response that will be appropriate.

Statements that extend thought either give or ask for additional information, or they provide clarification and elaboration of what has already been said. The level of thought, however, does not change as a result of this extension. The following exchange takes place at the level of specific information. The last four statements are extensions of the first.

1. C Malibu took money home with her.
2. T What did Malibu do with the money?
3. C She saved it.
4. C She put it underground.
5. C She put sticks and tin over it.

6. C   Before she did that, she put it in a little pot (Taba, Levine, & Elzey, 1964, p. 121).

Lifting occurs when the teacher or a child calls for an upward shift in the level of thinking. In the example cited here, the teacher attempts to lift the level from information to explanation.

1. C   They carried things in baskets on their heads.
2. T   Explain why.
3. C   I suppose they can carry more things that way (Taba, Levine, & Elzey, 1964, p. 121).

Controlling thought is a teacher function. It amounts to a teacher performing cognitive operations that should be performed by pupils.

A significant point for the strategy of improving classroom thinking is raised by Taba's observation that premature efforts by the teacher to lift the level of children's thinking in discussion results in a return by them to operations at the information level. Since her report does not make clear the regularity with which this occurs, nor does it specify the conditions under which lifts are premature, it is advisable to treat this observation as an intriguing and testable hypothesis, not as a conclusion.

Because of our extensive earlier concern with pupil participation, we may inquire about the distribution of participation in circumstances where the direct objective of the teacher is to foster thinking skills. Remember that the eighty lessons of this study were all cast as discussions between teacher and pupils; little monolog teaching was done. Taba's general impression is that the participation of pupils is higher than usual, and that participation tends to increase with grade level. Actually, over all classes and all lessons, total participation was 76 per cent. Participation ranged from a low of 33 per cent in one discussion to 100 per cent in several of the eighty discussions.

Teaching strategies and levels of thought. On the average, the pupils were responsible for fifty-eight per cent of all thought units; the teachers, for only forty-two per cent. Minor variations occurred in this ratio across grade levels or from one discussion to another. Pupils do little seeking, a fact which by now is well established; however, there was a trend for the percentage of thought-unit seeking done by the pupils to increase from the first to the final discussion.

What happens when teachers try to extend and to lift the level of thinking of their students? These seem to be among the most crucial questions we have to deal with in attempting to improve the quality of thinking in the classroom. There is a correspondence between the amount of extending and of lifting sought by the teachers and the amount expressed by the pupils.

Taba found that teachers sought extension at the same intellectual level in nineteen per cent of their moves, and pupils expressed extensions of thought 10 per cent of the time. Only 69 per cent of teacher requests for extension were responded to by the pupils, however. There is wide variation in the success enjoyed in this activity by groups of teachers. The first discussion in the second grades produced a corresponding response in only 24 per cent of the cases where teachers invited extensions. At the upper end, the fourth grade teachers achieved 90 per cent correspondence with pupils in the third discussion.

Teachers seek lifts in the level of thinking much less frequently than they do extensions of a thought. Teachers called for lifting of thought in only 2 per cent of their thought units; pupils likewise moved up the level of their thinking only 2 per cent of the time. Correspondence is not perfect; teachers enjoyed success 76 per cent of the time. However, the variation among teachers was much smaller than was true for extensions.

The frequency of higher levels of thought diminished across the cognitive tasks of differentiating, grouping, and categorizing. The data

> ... indicates that it is easier to perform the operations of grouping and classification and to give reasons than it is to make inferences in the light of consciously stated cause and effect relationships and to setting factual and logical connections between conditions and predicted consequences. In other words, as the cognitive skills involved in the task approach formal thinking the frequency of their use decreases (Taba, Levine, & Elzey, 1964, pp. 155–156).

With reference to our earlier discussion, we are not particularly surprised that Taba discovered an absence of relationship between measured intelligence of the pupils in the participating classes and either the frequency of their participation or the characteristic level of thought of their participation. However, a significant relationship does exist between the amount of participation a pupil engages in (when participation is dichotomized into high and low) and the level of his contribution (judged either high, middle, or low). Taba suggests that oral participation in group discussions that have a substantive purpose is a skill that develops with practice. Low participating pupils make a lower order intellectual contribution because of their lack of practice. While the data presented are correlational and do not permit us to make such an interpretation in any final sense, it seems a reasonable interpretation and one that holds out hope that teaching could help to improve matters for the low participators. However, without more conclusive evidence, the alternative interpretation (that high participators dominate the verbal scene because they know more and/or can think better) is equally acceptable. The matter is one worthy of careful pursuit and analysis.

Taba's Teaching Module

A subsequent investigation was conducted by Taba (1966) in which the strategies and procedures of the first one were extended and modified. Again the emphasis was upon the development of productive thinking of elementary school children, this time limited to students in the fourth, fifth, and sixth grades. Teachers of the experimental classes were given a training program aimed at providing them with strategies for helping children learn to form concepts, to draw inferences and make generalizations, and to apply principles to new situations. Once more the curricular area was the social studies, and again the principal data for the experiment were drawn from the tapescripts of four lessons taught at various times throughout the school year.

One of the most significant developments of this latter study was the *teaching module*. The teaching module is a sequence of teaching acts that occur in sequence and are identified as leading to the production of high-level thinking by a pupil or pupils. Modules may be of several forms. In general, they begin with a focusing question by the teacher to which the pupils respond with a prediction. The teacher follows predictions with requests for extension. That request may elicit one of several responses; a pupil may give another prediction, which the teacher either repeats or asks the child to support, or he may give an unsupported high-level response. The next round of requests for extension or support of an assertion or prediction is followed by a relevant high-level thought by the child or by factual support for his original prediction.

From an analysis of all the classes in her project, Taba determined that modules that led to high-level thinking by pupils were much more frequent in the experimental classes than in the control classes. At the same time, for all classes, high-level thought responses by a pupil tended to be preceded by a sequence of teacher-pupil interactions that fit the form of the module more frequently than not. That is, although the general form of the module leads to higher level thinking by students with some dependability, such an outcome can also be achieved by other (and at this time unspecified) means.

The Effect of Instructional Behavior on Productive Thinking

Gallagher and Aschner (1963) have examined the productive thinking of pupils in relation to the instructional behavior of their teachers. These examinations have been based upon an analytical system for coding such behaviors of teachers and pupils. The system represents a modification and application to classroom settings of the operations categories of Guilford's (1956) well-known structure of intellect. Thus, the cognitive components of classroom language can be identified as memory, convergent thinking, divergent thinking, or evaluation.

In one preliminary study, Gallagher and Aschner (1963) found relationships between one kind of teacher behavior and pupil responses evoked by it. Explicitly, they found that teacher invitations to pupils to respond divergently lead to such responses, and that only a minimal amount of such seeking is required to evoke an array of divergent pupil responses. Although clearly only a starting point, our ability consciously to plan strategies for the emission of thought responses of the kinds desired should improve markedly as continuing efforts of this kind are made.

SUMMARY AND APPLICATION

In this chapter we have suggested that skill in thinking productively is teachable. Moreover, various experimental projects seem to indicate that teachers, through the use of deliberate strategies of instruction, can foster productive thinking in some pupils. At the same time that we accept the hypothesis that teachers can influence the skill and level of thinking accomplished by students, we must point out that our knowledge of the relevant variables, and our knowledge of how to govern those variables, is primitive.

Taba divides teaching strategies into two large categories: generic strategies, which can be characterized with some precision, and individualistic or idiosyncratic strategies, which are unique to individual teachers. The latter category represents the role of art in teaching, or the personal element which depends for its shaping and its success upon the unique relationships between the personality of the teacher and the personalities of the class members. The ultimate validity of those categories is less important than the fact that at this time in eduational history we are unable to formulate instructional strategies that are altogether reliable, or that can be fully specified, or that avoid vagueness and imprecision.

What implications are there in the present discussion of classroom interaction and productive thinking for the behavior of the practicing teacher? We believe that it is possible for the teacher to identify one or more classes of teaching behavior that he wishes to improve in his own performance. Such a class of behavior might be explaining, or strategy for improving concept formation, or another alternative. We would suggest that it is possible for the teacher to identify the kinds of teaching behavior relevant to the skill in mind, and to practice the appropriate skill in his teaching, and subsequently to analyze and plan for its improvement.

If one conceives of the teaching process as a skill, then it is reasonable to anticipate that skill in teaching will improve more or less according to laws that describe improvement in other skilled performances. One of these concerns the role of practice. Ordinarily practice is most useful when it is directed at practicing the right combination of movements, responses, etc. Practice of many skills is aided by feedback to the performer about the quality of his performance. The army recruit firing at a distant target for the first time learns to try to reproduce on subsequent occasions the pattern of behaviors that led to a bull's-eye, and to alter drastically those that resulted in the humiliation of "Maggie's drawers."

Admittedly most teachers probably practice the skills of discourse as much as fifteen, perhaps twenty, hours a week. That is, of course, a great deal of practice. But the behavior of teaching is so complex, and feedback about its adequacy is ordinarily so delayed or so vague, that it probably is not reasonable to predict that teachers will improve their instructional repertoire very markedly as a function of teaching experience, that is, with practice as it ordinarily occurs in classrooms on a day-to-day basis. Moreover, it could be seriously misleading to overemphasize the role of feedback in improving teachers' instructional performance.

Even at a relatively simple level, the rifle instructor never relies solely on the feedback his student will receive from firing his weapon in the absence of tutoring. The student is carefully instructed beforehand in the skills of triangulating, zeroing his weapon, computing elevation and windage, and the proper art of "squeezing off the rounds" as opposed to pulling the trigger.

The golf professional teaches the novice the proper stance at the tee, the interlocking grip on the club, the proper form and feel of the backswing and follow through, the necessity to "keep your head down" and "swing inside out." Simply given a ball and a club, and left to his own devices, the average beginner would make little progress by swinging away. Eloquent testimony to the validity of that statement can be collected on any public golf course on any weekend morning during the golfing season.

Teachers receive virtually no directed practice of the kind we have described for riflery and for golf. We are trying to suggest that the teacher can provide precisely that kind of practice for himself by attempting to match his behavior more and more closely to the models of teaching strategies presented earlier.

Teaching has, historically, been a peculiarly private endeavor. Although teachers engage in verbal discourse with pupils all day long, five days each week throughout the academic year, the presence of an outsider, particularly another adult, in the classroom is typically a special event and one that is likely to create at least mild tension for most teachers. The author has frequently observed at lunch tables and in coffee lounges that teachers seldom discuss with one another the serious professional issues pertinent to the organization and communication of subject matter to their students.

We realize that many teachers may resist any effort to enlist their participation in group activities that involve the analysis of their instructional behavior. In today's schools, however, it is easy to make an occasional tape recording of one's lessons. The teacher can profitably listen several times to a lesson, keeping in mind particular questions. At points where his and/or his pupils' behavior fails to conform reasonably to the paradigm of, say, an explanation, the teacher might construct and rehearse alternative behaviors designed to meet the criteria appropriately. This technique has the added advantage that a teacher can conduct the enterprise entirely by himself, if that is his preferred style of operation.

REFERENCES

Chapter 7

Fawcett, H. P. The nature of proof. *Yearbook of the National Council of Teachers of Mathematics,* 1938, 13.

Gage, N. L., Belgard, Maria, Dell, D., Hiller, J. E., Rosenshine, B., & Unruh, W. R. *Explorations of the teacher's effectiveness in explaining.* Technical Report No. 4. Stanford, Calif.: Stanford Center for Research and Development in Teaching, 1968.

Gallagher, J. J., & Aschner, M. J. A preliminary report on analyses of classroom interaction. *Merrill Palmer Quarterly,* 1963, *9,* 183–194.

Glaser, E. M. An experiment in the development of critical thinking. *Teachers College Contributions to Education,* 1938, No. 843.

Guilford, J. P. The structure of intellect. *Psychological Bulletin,* 1956, *53,* 267–293.

Hudgins, B. B., and Ahlbrand, W. P., Jr. *A study of classroom interaction and thinking.* Technical Report Series No. 8. St. Ann, Mo.: Central Midwestern Regional Educational Laboratory, 1967.

Hughes, Marie et al. *Development of the means for the assessment of the quality of teaching in the elementary school.* Salt Lake City: University of Utah, 1959. (Mimeographed)

Rosenshine, B. To explain: a review of research. *Educational Leadership,* 1968, *26,* 303–309.

Smith, B. O., & Meux, M., et al. *A study of the logic of teaching.* Urbana: Bureau of Educational Research, University of Illinois, 1962.

Smith, B. O., Meux, M., Coombs, J., & Nuthall, G. *A tentative report on the strategies of teaching.* Urbana: Bureau of Educational Research, University of Illinois, 1964.

Smith, B. O., Meux, M., Coombs, J., Nuthall, G., & Precians, R. *A study of the strategies of teaching.* Urbana: Bureau of Educational Research, University of Illinois, 1967.

Smith, L. M., & Hudgins, B. B. *Educational psychology.* New York: Knopf, 1964.

Taba, Hilda. The problems in developing critical thinking. *Progressive Education,* 1950, *28,* 45–48, 61.

Taba, Hilda. *Teaching strategies and cognitive functioning in elementary school children.* San Francisco: San Francisco State College, 1966.

Taba, Hilda, Levine, S., & Elzey, F. F. *Thinking in elementary school children.* San Francisco: San Francisco State College, 1964.

Thomson, R. *The psychology of thinking.* Baltimore: Penguin Books, 1959.

CHAPTER 8

THE ART OF CLASSROOM QUESTIONING

Throughout our previous discussions it has been obvious that the question is the teacher's chief verbal tool for shaping and molding interaction in the classroom as well as a primary source of data for evaluating the substantive knowledge and intellectual skill of his students. By whatever term they may have identified it, the major investigators whom we have reviewed have all stressed the significance of classroom questions. For Smith, the entry is frequently in the form of a question. Bellack's solicitations are almost always in the grammatical form of questions. Taba readily acknowledges the centrality of good questions in facilitating appropriate intellectual development of children, and so on. In this short chapter, we shall try to summarize and integrate what has been implied previously about the centrality of questioning techniques and also examine the available evidence about how teachers use questions, and with what kinds of consequences.

For the most part, we have taken care to describe, analyze, and

The author wishes to acknowledge the contribution of two of his former students in emphasizing the crucial role of classroom questioning and in reviving some important but long-forgotten primary sources. For an extended discussion, see Hoetker and Ahlbrand (1969).

evaluate reports of research and other statements about classroom teaching. We are now going to depart from that custom to an extent. While we shall review a body of research and opinion about the question-asking behavior of teachers, we feel some compunction to go beyond that stage and to try to move in the direction of specifying a useful strategy for formulating classroom questions. This places us upon very shaky ground. Therefore, before we launch this discussion, a few words of explanation are in order—for the author's peace of mind, if for no other purpose.

One of the pitfalls of writing about teaching, which Smith (1951) calls a "practical science," is that one may become prescriptive in the absence of an empirical basis for prescription, thus tending to indoctrinate instead of to teach, or one may attempt to write as though one outcome of teaching were as valuable as any other or, indeed, as though questions of ends and values were irrelevant to discussions of teaching. Let us stress that whatever we say here is not to be construed as a set of rules for conducting classroom recitations. As surely as they become so regarded, the teacher will be left with a stereotyped set of behaviors that embody the worst offenses of the recitation procedures which the critics have so well catalogued.

Another danger is the temptation to infer the positive from a description of the negative. This is somewhat analogous to the confusion between teaching and learning. As we noted earlier, a frequent assumption is that teaching is a mirror image of learning. In other words, if we understand how people learn, we can deduce what teachers must do to insure learning, thus defining teaching by means of our knowledge of learning. We face a comparable problem in our ensuing discussion of question-asking behavior. What we will find is that there exists an extensive catalogue of unproductive behaviors of teachers. The easy but unsubstantiated conclusion is that productive behaviors will be those that are the opposite of the unproductive ones. To illustrate, it has been reported that teachers demand more or less immediate replies to difficult questions and that this tactic is associated with unproductive questioning. The implication exists that if teachers would permit longer periods of silence to ensue, the quality of pupil responses would be enhanced.

CHARACTERISTICS OF TEACHER QUESTIONING

Stevens authored a fascinating monograph on classroom questions published in 1912. As far as we know, she was the first person to study empirically the question-asking and answering behavior of high school teachers and their students. Her findings appear to describe today's teachers and students as accurately as it described those of 1910, upon whom her studies were based (Stevens, 1910). For example, she found that a sample of teachers whom she studied did 64 per cent of the talking in the classroom, asked questions at rates averaging between two and four a minute, and spent about 80 per cent of the class time engaging in what Bellack would identify as soliciting-responding-reacting cycles.

It is enlightening to examine Stevens' generalizations drawn from her findings.

> When I asked a school principal what he considered fair questioning activity for his teachers he replied, after reflection, that he supposed some of his teachers might ask forty-five questions in a forty-five minute period; that is, one question per minute. When I showed him the figures of a series of observations made in his school his reply was, *"Why, when do they think?"* a very good question for principals and teachers to answer (Stevens, 1912, p. 16).

The seven following points are abstracted from Stevens' more prolonged interpretation of her findings based upon 100 observations of teaching in the secondary school. All major areas of curriculum of that day were represented in her observations.

> *FIRST:* The large number of questions suggests the maintenance in the classroom, for considerable portions of time, of a highly strung nervous tension where there should be natural and normal conditions. This high-pressure atmosphere is always a creation or reflection of the manner of the teacher, with whom it is sometimes wholly temperamental and sometimes only assumed in the classroom for the purpose of gripping the attention of pupils. Attention once secured and the pace once established, it seems to be characteristic of classroom procedure to accelerate the tempo rather than to slow down to one that is more normal and more consistent with nature's own processes of mental activity.
>
> The teacher who has acquired the habit of conducting recitations at the rate of from one hundred to two hundred questions and answers per classroom period of forty-five minutes has truly assumed the pace that kills. It is deadly to the nervous organism that maintains it and, by reflection, injurious to the children who live in that atmosphere.

SECOND: The large number of questions suggests that the teacher is doing most of the work of the class hour instead of directing the pupils in the doing. One reason why one hundred and fifty questions *can* be asked in forty minutes is due to the fact that the teacher can think more rapidly and talk more rapidly than his pupils, and so, in order to cover a large amount of subject matter, he carries the trend of the lesson through his questions, the pupils merely punctuating the series with short answers from the text . . . (Stevens, 1912, p. 17).

THIRD: The large number of questions suggests that whenever teachers, either individually or collectively, preserve such a pace for any length of time, the largest educational assets that can be reckoned are verbal memory and superficial judgment. It is quite obvious that with the rapid fire method of questioning there is no time allowed a pupil to go very far afield in his experience in order to recall or to associate ideas in fruitful ways. He is called upon merely to reflect somebody else—the author of his textbook, generally—in small and carefully dissected portions, or to give forth snap judgments at the point of the bayonet (p. 23).

FOURTH: The large number of questions suggests that there is no time in the mechanics of the school room to cultivate the gentle art of expression. The query goes up from educators and thoughtful parents everywhere, "Why do our young people express themselves so badly?" "What are our schools doing to cultivate the powers of speech?" The only way to develop powers of speech is to give opportunity for their exercise under skilled guidance. When the day's work—yes, the week's work—is so largely given over to rapid questioning, there is no time for niceties of speech. When there are from two to five answers per minute, each supposedly reflecting a mental process, there is little time given to correction of crudities in utterance; furthermore, it frequently seems that the teacher is so gratified to catch a glimmer of an idea from a pupil, that he will promptly seize it, amplify it, clothe it fittingly, the pupil meanwhile thinking he has said something creditable. Why does the teacher do this? For some reason that is real or imaginary he has set himself a pace and he cannot allow the time necessary for a pupil to recall, associate and *express* an idea. If this happened occasionally one might consider it justified, but it is a very common situation with high pressure questioners (pp. 23–24).

FIFTH: The large number of questions suggests that there is little thought given to the needs of individuals. The teacher sets the pace in his questioning: the pupils follow as a body, or drop by the wayside. When pupils become interested in their work and begin to think for themselves, it is very natural for them to ask questions, and they will do it invariably if allowed to do so. In the elementary school, the children are encouraged to seek information,[1] but in high school there is no time apparently for individual initiative. Take what the text-book gives you and be satisfied, seems to be the watchword of many classrooms. A glance through the stenographic reports shows that few questions are asked by the pupils, and when asked, they are passed over apologetically or deferred to a more convenient season. The moment we admit that we ask from 75 to 175 questions in a class period, we commit ourselves as 'drivers' of youth instead of 'leaders'; drill masters instead of educators.

SIXTH: The large number of questions suggests that we are coming, more and more, to make the classroom the place for displaying knowledge instead of a laboratory for getting and using it. At the close of a class hour, the teacher assigns a lesson for the next day; the pupils take the books home for the purpose of learning the lesson; the following day the teacher gives the pupils the opportunity to display how much or how little they learned. In some classes this represents the process of class activity from the beginning of the year to the end. Hearing the lesson or, quite aptly, 'backing the book' is the function of education. There is little effort made to adjust or use knowledge so acquired, or to work it over with knowledge previously acquired.

SEVENTH: The large number of questions suggests that in actual practice there is very little effort put forth to teach our boys and girls to be self-reliant, independent mental workers. The

---

[1] We will deal with this point in fuller detail later. However, it seems appropriate to indicate at this point that Dodl (1965) found question asking by elementary school children in contemporary schools a rare form of behavior.

discrepancy between our theory and practice is nowhere more patent. With the tremendous pressure incident to the rehearsal of questions numbering from 70 to 170, for the purpose of covering every conceivable issue expressed in the pages of a text assignment, the teacher loses sight of the fact that he has a *youth* to teach through the medium of his subject. There is no time to teach him how to study: how to organize subject matter, how to judge relative worths of facts studied, what to memorize. Even if the teacher himself possesses a plan of work that is in itself a model of organization, its value is likely to be lost sight of in the rapidity and intensity of questioning activity. If there is no time for the teacher's own fine intellectual work to be made apparent it is not to be expected that time will be found for the slower process of forming and fixing habits of study with boys and girls.

There is no use in claiming to teach boys and girls how to study, and how to command their own intellectual forces by the current practice of keeping them at the point of the bayonet in rehearsal of text-book facts at the rate of two or four per minute (pp. 25–26).

A decade after the appearance of Stevens' monograph, Miller (1922) observed that high school teachers allow far too brief an interval between asking a question and demanding an answer. He had given an analogies test individually to high school freshmen, who had required, on the average, about fourteen seconds to supply a single-word answer to a fairly simple, straightforward problem and to do so in the presence of a single observer. According to Miller, teachers typically pose more complex questions (the data would not often support his assertion on this point), but they demand almost immediate replies, tending to be unaware of or for other reasons ignoring the burden imposed upon the student who has to construct a connected response and deliver it before perhaps thirty classmates as well as an impatiently waiting teacher. The following general description of teacher behavior is as apt today as it was in 1922:

If the answer is not given almost immediately, the teacher interrupts by meaningless remarks, by a needless repetition of the question, by passing the question on to some other pupil, or by answering the question herself. She can't endure the silence that must prevail while the pupil is thinking and organizing his material, and commonly feels that she must break the silence by making a remark of some kind, however useless and distracting it may be (Miller, 1922, p. 207).

We have fairly documented two characteristics of teachers' questioning behavior or, more aptly, two views of the same characteristic. The rate of question asking during the interactive phases of teaching tends to be high, averaging about two questions a minute. One inevitable consequence of this is that students have little time in which to think about an answer, usually only a very few seconds being allowed to elapse in silence.

QUESTION ASKING BY PUPILS

Pupils rarely ask questions as part of their classroom behavior. Any number of writers have remarked upon the strange role reversal between teacher and pupil that occurs when they enter the classroom. Would it not seem natural for the untutored member of the pair to express his ignorance and his desire for edification by calling upon the older and wiser member to answer his questions? Stevens, in fact, discriminates between *natural questions,* which are of the kind just described, and *formal questions,* characterized by the fact-checking query of the teacher. In this connection, Stevens recounts a poignant story about the different fates encountered by two small boys who asked natural questions.

Within a few months, I have chanced to hear two conversations carried on in front of a window through which students could be seen modeling in clay. In one instance the conversation between child and father ran thus: "What are they doing down there, daddy?" "They are modeling in clay." "What are they doing that for?" "Well, they want to learn how to make a statue that looks like somebody." "Is the somebody there?" "Yes, he is probably sitting in the corner." "What are they making it of?" "Of clay. We will walk around on 116th Street, if you like, and I will show you a statue that was made by a sculptor who began it just as these students are making that one." We can picture the child's introduction to Daniel French's Alma Mater in front of the Columbia Library and the unfolding of his intelligence regarding its construction as the boy plied his questions, and received stimulating answers. A few days later, standing before the same window another child asked practically the same initial question of his nurse, who gave the response, "O, making mud pies, I guess." "What are those big people making mud pies for, Mary?" "O, don't bother me now with any more questions." Whereupon the child turned his attention and his activities to teasing his dog. In both cases the questions were "natural," that is, the would be learners were the questioners. The educational opportunity was the same: in the first instance the learner's initiative was judiciously guided; in the other it was killed outright (Stevens, 1912, pp. 72–73).

We earlier noted Stevens' supposition that elementary schools are much more "natural" in their concern for interests of pupils than are the secondary schools. But this presumption seems not to bear up too well under careful scrutiny. Dodl (1965) observed fourteen intermediate grade classes with the explicit intention of studying the kinds of questions pupils ask, and the conditions of teacher behavior that are conducive to such questioning. In general, his findings support other contentions (Bellack, Kliebard, Hyman, & Smith, 1966) that the pupil's classroom role does not include question asking. Less than 2 per cent of the behaviors coded were questions asked by pupils. Dodl concluded that elementary teachers do little to encourage children to ask questions.

The Bellack data inform us in a statistical sense about the infrequency of student question asking. But findings reported by Corey a generation ago help us to understand some of the implications of this behavior for individual students on a day-to-day basis. Half a dozen science classes were each observed for a full week and verbatim language records were taken. The following analysis concerns the questions asked by pupils:

> The 169 pupils, for the five day period, asked less than an average of one question each. Fahey found that the median number of questions asked by the pupils during two consecutive semesters was eleven. During the course of the year seven of the children asked no questions whatsoever.
>
> Neither the questions nor the answers were long enough to express involved concepts. The difference between the length of the questions of the teachers and the pupils was rather marked, as was the variation from class to class in the length of questions asked by pupils. In the eleventh grade English class the one question asked by a pupil was a monosyllabic "What?"
>
> If talk is a type of activity which results in learning on the

part of the speaker, it might be reasonable to assume that the greater part of the class time should be consumed by pupil talk. . . . The variation from class to class is significant. In seventh grade science the pupils talked 20 per cent of the time, while in eleventh grade English, largely because of oral reading, the pupils were . . . talking approximately half of each period. Speaking in terms of averages, the chances were about sixty to one that the teacher of a class rather than a particular pupil would be talking at any one time, and about two to one that teachers rather than pupils would be talking.

The pedagogical significance of these data depends somewhat on one's philosophy of instruction. If it is contended, first, that questions asked in class should require pupils to reflect, to make inferences, and to develop generalizations, it is clear that most of the oral questions asked by the teachers of these classes were not satisfactory. Second, if the number of spontaneous questions asked by pupils reflects their interest in, and need for, the learning being offered them, such experiences in the classes observed were not particularly stimulating (Corey, 1940, pp. 751–752).

THE IMPROVEMENT OF CLASSROOM QUESTIONING

We obviously need some criteria for determining "improvement" in questioning techniques. It is possible to state some such criteria which will meet with general agreement; to meet the criteria will be more problematic. In some cases, empirical data not currently available would be necessary to tell us whether the demands of the criterion have been fulfilled. However, we shall endeavor to be as concrete as possible about procedures for effective questioning.

First, *in general, work toward reducing the number of questions asked of pupils.* Stevens' conclusion on this point is instructive: "A large number of questions is an indisputable index of bad teaching (except in some modern language and developmental lessons). A small number of questions does not necessarily indicate good teaching" (Stevens, 1912, p. 71).

Second, *make a deliberate effort to allow pupils a reasonable period of time in which to construct responses to questions.* It would seem that this interval should somehow increase with the complexity of the desired answer, and with the independence of the answer from any formal preparation the student may have been expected to make. It is true that this recommendation sounds a bit like the famous recipe for tiger stew (First, catch a tiger). That is, the compelling and controlling forces of classroom behavior are often social, shaped by the presence of many people in close proximity to each other, and the seeming impropriety of extended silences during designated periods of interaction. Bloom and Broder (1950) found that college students who were poor problem solvers were characterized by an attitude of assuming that if they did not immediately know the answer to a problem (question), an attempt to reason it through was unlikely to achieve positive results.

If the teacher behaves as though his questions are to be thought about, that silent cognitive activity is a respectable way for teachers and pupils to spend their class time intermittently, he may discover that pupils follow suit and will use intervals of silence to sally forth into productive thinking. However, this point must not be taken too literally. Taba (1966) learned that high levels of pupil thinking depended in part upon the teacher's sense of timing of questions, and the sequence with which they are posed. Repetition and restatement of the children's predictions or of the teacher's questions seemed often to play a significant part in developing children's thinking.

Third, *analyze the cognitive level appropriate to the task at hand.*

Some years ago Bloom and others (1956) produced the first of a projected three-volume *Taxonomy of Educational Objectives.* That first book, *Cognitive Domain,* represented an effort to divide intellectual skills into five categories. These, plus a broad and important category of knowledge (memory), define the range of cognitive activities in which students might engage. The intellectual skills specified by the taxonomy are comprehension, application, analysis, synthesis, and evaluation. The authors of the taxonomy emphasize that teaching and examining tend to be too narrowly confined to issues of knowledge or memory, with insufficient attention directed toward the development of intellectual skills.

More recently Sanders (1966) has produced a guide for teachers to assist them in asking questions at a variety of levels. Based upon the earlier mentioned taxonomy of educational objectives, Sanders' volume provides many concrete suggestions to teachers for formulating questions that accomplish more than the elicitation from students of memorized facts.

Sanders suggests as a rule of thumb that teachers aim at devoting at least one-third of the class time to questioning at levels above memory. Certainly the selection of one-third is arbitrary (and impossible to defend logically as being superior to one-fourth or one-half), but it does not seem an unreasonable goal, if only because potentially attainable by most teachers.

Sanders makes several excellent general points relevant to developing higher order questions. First and foremost is his assertion that greater breadth and depth of understanding of the subject matter is required of the teacher when he attempts to concentrate on questions that are more intellectually demanding than simply factual recall. If the teacher is content to ask questions principally at the memory level, he need not have much more subject matter sophistication than the array of information presented by the textbook.

A brief episode in Herman Wouk's (1951) classic novel of the Second World War, *The Caine Mutiny,* illustrates the point. Willie Keith, a midshipman, has delighted in discovering that his training manual characterizes the submarine as principally useful for coastal defense because of its limited cruising range. This was at a time in 1943 when the Germans were regularly sinking American merchant marine vessels only a few miles off our own coast. The next day in class, the instructor called upon Keith to identify the chief use of submarines. After trying to ascertain whether the teacher wanted an answer based upon actual events or upon Navy doctrine, Willie replied in the following words:

> "Submarines, because of their small cruising range . . . are chiefly suitable for coastal defense."
>
> "Correct," said Ensign Brain, writing down a perfect mark. "Why all the stalling?" (Wouk, 1951, p. 27.)

Textbooks have the merit of presenting large bodies of systematically organized content to students, but ordinarily they are poor vehicles for generating good questions or provoking thinking. More than a single set of ideas must be presented to students in order to make possible the kind of questioning activity advocated.

Finally, teachers need to be aware that questions or problems posed to students may contain potential sources of error that are largely irrelevant to the skill under question. If the teacher wishes to promote skill in evaluating, for example, he must take some steps to insure that the factual argument which is the basis of the evaluation is known by the student, or is somehow made available to him.

Fourth, *adjust the cognitive level of questions to information that students already possess.* Aschner (1961) pointed out a common difficulty that teachers face as they ask questions, namely, that the level and complexity of intellectual gyrations demanded of a student depend heavily upon what he already knows, and the form in which he knows it. For instance, the teacher may ask his students to compare and contrast the basic philosophical tenets of the two major U.S. political parties with the expectation that the question will force the students to select and organize a variety of information at their disposal and present it in a form that is somewhat new and different from their previous organization of it. However, if the textbook read the night before provides just the kind of synthesis that the teacher's question calls for, the student's response may be nothing more than the recollection of a set of facts.

Rodgers (1968) reported an unusual and interesting study relevant to this problem. His findings suggest that the relationship between the student's prior knowledge and the question asked of him is further complicated by the fact that students consult various sources for the answers to even apparently straightforward and unambiguous questions, and that teachers cannot depend very heavily upon all the students in a class arriving at the same answer, or the answer that the teacher expects. He observes also that as questions call for more reasoning by students, the diversity of responses increases.

Aschner and Rodgers are in agreement that, to the extent that questions are clearly and precisely formulated, the teacher can more successfully focus the learner's attention on the intellectual task intended. It should be clear that the precision with which questions are asked does not limit their level of cognitive demand. On the contrary, we would expect vague and ill-structured questions to lead to little thought on anybody's part.

Throughout our discussion of classroom questioning, we have implied that teachers can assist students in achieving important educational goals if they work at the improvement of question asking. In large part, we have suggested that improvement means asking questions at higher levels of intellectual functioning; more questions that involve reasoning, judging, and creative thinking; and fewer that call for only remembering, to use the simple categories provided by Aschner (1961). Does this claim have any validity?

A piece of research reported by Huckins (1968) illustrates the kind of evidence needed to support our contention. By itself, of course, a single study hardly constitutes incontrovertible proof. Huckins conducted an experiment with several sixth-grade social studies classes. He developed two sets of study questions. One set emphasized knowledge or remembering and the other, analysis and evaluation. Each child who participated in the experiment devoted about thirty minutes a day for four school weeks to studying his regular social studies text material and relating that study to answering the questions specially constructed by Huckins. At the end of the four-week period, all the children (about 250 of them) took an achievement examination based upon the social studies material they had been studying during the experimental period. Two major results appeared. The children in the classes that had answered evaluation and analysis questions made higher achievement scores than those in the other classes. The better readers in all classes also made higher achievement scores.

Huckins' interpretation is that the higher order questions led to more active involvement or interaction of the pupils with the instructional materials and, therefore, to improved achievement. Unfortunately, Huckins' research report does not include samples of the achievement test. Although we favor his interpretation, the possibility exists that items on the final test were more like the items the experimental children had studied for the previous four weeks, thus giving them an advantage over the others.

Formulating questions that help students to think better is a difficult job. The beginnings that have been made in the systematic study of this task hold promise that more dependable knowledge applicable to classroom teaching will be produced. At this time, we can begin to see the outline of some of these strategies and we have attempted to describe them with some thoroughness.

REFERENCES

Chapter 8

Aschner, M. J. McCue. Asking questions to trigger thinking. *NEA Journal,* 1961, 6, 44–46.

Bellack, A. A., Kliebard, H. M., Hyman, R. T., & Smith, F. L., Jr. *The language of the classroom.* New York: Teachers College Press, Columbia University, 1966.

Bloom, B. S., & Broder, Lois J. *Problem-solving processes of college students: an exploratory investigation.* Chicago: University of Chicago Press, 1950.

Bloom, B. S. et al. *Taxonomy of educational objectives. Handbook I: cognitive domain.* New York: Longmans, Green, 1956.

Corey, S. M. The teachers out-talk the pupils, *School Review,* 1940, 48, 745–752.

Dodl, N. R. Pupil questioning behavior in the context of classroom interaction. Unpublished doctoral dissertation, Stanford University, 1965.

Hoetker, J., & Ahlbrand, W. P., Jr. The persistence of the recitation. *American Educational Research Journal,* 1969, 6, 145–167.

Huckins, F. P. The influence of analysis and evaluation questions on achievement in sixth grade social studies. *Educational Leadership,* 1968, 25, 326–332.

Miller, W. S. The administrative use of intelligence tests in the high school. In Intelligence tests and their use. *Yearbook of the National Society for the Study of Education,* 1922, 21, 189–222.

Rodgers, F. A. Effects of classroom questions on the selection of resources and responses by undergraduate and sixth grade students. *Educational Leadership,* 1968, 26, 265–274.

Sanders, N. M. *Classroom question: what kinds?* New York: Harper & Row, 1966.

Smith, B. O. New approaches to pedagogical science. *Educational Theory,* 1951, *1,* 79–86.

Stevens, Romiett (Ed.) Stenographic reports of high school lessons. *Teachers College Record,* 1910, *11,* 235–300.

Stevens, Romiett. The question as a measure of efficiency in instruction: a critical study of classroom practice. *Teachers College Contributions to Education,* 1912, No. 48.

Taba, Hilda. *Teaching strategies and cognitive functioning in elementary school children.* San Francisco: San Francisco State College, 1966.

Wouk, H. *The Caine mutiny: a novel of World War II.* New York: Doubleday, 1951.

SECTION 4

MATERIALS OF INSTRUCTION
INSTRUCTION
INDIVIDUAL DIFFERENCES
INSTRUCTIONAL
INNOVATIONS

CHAPTER 9
INSTRUCTIONAL MATERIALS

Instructional materials clearly play a central role in the instructional process. Teachers often depend upon textbooks or other written materials to provide pupils with the basic knowledge needed to further their learning, to participate actively in class discussions, to make critical judgments about an issue, and so forth.

In this chapter we will look at several of the major kinds of instructional materials that either are in general use in classrooms throughout the nation or seem to be in a position to alter materially what has traditionally occurred in classrooms. In the latter category, we have particular reference to programmed instruction and to computer-assisted instruction. Among the more traditional aids are textbooks and other written materials, and educational films, including educational television.

Any educational method or material is susceptible to abuse. We have already described certain abuses of the textbook method of teaching. Some readers may have had teachers who made overly extensive use of educational films, for example, expecting the films to carry the major load of teaching without respect to their limitations as teaching tools. In the hands of a skillful and professionally competent teacher, instructional materials of all kinds come to life and make the educational contributions for which each was designed. Just as teachers themselves can make a significant contribution to the learning of their pupils by being able to make effective and appropriate explanations of subject matters, so textbooks and other instructional materials, when used wisely, can materially assist the teacher in achieving his instructional or expressive objectives.

Our purpose is to give the reader a clearer comprehension of how various materials are to be used, the purposes which they can be expected to help achieve, their major limitations, and their chief properties or characteristics. Our discussion will be organized around three types of materials: textbooks and other printed materials; films and educational television; and programmed and computer-assisted instruction. Specific characteristics of good examples of various kinds of instructional material will be noted; chief uses and potential abuses vis-à-vis the classroom setting will be discussed; and research findings pertinent to particular types of instructional materials will be reported.

While a certain unevenness is inevitable due to the discrepancy in available information regarding the functions and uses of the various materials, we shall make every effort to keep the discussions as parallel as possible for ease of comprehension and comparison.

INSTRUCTIONAL MATERIALS
AND INSTRUCTIONAL THEORY

It has sometimes been observed that there is nothing more practical for the guidance of human activity than a good theory. Such a theory, were it available at this time, would stand us in good stead as we begin our discussion of instructional materials and their place in classroom teaching. The absence of a theory prevents us from extending generalizations across the various kinds of media that we must deal with under the general rubric of instructional materials. The existing conceptual boundaries are relatively narrow, tending not to encompass both books and films, or filmstrips and encyclopedias, for example. However, we shall try to compensate somewhat for the lack of general theory or conceptual structure by referring to theories at a lower level of generality and then trying to extend their applicability to related types of instructional materials where warranted.

There have been many research investigations conducted into the nature and operation of instructional materials, especially since the advent of educational films and radio in the 1930s, followed by educational television a generation later. Unfortunately, most of that research has been highly empirical in the sense that studies have been individual rather than part of an overall research program, and frequently the questions asked by the researcher have been highly specific to a given film, etc., thus negating any generalized use. Only rarely have investigations of instructional media been guided by an overarching theory or conceptual structure about the nature of communication, teaching, or learning. Fortunately, this indictment is less true for the more recent investigations of programmed instruction and computer-assisted instruction.

Strangely, written instructional materials, surely the most widely used classroom tools even in this audiovisual age, have received less attention from researchers than other kinds of media. This, too, seems to be changing. Possibly in the near future, a chapter similar to this may be increasingly specific and definitive about the properties and appropriate variables of written materials that affect the learning of students.

At the present time, the theory of reception learning propounded by Ausubel (1963, 1968) furnishes the best guide to the construction and use of such materials. In our discussion of textual and other written materials we shall take advantage of the basic concepts of Ausubel's system to organize that presentation. Similarly, our analysis of motion pictures and educational television will lean heavily on the organizing concepts of Miller (1957), which in turn were derived from the drive-reduction theory of learning which Miller and Dollard (1941) created in the early forties. The use of two theoretical structures that are, at least on the surface, so different to examine two bodies of instructional materials that are, again at least superficially, so similar is not a particularly desirable state of affairs. It is, however, preferable to no organizing concepts at all, and so we proceed, looking hopefully to the future for a set of broader concepts about communication that will provide more order and system to the welter of data that these fields now contain.

TEXTS AND OTHER PRINTED MATERIALS

Although we might seldom think about it, textbooks represent one, possibly the major source, through which students gain formal knowledge about the several subject-matter areas typically studied in school. To the extent that this assumption is tenable, an obligation devolves upon authors, publishers, and users of textbooks to inquire into the principles of their construction and use that affect what students learn from them. We have already suggested that surprisingly little systematic knowledge has been developed in this regard. We shall try here to present a conceptual scheme (borrowed from the work of Ausubel) for the analysis of text materials, to review the available research evidence pertinent to such materials, to inquire into ways in which these written materials are used in classrooms, and to analyze the consequences for pupil learning.

Ausubel's theory of reception learning was presented in chapter 2 as one of the major prevailing views of classroom learning. The reader will recall that the aptness of the theory lies in its assumption that students' classroom learning is largely controlled by verbal materials of instruction, such as teachers' lectures, textbooks, educational television or films, and so forth. His purpose was to develop a set of concepts that would be helpful to the teacher or the writer in producing such materials, whether they be written or oral. The system also assumes that the goal for the student is to master large bodies of such knowledge in a meaningful way, which means essentially being able to remember and use his knowledge over relatively long periods of time.

The following concepts and arguments from Ausubel's theory appear to be particularly relevant to a consideration of text materials for instruction.

1. Text materials should follow the principles of progressive differentiation and integrative reconciliation. In turn, these two concepts demand that the text writer begin by introducing a selected set of the most general concepts from the domain of knowledge about which he is writing. Such fundamental concepts, particularly as the relationships among them are explicated, tend to provide a skeletal outline of the topic or area under discussion. The writer begins by identifying, defining, and perhaps illustrating those most basic concepts. The principle of progressive differentiation demands that the writer subsequently introduce less important concepts, and continue to indicate the ways in which they differ from each other and from the more overarching concepts previously introduced. Ausubel argues that those major concepts provide a kind of ideational anchoring, a clarity, and a stability for the learner to hold onto as he learns lower order and less general elements of the lesson.

   Integrative reconciliation is a term used by Ausubel to refer to the repeated reference to the same concepts as the discussion of an area of knowledge proceeds. It is his contention that textbook writers compartmentalize knowledge and write as though one topic, once it has been presented and developed, need never again be thought about, and has no relationship to other concepts or topics within the same domain of knowledge. On the contrary, as Ausubel points out, knowledge is not typically so compartmentalized, and textbook writers would perform a more effective service to learners if they attempted to avoid the fragmentation of isolated chapters and utilized the principle of integrative reconciliation more frequently and more appropriately.

2. Text materials should be organized so that the basic concepts of the subject matter, those with the widest and most general explanatory power, are used as bases around which to present the less general, more detailed aspects of the subject.

3. The presentation should show conformity to the structure of each subject matter (to the extent that such structure exists or can be discovered); the discussion should be organized with regard for the logic of the material and the strategy of learning the given subject matter.

4. There needs to be a systematic, sequential organization of material with some attention paid to the gradation of the level of difficulty of the discussion as more and more of the content is developed.

5. The textbook writer should consider the use of concrete empirical props and of relevant analogies when they are appropriate to the developmental level of the learner.

6. Text materials should be written so as to stimulate the active, critical, reflective, and analytic involvement of the learner. They should enable him to reformulate the terms of the text material in his own words and in terms of his own experience. Thus, text material is not to be learned verbatim (except perhaps in the rarest of cases) but is to be learned in a meaningful way by the pupil so that it can be incorporated into his cognitive structure and remain available to him for use in future situations.

7. Advance organizers should accompany units of new instructional material to provide the needed ideational scaffolding and ease the problem of relating the new subject matter in a meaningful way into the learner's existing cognitive structure. Advance organizers are brief statements written at a high level of inclusiveness and generality that precede the detailed text statements. Organizers are of two chief kinds, expository and comparative. Comparative organizers are presumed to be more useful to the learner when they precede passages of text material that are closely related to previously learned,

highly familiar content, where the likelihood of psychological interference between the two is great. Comparative organizers are written with the intention of comparing the familiar and the new, of emphasizing the differences between them in order to make it easier for the learner to understand and remember the differences when he studies the later, longer, and more detailed substantive discussion.

Ausubel and his associates have produced a considerable body of research evidence about the role played by organizers in learning of the kind we have described here. In general, organizers do seem to be helpful to learners. They are of particular assistance to the less able learner, apparently because the more able student performs for himself some organizing operations that the organizer tends to perform for the less able student.

In 1955, a group of educational researchers drew attention to the absence of definitive research about the composition and use of textbooks:

Strangely, there has been an almost total absence of . . . research on the more ubiquitous text, even though the text is a source of dissatisfaction and a subject of controversy. Very little research has examined the contribution of text materials; this work has been scattered, inconclusive, and often trivial. Philosophical study of texts has led to equally insubstantial results (Cronbach, 1955, p. 4).

At the same time, these investigators point out, teachers have heard the criticisms of textbooks and would undoubtedly like to see them improved and the principles for their improvement carefully specified. However, despite the criticisms of the experts and the plea for other instructional materials as effective substitutes for textbooks, teachers have persisted in using texts.

Surely most educators have been aware that the problems of the text need sober attention. The classroom teacher has heard the attacks on the text, but even so he has refused to discard it, because his daily experience shows him that the text is useful. Teachers have not had sufficient confidence in the substitutes offered for the text to abandon their old standby. For these reasons the issue of whether or not texts should be used is probably a false issue. Distracted by this dispute, however, educational leaders have failed to grip the real problem, namely, to find specific ways of improving printed materials of instruction (Cronbach, 1955, p. 4).

Characteristics of Textbook Writing

The Cronbach monograph from which we quoted carries the grandiloquent subtitle, *A Comprehensive Theory and Platform for Research*. The contents meet the expectations set by that subtitle extremely well, but the harvest of research studies on text materials that has appeared in the ensuing years is disappointingly meager. Still, we have learned some things empirically about textbooks and their uses, and we shall discuss those findings subsequently. At the moment, it will be instructive to consider the analyses of textbook writing produced by McMurray and Cronbach (1955). Throughout this discussion of the Cronbach monograph, it should be kept in mind that the analyses and suggestions referred to are directed principally at textbook writers. However, many of the points have relevance for the teacher's use of texts in the classroom, or as points to be considered by textbook selection committees, on which many teachers serve at one or another time.

Four kinds of writing can be used in textbooks, and each of them has some clearly specified functions.

1. Narration and description. Narratives provide an essentially story-form account of whatever experience the text writer is attempting to communicate. Although little used in textbooks, narrations could be helpful in developing pupil attitudes, according to McMurray and Cronbach. Descriptions allow the pupil to learn vicariously the properties of an object or an event. Both narration and description are artistic forms of communication.

2. Prescriptive and directive text materials. The use of prescriptive or directive writing in texts seems to be advantageous for specified purposes and to achieve particular kinds of instructional goals. A major characteristic of such writing is that it leads to direct action. Another characteristic is that prescriptive writing tends to encourage the reader to rely more upon the author's reasoning than upon his own creativity. To the extent that the knowledge upon which prescriptions are based is finished and unlikely to change in the future, prescriptions for action can be highly useful. They conserve the time and intellectual energy of the learner. However, if that general condition cannot be met, prescriptions are dangerous because they do not transfer well to future situations that depart to any considerable degree from the circumstances under which the prescription was learned originally. Also, learners are likely to interpret future settings as being similar to those in which the prescription was learned. Thus, the child who learns conformity as a prescription for his social behavior tends to continue to conform as an adult even in political settings where such conformity is contrary to his own best interests and those of his fellows.

3. Generalizations in text materials. Generalizations are statements about lawful relationships between or among events. They are of a different level of abstraction than narration or prescription. Because generalizations tend to order and systematize large numbers or amounts of specific facts or observations, their educational value is high. Consequently, they hold an important place in the considerations of textbook writers.

Authors typically select particular generalizations for inclusion because of their presumed importance. However, that importance may be far more apparent to an individual who is thoroughly schooled in a discipline than it is to a child or adolescent encountering it for the first time. To assert to the child that he is to learn the generalizations because "someday he will see their importance" is to provide a set for the child which will be ineffective in bringing about the learning that we wish him to achieve. If at all possible, the relevance of generalizations to the learner's present life should be stressed. This does not mean that only generalizations that can be used by learners to solve problems here and now should be taught. Rather, it suggests that generalizations be presented in ways that help the learner to understand how his knowledge of them can facilitate his comprehension, and appreciation, of the environment in which he lives.

This idea of presenting generalizations so that they contribute to increasing intellectual mastery or competency is quite consistent with Ausubel's overarching concepts pertaining to the elaboration of the learner's cognitive structure. As new generalizations emerge in cognitive structure, they provide increased differentiation of a previously undifferentiated component of the universe. At the same time, they enable the learner to "forget" a welter of detailed facts and instances (that is, to allow them to undergo obliterative subsumption) without in fact losing any critical information.

4. Systematic knowledge in text materials. By systematic knowledge, McMurray and Cronbach have reference to the basic concepts, laws, and generalizations of a field of knowledge—to what, although the term came into popular educational usage some years after their formulation, is currently identified as the *structure* of a discipline. Systematic knowledge is presented in textbooks not simply, or even fundamentally, to lay out the body of facts which have been developed within the field, nor even to teach the language system of, say, physics or biology or grammar. Rather, the intention of teaching a system is to provide the learner with a new way of asking questions about the universe.

The position adopted by McMurray and Cronbach refutes an earlier view widely held in the years of progressive education. That view maintained that the laws and theories of the various domains of systematic knowledge are so remote from the concrete experiences of children that only empty verbalisms result from exposing learners to them. Simply providing children with concrete experiences and opportunities to manipulate objects in their environment may provide a better base of readiness for systematic learning, but it is not a substitute for the teaching of systems of knowledge. Again, this argument is consistent with the later contention of Ausubel (1963) that younger children may require the use of concrete props in order to learn meaningfully about the universe; however, by the years of early adolescence and beyond, learners have acquired a sufficiently wide array of experiences with the environment that such empiric exposure is seldom required antecedent to or even concurrent with the presentation of systematic knowledge.

One way to evaluate texts and other written materials used in classrooms is to determine the purposes that govern what is to be taught. Each of the four kinds of writing specified by McMurray and Cronbach may be used appropriately by text writers but, as we have seen, some objectives of teaching are served more effectively by one type than by another. For the teacher who is responsible for the selection of classroom materials, an analysis of the kinds of writing and the relative proportions of each contained in the materials under consideration seems to be one valid guide to choosing instructional materials that will be of value for his teaching.

The Role of Textbooks in Planning for Instruction

Cronbach (1955) has also provided us with one of the most comprehensive statements concerning the role of text materials in American education. One of the topics to which he attends is the use of textbooks in the classroom, particularly their use by the teacher in planning for teaching. We have already noted the part textbooks play in reducing the planning burden imposed upon the teacher. Cronbach refers to a conceptual scheme proposed by Herrick (1950) which identified three levels of teacher planning. Level I places the heaviest burden of responsibility upon the teacher, and Level III, the least. In Level III, the teacher depends almost entirely upon the textbook and related materials to carry the load of planning and sequencing his classroom activities.

Cronbach argues that leaders in the field of education, including professors, urge the masses of teachers to operate at a level close to Herrick's Level I. However, these leaders are not realistic about the capabilities or strivings of the large number of run-of-the-mill classroom teachers. In an occupation that employs more than one million practitioners and which must contend with making up teacher shortages rather than winnowing out the least qualified members (remember that this was in 1955), it must be expected that many of these practitioners will be very much like the average American citizen. Therefore, it may be more reasonable, and may result in better quality teaching, to place in the hands of most teachers text materials that have been constructed with great care to perform the basic functions of teaching.

According to Cronbach, textbook publishers, whose representatives contact teachers in all types of communities throughout the nation, are probably more realistic about the talents of the average teacher, and they tend to build textbooks that can be used productively by teachers who rely on the textbook "package." The views of textbook publishers themselves on this issue are captured in the following excerpts from *Textbooks in Education,* a 1949 publication of the American Textbook Publishers Institute from which Cronbach quotes.

> . . . The really best way to judge a promising textbook is to try it out with your class. . . . But when I say try it out, I mean something pretty special, not what a great many teachers are likely to think I mean. You don't really try a book out unless you use it in the way the author intended it to be used. . . . When you buy a new washing machine, the first thing you do before using it is to read carefully the manual of directions that comes with it. You want to know how the engineer who built it expects it to be used for best results. Furthermore, you wouldn't think of complaining to the company about the way it works if you hadn't operated it strictly in accordance with those directions. Certainly you wouldn't try to wash dishes in a machine made for washing

only clothes and then conclude that the machine was no good because it smashed all your dishes.

Yet that is almost precisely the way many a teacher has treated the textbook. She's used it as a reference book, as a source of problem material, she's skipped around from one place to another, she's even told her children not to read the explanations of the text ("I don't teach it that way"), and then she has complained that the book is not satisfactory. For what? To be sure, it's not entirely her fault. In her formal professional education she has probably had little or no training in the function and use of textbooks. Chances are good that she has been impressed with the idea that one way to demonstrate her originality, her "progressiveness," her general teaching ability, is to disregard the textbook and certainly under no circumstances to be caught "following" it (Cronbach, 1955, p. 195).

Another quotation from the same source amplified the Institute's position on the role of textbooks in classroom teaching.

The modern textbook is more and more thought of as an "assistant teacher in print" . . . [The author] sets up as clearly as possible the aims which his teaching is to accomplish.

. . . [He] does this, not on the spur of the moment, nor in any catch-as-catch-can impromptu way, but thoughtfully and deliberately, with time to check and recheck, test, revise, and actually try out his material.

. . . He assumes that [classroom teachers] will cooperate with this teacher in print, using all their teaching ingenuity to make it work for them and for their pupils.

This calls for no sacrifice of responsibility on the part of the teacher. With all they have to do, there is no reason for them to plan the organization of the course in detail. The author of the textbook can do that for them. There is no need for them to think up all the precise instructional language . . . nor should they have to rely entirely on their own resources for the planning of class activities. . . . The author of the textbook can do these things better than any but the ablest teachers can.

The author, however, can never fully . . . provide for individual differences [nor capitalize] on opportunities in a particular locality. He can only set the stage, assuming that . . . the teacher will be the director . . . and will use his script sympathetically . . . (Cronbach, 1955, p. 196).

Cronbach proposes that alternate forms of textbooks might be produced that would be of service to teachers who operate at a level higher than Level III or that would encourage many more teachers to operate at such a higher level. Cronbach has in mind the publication of multiple, brief texts, for example, which view common substantive issues from different perspectives, or text materials that have thought-provoking questions implanted in the body of the text in places where they are easily seen by pupils and not easily avoided by teachers.

The purpose of Cronbach's proposal is to provide sets of instructional materials that will place greater reliance upon the teacher's knowledge and ability to develop strategies of teaching, and depend less heavily upon the textbook as a master of the teaching situation. There are obvious practical issues involved in this recommendation. For example, if it is true that a large proportion of classroom teachers do not have the ability to teach effectively beyond a level where the textbook performs most of the intellectual and planning functions of teaching, text publishers will be reluctant to produce large quantities of books that are not usable by great numbers of teachers of social studies, mathematics, or the language arts, as the case may be. At the same time, that risk may be counterbalanced by the possibility of school districts being willing to adopt series of texts that offer some viable alternatives to teachers.

It is a sad commentary upon the state of our educational knowledge that the investigations into the ways in which teachers use textbooks, which Cronbach called for in the mid-1950s, have not been conducted even as late as the 1970s. We have relatively little firm knowledge about effective uses of texts in teaching situations, and we can do little more than urge teachers to study their own practices in the use of text material and to try to modify those practices intelligently to serve the learning needs of the particular individuals whom they teach.

AUDIOVISUAL MATERIALS OF INSTRUCTION

The term *audiovisual materials* could obviously include a broad gamut of materials of instruction, but typically it excludes such traditional forms as teacher lectures, textbooks, and most other printed materials. We might very well have included programmed instruction and computer-assisted instruction, but because of their relative newness on the educational scene and their theoretical departure from the older media, it seemed more appropriate to consider them separately. By materials of audiovisual instruction we shall mean essentially educational films and educational television. There are other media, such as filmstrips, still pictures, three-dimensional materials, etc., to which we have not attended.

Many of the variables referred to in our discussion of textbooks probably also affect the course of learning from films. Miller (1957), in a widely cited review of research evidence on instructional films, attempted to subsume large components of such research under the more general headings of the central variables in his theory of learning, that is, drive, cue, response, and reward (Miller and Dollard, 1941). Miller hypothesizes that pupils learn from instructional films if the following conditions are met: "Drive: the student must want something," "Cue: the student must notice something," "Response: the student must do something," and "Reward: the student must get something he wants" (Miller, 1957).

Miller also identifies several film variables that appear to influence how much pupils learn from viewing films. These variables are obviously very similar to some of those identified by Ausubel as critical for effective mastery of verbal learning materials. As Miller comments, logical material is better learned and retained than material learned by rote; related to this, and partly because of it, material that is meaningful is superior for purposes of instruction, and its mastery is enhanced to the extent that it is well organized.

Audiovisual materials provide every teacher with an opportunity to extend his effectiveness in teaching. Educational films enable him to bring into the confines of his classroom views of the world which he cauld never otherwise accomplish. The quality of many of today's educational films, including color, sound, and clarity of the picture, is extremely high. Educational television programs frequently bring students in the classroom into contact with a teacher in the studio who was selected because of his ability to communicate effectively, and whose lectures or demonstrations have had the benefit of painstaking preparation and polishing not only by the teacher but often by technicians involved in photographing the demonstration materials, etc. In short, audiovisual materials are typically the product of careful craftsmanship by educational and cinematographic professionals.

When used in the classroom with reasonable attention to preparation for their viewing, and when subsequently related to the broader aspects of the curriculum, audiovisual materials provide a vital asset to the quality of education that teachers and schools can offer to children. At the same time, the impact of audiovisual materials can be neutralized by inappropriate or too frequent use, without regard to the relationship between what is being viewed and the central themes and topics that the class is pursuing. Audiovisual materials are, like texts and other printed materials, tools of instruction to be utilized by the teacher to serve some worthwhile educational purpose. When they are used indiscriminately, to entertain rather than to educate, or to fill empty periods of time, they are being perverted, and little can be expected to ensue from such misuses of these or other instructional materials.

We might mention, also, that one of the chief inhibitions to the use of audiovisual materials of instruction in classrooms is to be found in teachers' unfamiliarity with operating equipment and, consequently, their apprehension about it. Other inhibiting factors include malfunctioning equipment and delays in obtaining materials or equipment that consume the teachers' time and energy, often fruitlessly, and destroy his plans for teaching. There are few events in a teacher's life more disheartening than finding, at the time he is due to show an educational film for which he has prepared his class, that (1) the student projectionist who was to handle the viewing is not in school today, (2) the film did not arrive from the audiovisual department, and/or (3) the 16-millimeter projector is (a) broken, or (b) in use by another class.

Teachers, schools, and audiovisual departments share the responsibility for insuring that teachers can use the materials of instruction in effective ways, including being able to plan for the use of such materials and to depend upon their being available at the planned for time. Teachers must know each piece of audio-visual equipment assigned to their school building and know how to use it themselves. Ordinarily, there is an audiovisual coordinator in the building who is knowledgeable about such equipment and who is available to provide instruction to novice colleagues. Teachers similarly have a responsibility to order materials that they need from the audiovisual department early enough to allow that department a reasonable time to deliver the materials or to indicate that they are not available for the requested time. Thus, the effective use of these materials involves close coordination and teamwork between the teacher, his building coordinator, and a department or division of audiovisual materials.

As with all human organizations, the school's efficiency is less than perfect, and the result from time to time will be frustration for the teacher and spoiled plans for teaching. The solution to the problem, to the extent that there is one, seems to lie in keeping communication and movement of material among the participants as open and as swift as possible, and in careful planning by teachers. In addition, a modicum of empathy for the problems of fellow staff members represents a useful ingredient for this solution.

Educational Films

Educational films, either projected in the classroom or shown over educational television channels, make it possible for teachers to broaden the intellectual horizons of their pupils far beyond the physical boundaries of the school.

Research evidence. The advent of the motion picture for educational purposes and of the radio "schools of the air" seem to have been the occasion for an intensive inquiry into their impact upon pupil learning. The quality of these inquiries is mixed, and their generalized usefulness is often quite limited. However, through the years, certain trends about the effects of educational films have become apparent from the hundreds of investigations that have been conducted. In the following paragraphs we will try to summarize the principal findings of those studies.

Allen (1960) concluded that educational films can be employed to teach factual knowledge to students effectively over a wide range of subject matters, ages of pupils, ability levels, etc. In general, it seems that films can teach facts about as effectively as teachers in the conventional classroom setting. Factual teaching of this sort would seem to be equivalent to the category of description which we used in relation to text materials. On the whole, films probably can teach sets of facts about as well as texts or teachers and might be used to free the teacher from factual imparting of information. There would seem, also, to be many kinds of subject matter for which the movie camera can provide descriptive coverage superior to the most detailed lecture or written account.

Contrary to popular belief, educational films have been found to be capable of eliciting active intellectual involvement of pupils, not just passive viewing. In this connection, there is some limited evidence that educational films can be used to teach concepts as well as factual information (Rulon, 1933; Vernon, 1946). May and Lumsdaine (1958) found that when questions designed to provoke thought and arouse curiosity were inserted into a film, they tended to enhance its teaching effectiveness.

Cronbach (1955) argues that text material can employ narrative style to influence pupil attitudes in positive directions. There is evidence cited by Allen (1960) that educational films can accomplish a similar objective, at least to a limited extent. Allen argues that educational films are useful for modifying attitudes, interests, and beliefs of viewers, providing the content of the film tends to reinforce what is already basically believed. In other words, evidence does not suggest that films can be used effectively to induce changes that are contrary to the viewer's existing structure of beliefs or attitudes. On the contrary, several investigations have demonstrated a boomerang effect from the viewing of films intended to ameliorate attitudes toward minority racial groups, religions, or political beliefs. When the viewers held attitudes that were negative toward the purposes of the films, their attitudes were strengthened rather than softened by viewing the film.

Films as unique instructional materials. Motion pictures have some unique properties as instructional materials. The most obvious of these concern the graphic nature of films. No other medium available to the school has the capacity for bringing the reality of remote parts of the world into the classroom. We have already alluded to this characteristic and, in a sense, it is obvious. There are, however, other unique elements of films that have not been so thoroughly exploited.

For example, Lumsdaine (1963) cites the use of slow motion techniques with film as a presumably ideal means for teaching perceptual-motor responses. Such acts, whose forms are ordinarily affected by the speed with which they are performed, can be accurately captured on film and then shown at an appropriately slowed down speed. According to Lumsdaine, what little relevant evidence there is tends to support the use of slow motion films as an aid to the learning of simple motor performance.

Similarly, little is known about the relative merits of motion pictures and still pictures. Lumsdaine (1963) cites a single study by Roshal (1949) in which movies and still pictures were used to demonstrate knot tying to young sailors. The filmed version was more successful as a teaching device for that particular task than was a series of still pictures which illustrated the various critical stages in tying the knots. We must be careful not to draw firm conclusions from a single experiment, and Lumsdaine cautions that whether motion pictures will be more effective than still pictures seems to depend upon several variables specific to the tasks under study.

The studies cited above are suggestive for the teacher. Although he ordinarily has little or no control over the construction of audiovisual materials, especially of films or videotapes, he is in a much stronger position to assess what kind of materials will accomplish his instructional objectives, and to select them accordingly.

Recommendations for selecting and using films. The methods that the teacher uses to prepare himself and his class for viewing a film, for the showing itself, and for follow-up activities, all appear to influence how well pupils profit from the film. In the following discussion, each of these aspects is presented in the context of research evidence and current, approved professional practice. While the use of educational films can be a rewarding experience for the teacher and for the class, it is clear that the teacher's job is made more demanding and more complex if the effort is expended to use films appropriately to provide educative experiences for pupils.

We begin with the question of how teachers should select films. Attention should be given first to the teacher's objective in showing the film. In most school districts, some provision is made for making available catalogues that enable the teacher to find descriptions of films in terms of topics, length, general coverage, appropriate grade-level range, whether sound or silent, color or black and white, and whether it has a film guide (most films do). Sometimes general evaluations are given, but individual teachers probably do well to evaluate films as they use them. The teacher is well-advised to keep a card file of audiovisual aids that he has used in the past with some notes to himself as to the adequacy of each, whether he should use it again, or for what purposes it seems to be best suited.

Once the film has been selected and received, the following general procedures are recommended. Although there may be little in the way of firm evidence to support these recommendations, their reasonableness insofar as the preparation of the teacher is apparent. Prior to showing the film to students, the teacher should preview it himself. Some experts in audiovisual education recommend that the teacher invite several of his pupils to share the preview with him in order that their perceptions of its appropriateness, adequacy, and general merit can be added to his own in making a final decision whether to show the film, or how to use it with the total class. Ordinarily, films have accompanying teacher guides which review the content of the film and identify new or special terms that are used which are likely to be unfamiliar to learners. Sets of questions covering the content of the film also are frequently included, and sometimes a transcript of the sound track is enclosed.

Research evidence does suggest that the teacher can increase the pupils' motivation to attend to the film, and consequently increase what they learn from it, by introducing the film prior to its showing. In preparing the class to view an educational film, Allen (1960, p. 125) found that the following factors seem to be involved in increasing pupil learning from the film:

1. Study the difficult words and phrases to be used in the film.
2. Study questions and problems relating to the content of the film.
3. Provide a list of points to look for in the film.
4. Have pupils read a brief descriptive story of the content.
5. Emphasize the importance of pupils' learning the content of the film. Simple motivating devices, or anxiety-producing statements, announcing that a quiz or test will follow the film, have been found effective.

It also matters what pupils are doing as they view the film. The set that the teacher has established with his introductory comments and emphases should direct pupils to look for and listen to particular elements of the film. In addition, it has been found that pupils' learning is enhanced when they are required to verbalize at specified points in the film or filmstrip, such as answering a question or summarizing what has occurred. The evidence for this is less convincing with respect to learning motor skills than for verbal learning. Pupil learning also tends to be positively influenced when the teacher or a test provides him with knowledge of results, that is, how accurately he has answered questions. There is also some evidence that mental practice of a skill during the viewing of a film is a relatively good substitute for physical practice of it when the latter is impossible or inconvenient because of lack of equipment, space, or for some other reason. It has been found that the practice of pupils' taking notes during viewing is not helpful to their learning, probably because the note taking interferes with watching the film and interrupts the continuity of pupils' thought processes.

After the film has been viewed, the teacher has several options available which have generally been proven to enhance pupils' learning from the film. One of these is simply to show the film a second time, without discussion. Of course, teachers frequently have specific purposes in re-showing a film, and neither this nor other postviewing options are intended to be prescriptive. Summaries or reviews after the showing are less effective if they are given by the teacher than if they result from discussion in which various members of the class or audience participate. Quizzes or examinations, if announced in advance of viewing the film, have also demonstrated their utility in enhancing what pupils learn from educational films.

Tape Recorders and Language Laboratories

Carroll (1963) provides us with a succinct critical review of the uses of and research on tape recorders and language laboratories in the teaching of foreign language to about 1960. In general, he believes the tape recorder to be one of the most useful devices ever invented for language teachers. The results of one study cited by Carroll (Pickrel, Neidt, & Gibson, 1958) demonstrated that four classes of junior high school students taught by regular classroom teachers who were not trained in Spanish but who made use of tape recordings prepared by a fifth teacher who was a qualified teacher of Spanish, learned about as much Spanish as students in the class of the trained Spanish teacher. Carroll is obviously unwilling to conclude or to suggest that untrained teachers, armed with an appropriate collection of tape recordings, could substitute effectively for teachers trained in the language. However, the study cited provides dramatic testimony to the flexibility and potential effectiveness of tape recordings in language teaching and learning.

The studies of language laboratories reviewed by Carroll do not demonstrate that students who work in language laboratories are better trained in the language than students who learn in conventional classroom formats. However, he does cite evidence that college students report greater satisfaction with the laboratories, and that the laboratories make fewer demands upon the instructional time of the faculty.

Materials Aimed at Individualizing Instruction

Although we have not referred to the issue of individual differences previously in our discussion of instructional materials, it is obvious, when we reflect upon it, that the more traditional forms of material, such as texts and films, are not produced with the objective of accommodating individual differences. For the most part, they are developed to fit the learning rates of a presumably large average proportion of pupils. Little or no provision is built into textbooks, for example, to handle the problem of a child who, having read a paragraph or a page or having studied an explanation or a procedure for doing something, is still unable to comprehend what he has studied. Certainly the pupil can read and reread passages of text which he fails to grasp and, in principle at least, he can view a film or filmstrip as often as necessary until he does understand its message.

However, such instructional materials, particularly textbooks, are geared to methods of teaching that deal with groups of learners simultaneously. Critics frequently use the phrase "lockstep learning" to refer to the group-instruction method. More is involved than simply a common pace through instructional materials. For the most part, the entire class is expected to perform the same tasks in the same sequence at about the same time. The inability of children to accomplish learning in such a uniform manner, coupled with the long-term unwillingness of educators and producers of instructional materials to provide means for effectively teaching children as individuals, has probably retarded the educational achievement of generations of American children.

The development of teaching as a profession, moreover, has been hampered in the same way. For, as long as teachers can perform with moderate success with large groups of pupils without the demand for clear and effective individualization of instruction, the role of teacher itself will fail to develop the skills, abilities, and expertise in diagnostic and prescriptive functions that would differentiate the teacher as a professional practitioner from the teacher as a group leader, which is his current chief role. Fortunately, two innovations in the technology of education show some promise of helping schools to provide educational experiences to learners on an individual basis never before possible. These two innovations are (1) programmed instruction and (2) computer-assisted instruction.

PROGRAMMED INSTRUCTION

An essentially new form of textual material entered the educational arena in 1954. This new form was what is now called *programmed instruction,* and it is possible to specify its introduction in Skinner's classic paper of that year, dealing with the science of learning and the art of teaching. Skinner's thesis was that much teaching of basic facts and concepts, such as operations in elementary arithmetic (which he used as illustrations for the article), could be achieved more effectively by a teaching program administered mechanically than by the classroom teacher. Furthermore, this use of technology in the classroom would free the teacher for those kinds of teaching and interaction with students that are more human and, presumably, that are more befitting the role of a teacher.

The concept of programmed instruction has probably found a permanent or semipermanent position in the catalogue of instructional materials. The "teaching machine," which was emphasized by Skinner and others in the beginning, has fared less well, and his early insistence upon programming as a direct application of operant-conditioning principles has not been upheld. Nonetheless, the whole teaching-machine movement was successful in drawing the attention of educators and psychologists to the precise contingencies that can be established between small elements of instructional materials and the responses that they are to elicit.

For probably the first time in the history of education, people who were responsible for the production of instructional material were required to look closely at the cognitive activity of learners engaged in the processes of school learning. This not only has altered the technology and manufacture of programmed instruction and related curriculum innovations, it has also strongly influenced investigators of the instructional process. In recent years, these investigators have tended to study events of teaching and learning at the level of specific classroom interactions and communications of teachers and children. This is in sharp contrast to the grosser level of educational experiment characteristic of an earlier generation of educational research in which two or more gross methods of teaching competed, with evaluation based on achievement test scores.

We began this section by stating that programmed instruction is a new form of textual material. To help clarify that statement, we have reproduced a brief sample of a program, which we borrowed from Scriven (1969, pp. 4–5):

1. In a programmed text, the educational material is broken up into small portions called *frames*. If you read these carefully you will be able to fill in any gaps in the *frames*. You are now reading the first fr_____ of a specimen program.

   (fr)ame

2. Each frame involves some questions, or several questions, or blanks to fill in. The whole collection of frames makes up the program or _____med text.

   program(med)

3. If all students of a programmed text have to go through all the _____, we call this a *linear program*. The other kind of program is called a *branching*

   frames, questions

program. When some students read
different parts of a program from
others, we call this a _____ pro-   branching
gram.

4. The contents of a programmed text,
   which we call the _____, could be   program
   put onto a film or paper strip. A device
   for presenting this, one frame at a time,
   is called a *teaching machine.* This
   teaching machine is then, technically
   speaking, using the same _____   program, material
   as a programmed text.

5. Is this true or false: "A teaching machine in which all the students go
   through all the frames is using a *linear*
   program, by contrast with a *branching*
   program."   true

In general, programmed materials are of one of two kinds: either
linear, of which the Scriven excerpt is an example, or branching. The
branching program differs from the linear in that learners begin at
the same point of instruction but do not necessarily go through
precisely the same steps in completing the instruction. Branching
programs assume that learners will be differentially knowledgeable
about an area of instruction, and they make it possible for a student
who demonstrates that he already knows a given unit of content to
move on to a more complex level, or to a different topic. Linear programs, on the other hand, require all learners to study the same sets
of frames of a program, and to proceed through exactly the same
sets of questions and answers and other exercises.

One characteristic shared by both kinds of programs is active responding by the learner. Although individual programs vary in the
ways they demand the student to respond, such as writing or some
other overt response or simply covertly answering to himself, the
programs do force the student to remain alert and attentive to the
content to which he is being exposed. This is one of the major advantages that programmed instruction has over typical text materials.

Few texts are constructed so as to insure the reader's continuous
attention to the material being presented or to heighten the likelihood that he comprehends what he is being taught. Writers such as

Cronbach (1960) and Rothkopf (1966) have used and recommended the use of questions embedded in the content of text materials. Rothkopf, for example, found that such questions, if occurring after approximately every one thousand words of text, have a facilitative effect upon the content just read. He refers to the behavior engendered by such spotted questions as *mathemagenic behavior,* that is, behavior which gives birth to new learning. At any rate, it seems clear that a pupil's attention is heightened when at frequent intervals in the course of instruction he must actively respond to the material that he is studying.

The results of investigations in which programmed instruction has been tested are complex and, to an extent, contradictory as well. The early emphasis upon the mechanical aspects of programmed instruction has largely disappeared. The logic and structure of the programmed material seem obviously much more effective in controlling learning than the pacing of the material, which was possible with a machine. Similarly, how the student responds, that is, whether he writes out each missing answer, says it aloud, or merely reads the correct response in the body of the program, does not seem to be crucial in learning the material, as was originally believed by proponents of teaching machines.

Comparisons of programmed instruction with other more traditional forms of instruction have not produced consistent results. Programs have sometimes been shown to produce better learning than conventional lecture situations. As Cronbach (1966, p. 80) has observed, however, it would be extraordinary if a team of programmers, given one or two years to produce a carefully prepared instructional program, were not able to "outteach" the harried classroom teacher or lecturer, bound by all the constraints of time and lack of resources for preparing his courses.

Computer-assisted instruction. Among the newest entrants into the field of instructional materials is the high speed computer. Despite its recent introduction, however, scientists, technologists, and educators, working together, have already demonstrated the mighty potential of the computer to contribute to the work of instructing students and, equally important, to aid in the development of theories about teaching and about classroom learning. Because of its high speed operations and flexibility in the amount of data that it can remember and process, the computer has enabled curriculum designers to plan curricula with greater regard for the needs of individual pupils than has been possible in the past.

An excellent example of how computers are being used to facilitate and to study the process of teaching has been reported by Atkinson (1968). The particular program which he describes is in beginning reading. A group of Stanford University educational research workers, of whom Atkinson is one, have been investigating approaches to teaching reading to first-grade children by means of high speed computers.

Seated at his station, the child has before him a cathode ray tube (CRT), which is much like a television screen; a light pen, which is a probe for indicating his responses to questions on the CRT; and a typewriter-like keyboard, also used for responding. Stimulus items are presented to the child from the computer terminal in the form of written or graphic material that appears upon the CRT, or they may be audio messages. In general, the child responds to the stimulus by placing his light pen upon a given response on the CRT or by using his keyboard to punch out an answer; the computer is programmed to evaluate responses in either form. The computer then provides the child with the next step he must take, which may be to move on to the next problem; or shows him the correct response and asks him to identify it; or demands that he repeat the problem.

Because of the great flexibility of the computer and the care and analytical skill with which Atkinson and his associates have developed the curriculum for beginning readers, each response made by an individual child triggers the presentation of the item which is theoretically determined to be optimal for him at that particular stage in his career of learning to read. The instructional theory as it stood in 1968 was obviously not a finished one, although it involved a number of useful decision-making rules. The important point is that the data generated by the responses of the pupils who were learning to read with the help of a computer were being systematically analyzed and stored, thereby helping to improve the theory of instruction for beginning reading. If for no other reason, the computer would seem to earn its keep as a device for providing instruction because of its great capacity for storing and retrieving information that will contribute to the construction of sophisticated theories about individual learning rates and sequences.

As to the specific effects of the computer program upon the acquisition of beginning reading skills, Atkinson has provided a partial report about the results of the year's program during the 1967–68 school year. An elementary school close to Stanford University that had a sizable number of first grade children enrolled—somewhat more than one hundred—was selected. This school is located in a "culturally disadvantaged" area of the community, and the tested intelligence of the children is not high. The average IQ of the group was 89. The first year's program was established on an experimental basis, with half the children being taught reading by the computer and the other half remaining with the first-grade teachers for more traditional instruction. It is worth noting parenthetically, however, that the control children were studying arithmetic under computer tutelage, so therefore biases in the findings which might ordinarily be the consequence of some children's receiving more special attention probably would not operate in this situation.

Several results of the first year's use of computer-assisted instruction (CAI) in beginning reading seem to be worth summarizing. On tests of vocabulary, pronunciation, and word recognition, among others, the children in the experimental treatment, that is, those who received assistance from the computer program, scored significantly higher than the control children. Of the various comparisons made between the two groups at the close of the year, only the scores on the Comprehension subtest of the California Achievement Test failed to reflect meaningful differences between the two groups of first graders.

In the early primary grades, girls, on the average, show higher achievement in reading than boys do, presumably as a result of two factors: (1) the typical social and reward structure of classrooms, mediated by the values of women teachers, and (2) the superior visual memorization abilities of girls. Atkinson reports that no significant sex differences appeared in the first year of the computer-assisted program, probably because of the altered environment in which such instruction occurs and because the program is designed to stress analytical rather than memorial skills.

One of the most striking and important results of the first year's work concerns the modification of program in terms of the individual differences among children. Atkinson's reading program contains a central core of problems known as "main line problems." Those are the problems over which the pupil must somehow exert mastery. Between the beginning of the program in mid-November and its termination seven months later, the difference in the number of main line problems completed by the fastest and the slowest pupil in the experimental group was over two thousand. This difference is not a function of the rate of responding, which was relatively constant among pupils, tending to average about four responses per minute. The difference lies principally in the branching flexibility of the program and the variations it provides in the amount of remedial practice, optimization routines, and acceleration.

Obviously, both the physical and social environment of the classroom change when instruction is provided by computer. The child moves to a different physical location, and he is much more on his own than in the usual classroom setting. Atkinson indicates that preliminary reports about the social effects of CAI reveal positive responses from those who are involved in the program—students, their parents, and teachers. However, there is much more to the impact of a new innovation upon the lives of children and teachers than is told or implied by those reactions.

Atkinson (1968) points out from his own experiences some of the problems involved in starting the program on time (it was mid-November rather than early September by the time the Stanford program was functioning). Problems which result from breakdowns and other difficulties in the operation of the equipment are intense although transitory, tending to disappear as systems are properly installed and finally functioning. Whatever the current difficulties associated with it, however, we would guess that computer-assisted instruction will be on the educational scene for a long time as both an instructional and a research instrument.

REFERENCES

Chapter 9

Allen, W. H. Audio-visual communication. In L. W. Harris (Ed.), *Encyclopedia of educational research* (3rd ed.) New York: Macmillan, 1960. Pp. 115–137.

Atkinson, R. C. Computerized instruction and the learning process. *American Psychologist,* 1968, *23,* 225–239.

Ausubel, D. P. *Psychology of meaningful verbal learning.* New York: Grune & Stratton, 1963.

Ausubel, D. P. *Educational psychology, a cognitive view.* New York: Holt, Rinehart & Winston, 1968.

Carroll, J. B. Research on teaching foreign languages. In N. C. Gage (Ed.), *Handbook of research on teaching.* Chicago: Rand McNally, 1963. Pp. 1060–1100.

Cronbach, L. J. (Ed.) *Text materials in modern education. A comprehensive theory and platform for research.* Urbana: University of Illinois Press, 1955.

Cronbach, L. J. *Essentials of psychological testing.* (2nd ed.) New York: Harper & Bros., 1960.

Cronbach, L. J. The logic of experiments on discovery. In L. S. Shulman & E. R. Keislar (Eds.), *Learning by discovery, a critical appraisal.* Chicago: Rand McNally, 1966. Pp. 77–92.

Herrick, V. E. The concept of curriculum design. In V. E. Herrick & R. W. Tyler (Eds.), *Toward improved curriculum theory.* Chicago: University of Chicago Press, 1950. Pp. 37–50.

Lumsdaine, A. A. Instruments and media of instruction. In N. L. Gage (Ed.), *Handbook of research on teaching.* Chicago: Rand McNally, 1963. Pp. 583–682.

May, M. A., & Lumsdaine, A. A. *Learning from films.* New Haven: Yale University Press, 1958.

McMurray, F., & Cronbach, L. J. The proper function of text materials. In L. J. Cronbach (Ed.), *Text materials in modern education.* Urbana: University of Illinois Press, 1955. Pp. 28–58.

Miller, N. E. et al. Graphic communication and the crisis in education. *Audio-Visual Communication Review,* 1957, *5,* 1–128.

Miller, N. E., & Dollard, J. *Social learning and imitation.* New Haven: Yale University Press, 1941.

Pickrel, G., Neidt, C., & Gibson, R. Tape recordings are used to teach seventh grade students in Westside Junior-Senior High School, Overby, Nebraska. *National Association of Secondary School Principals Bulletin,* 1958, *92,* 81–93.

Roshal, S. M. Effects of learner representation in film-mediated perceptual-motor learning. Pennsylvania State University Instructional Film Research Program. Port Washington, N.Y.: U.S. Naval Training Device Center, Office of Naval Research, Technical Report No. SDC 269-7-5, 1949.

Rothkopf, E. Z. Learning from written instructive materials: an exploration of the control of inspection behavior by test-like events. *American Educational Research Journal,* 1966, *3,* 241–249.

Rulon, P. J. *The sound motion picture in science teaching.* Cambridge: Harvard University, 1933.

Scriven, M. The case for and use of programmed texts. In A. D. Calvin (Ed.), *Programmed instruction, bold new venture.* Bloomington: Indiana University Press, 1969. Pp. 3–36.

Skinner, B. F. The science of learning and the art of teaching. *Harvard Educational Review,* 1954, *24,* 86–97.

Vernon, P. E. An experiment on the value of the film and film-strip in the instruction of adults. *British Journal of Educational Psychology,* 1946, *16,* 149–162.

CHAPTER 10

INDIVIDUAL DIFFERENCES AND CLASSROOM PRACTICES

An obvious but nonetheless critically important fact of life is the broad range of differences among individuals. Individual differences occur among all species, although we shall discuss only human differences, and among many kinds of abilities, although we shall limit our interest to those that are of use to teachers and schools—principally, individual differences in intelligence and in academic achievement. It is not our purpose to pursue issues in the definition or measure of intelligence, except in passing, since that is properly the function of psychological analysis. Instead, it will be our concern to try to sketch out and communicate in some meaningful ways the dimensions of the problems of individual differences that teachers confront.

Our intention is, however, somewhat broader than a simple categorization of the range of individual differences in abilities and capacities that are of consequence in making decisions for teaching. An effort will be made to present some of the value questions that teachers answer, with or without awareness, and to suggest some of the possible results that can ensue from one or another decision made about the treatment of individual differences. In this connection, we shall discuss and attempt to analyze some of the more commonly employed procedures for handling the challenge of individual differences.

Let us concede at the outset that psychologists have been more successful in delineating the dimensions of individual differences among children and adolescents than educators have been in proposing or in implementing methods to accommodate the differences. This is easy enough to understand; the solutions to problems typically are more elaborate than statements of the problem, although a clear understanding of the nature of the problem seems to be an indispensable step towards its solution. The first issue that we confront involves the need to know something about the range of relevant differences among pupils and what happens to that range as instruction enters the picture; that is, we have quite different phenomena depending upon whether instruction levels or sharpens differences among individuals. Although the answers to both questions seem to hinge upon the acquisition of empirical data, the matter is not as simple as it may appear. Even today, the question of the relationship between instruction and range of differences is unsettled.

Now, if we couple that empirical uncertainty with indecision or vacillation with respect to the central value issue (Should the school strive to maximize or to minimize individual differences?), we can see that the initial clarity we thought we had disappears into murkiness with alarming speed. It would then hardly be surprising to find that knowledge about how to proceed in order to achieve a specified end is imperfect, especially when we also find that ambiguity exists in the realms of both fact and value about what is to be achieved with respect to individual differences.

None of the foregoing is intended to suggest that viable and complete solutions to problems of individual differences are going to emerge once the answers to two reasonably straightforward questions are formulated. On the contrary, it is probably true that the teacher's life becomes more complicated as he attempts to struggle intelligently and earnestly with the problem.

To illustrate the seriousness of the problem of individual differences, we will assert that, at the level of the classroom, provisions for individual differences represent the broader social issue of equality of opportunity. When a teacher demands high and uniform standards of academic performance from all of his pupils despite the range of differences in their ability, which at the concrete level of performance means that some pupils cannot attain the expected level, the consequences for the pupils are the same as though the teacher held certain values about students, whether he does so consciously or not. Similarly, a teacher may verbalize a value of treating all pupils equally and translate this behaviorally as dividing his time and energy equally among his students. We believe that teachers and students alike would benefit immensely if teachers would attempt to verbalize and systematize their own values about individual differences, and try to assess the extent to which their behavior is consistent with the expressed values.

RANGES OF INDIVIDUAL DIFFERENCES

A great deal of knowledge has been accumulated about the growth and development of human beings, such that it is possible for the interested professional or layman to ascertain quite careful estimates of average heights and weights for a given age, or data on ages of walking, first word spoken, and so forth. But the fact that the *average* child utters his first recognizable word at, say, ten months of age is only one part of the information we need to understand when children begin to talk. The other is a concept of variability.

Most psychological characteristics of human beings have been found empirically to approximate a normal distribution. Thus, a few children may utter that historic first word at six or seven months, and some may not speak at all until perhaps fourteen or sixteen months of age. We must expect to find that people differ widely from one another on many important dimensions of physical structure and behavior. All or most of these may have some relevance for teachers, but some are more proximate to classroom concerns than others. We will deal only with those most central to the business of the classroom. For example, physical growth is not a matter of special interest to teachers and schools. It is not an issue about which teachers ordinarily are the most competent professionals available. But for a fifteen-year-old boy who is a junior in high school and who is physically small for his age and immature relative to his age and grade mates, the major consequences of his slow physical growth may be educational rather than medical or other health problems. Put very simply, his "difference," which will surely be perceived by both him and his peers, can have a variety of consequences for him, ranging from failure to compete successfully in physical activities to possibly social maladjustment and rejection. School personnel have some responsibility to be alert to and sensitive about problems of this order that beset children and adolescents, but it is not in this sense that individual differences represent major issues to teachers.

Instruction and learning are the major areas in which the teacher's specialized professional knowledge centers. Individual differences in pupils' level of knowledge at the beginning of instruction, rate at which they learn, and range of achievement at completion of the instructional period are very much within the province of the teacher's specialized area of performance, since it is these individual differences that help to shape the kind of planning, instruction, and evaluating in which the teacher engages. The teacher who behaves as though all his students are identical in knowledge and in their ability to acquire new knowledge is simply ignoring one of the important areas about which it is possible for him to have knowledge and which sets off the professional teacher from an intelligent and otherwise well-educated lay person who might offer instruction to children.

On the following pages there appear a series of tables and figures that illustrate the range of differences in school—relevant ability and achievement among individuals and within the same individual. We have adapted these data from Thomas and Thomas (1965). The first three sets of data represent test performances of children in a fifth-grade class. The school attended by these children is located in a working class neighborhood. Some of the pupils are Negro, some are of Italian descent, others are of Anglo-European ancestry. In other words, a number of the major American racial and ethnic groups are represented among this small group of fifth graders. Figures 10.1 and 10.2 reveal the levels and range of differences among these children in verbal and mathematical aptitude and in achievement in the basic skill and information areas of the elementary school.

The reader may ask whether it is sensible to refer to this group as a fifth-grade class. The term clearly is only nominal, a means of differ-

FIGURE 10.1 GRADE-LEVEL STANDING OF FIFTH GRADERS IN APTITUDE TEST

ESTIMATED GRADE LEVEL BASED ON NATIONAL NORM	VERBAL APTITUDE TEST	MATHEMATICS APTITUDE TEST
Grade 9		O
Grade 8	OOO	OO
Grade 7	OO	OO
Grade 6	OO	OO
Grade 5	OOOOOOO	OOOOOOOOOO
Grade 4	OOOOOOO	OOOO
Grade 3	OO	
	O = 1 Student	

Source: Thomas and Thomas (1965, p. 5).

FIGURE 10.2 GRADE-LEVEL STANDING OF FIFTH GRADERS ON ACHIEVEMENT TESTS

ESTIMATED GRADE LEVEL BASED ON NATIONAL NORM	READING TEST	MATHEMATICS TEST	WRITING	SOCIAL STUDIES	SCIENCE
Grade 12	O				
Grade 11				O	
Grade 10			O		OO
Grade 9	O	O	O		
Grade 8	OOO	O	O	O	
Grade 7	O	OOOOO	O	OO	OOOOO
Grade 6	OOOO	OO	OOO	OOOO	OO
Grade 5	OOO	OOO	OOOO	OOOOOOO	OOOO
Grade 4	OOO	OOOOOO	OOOOO	OOOOO	OOOOOO

O = 1 Student

Source: Thomas and Thomas (1965, p. 6).

entiating this from other groups in the school. Except for the Mathematics Aptitude Test, on which half the pupils score at the designated grade level, more pupils achieve at different grade levels than at the fifth-grade level. Here, as in most other instances, *fifth grade* is a meaningful term only if we understand it to indicate that a typical fifth-grade class will contain some pupils whose achievement is one, two, or perhaps even three grades lower than that designated for fifth grade, some whose scores would place them within the fifth grade, and others whose achievement is well above that level—perhaps as much as four to six years superior to typical fifth-grade performance. Of course, much the same findings occur at other grade levels, with the single qualification that the dispersion increases with advancing grade level.

Examine Figure 10.3. It contains the grade level equivalent in reading and mathematics for a group of ninth-grade students. Just as one

FIGURE 10.3   GRADE-LEVEL STANDING OF NINTH GRADERS ON READING AND MATHEMATICS TESTS

		READING TEST SCORES	MATHEMATICS TEST SCORES
	College Junior		OOO
	College Sophomore	OOOO	OOOO
	College Freshman	OOOOOOO	OOOOOO
	Grade 12	OOOOOOOOOOOOOOO	OOOOOO
	Grade 11	OOOOOO	OOOOOOOO
	Grade 10	OOOOO	OOOOOOOOO
	Grade 9	OOOOOOOOOOOOOOO	OOOOOOOOOO
	Grade 8	OOOOOOOO	OOOOOOOOOOO
	Grade 7	OOOOO	OOOOO
	Grade 6	OOOOOO	OO
	Grade 5	OOOOO	OOOOOO
	Grade 4	OOOO	OOOOO
	Grade 3		OOOOO

ESTIMATED GRADE LEVEL BASED ON NATIONAL NORM

O = 1 Student

Source: Thomas and Thomas (1965, p. 31).

might have concluded from the data of Figure 10.2 that the test scores represented achievement of a third-grade class, so here we might almost think that a twelfth-grade instead of a ninth-grade group is depicted. Again, as in Figures 10.1 and 10.2, the dispersion is great and, as we anticipated, the range of differences surpasses that of the fifth-grade class. Thus, some of these students read only as well as the average fourth grader and a few others read as well as college students!

Look now at Table 10.1. That table presents the scores, in percentiles, of four pupils enrolled in the fifth-grade class we have described. The purpose of this table is to demonstrate something of the flavor of intraindividual differences in aptitude and achievement. Two of the students, Mario and Pat, show excellent ability, but Pat's profile is more varied. Although she is outstanding in most respects, Pat's social studies achievement, while well above average, is not excellent. Mario, on the other hand, appears to be an almost uniformly superior student. Don approximates what we might think of as a truly average fifth-grade pupil in his aptitude and achievement profile. Many of his scores hover near the fiftieth percentile. In quantitative aptitude and reading ability he is comfortably above average, while his writing skill is very low. Lois's profile is that of a weak student in general, who has well above average quantitative aptitude. And so it goes. These four profiles do not begin to systematize our knowledge about academic individual differences, but they suggest an important generalization: that intraindividual variability is the rule.

TABLE 10.1 INTRAINDIVIDUAL DIFFERENCES OF FOUR PUPILS ENROLLED IN THE SAME FIFTH-GRADE CLASS

				TESTS			
	Verbal	Quantitative	Reading	Mathematics	Social Studies	Science	Writing
PUPILS							
Pat	88	99	95	95	71	95	96
Lois	11	69	9	10	6	34	6
Mario	93	99+	99+	98	96	97	91
Don	49	69	64	60	46	50	19
		(Percentiles Based on National Norms)					

Source: Based on data from Thomas and Thomas (1965, p. 7).

Suppes (1964) dramatically illustrates the range of individual differences in solving arithmetic problems. A group of gifted first graders was selected for special instruction in arithmetic. Allowed to proceed at their own rate, with sufficient instructional material, graduated in difficulty and available for that purpose, the fastest of these forty children had solved about thirty-four hundred problems after seven weeks, and the slowest had solved only about twenty-two hundred (see Figure 10.4).

FIGURE 10.4 PROGRESS OF FASTEST AND SLOWEST OF FORTY GIFTED FIRST-GRADE PUPILS IN MATHEMATICS

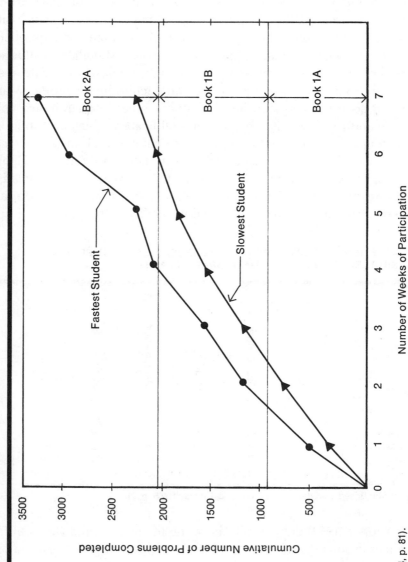

Source: Suppes (1964, p. 81).

At the end of the seventh week, these two bright first graders are already separated by almost a third of the second-grade curriculum. For understandable reasons, we are reluctant to forecast the maximum separation after this class has continued for another couple of years. The rate at which these bright children are working problems and proceeding through the curriculum is most surprising. It has certainly exceeded our initial expectations. We are not encouraging a speed contest; in fact, the teachers are making a decided effort to discourage intensive competition. These comparisons are, I think, a fair representation of the very large differences to be expected among even very bright children when the rate of progress of the individual child is not tied to that of the group (Suppes, 1964, pp. 80–81).

Although the existence of individual differences in rates of learning is a well-established psychological generalization, Suppes considers it ". . . the most important principle of learning as yet *unaccepted* in the day-to-day practice of subject-matter teaching in the classroom" (Suppes, 1964, p. 79).

Suppes further demonstrates his point by recounting a recent experiment in which thirty-eight kindergartners were taught some preliminary vocabulary recognition tasks. The children first learned fourteen simple words, and then learned to recognize two-word phrases, three-word phrases, four-word phrases, and finally five-word phrases, all built on the basis of the original fourteen words. The children who participated in this experiment had not been selected on the ground of ability, and the range among them, expressed as the number of trials required to reach the mastery criterion, is extremely large. The fastest learner reached criterion after 196 learning trials; the slowest child required 2,506 trials to learn the task. For the total sample of 38, the mean number of trials was 967.4, with a standard deviation above 400.

Cutts and Moseley (1960) describe the range of individual differences in somewhat different terms but the effect is the same.

This [sixth grade] class is very similar to hundreds which we've visited in all parts of the United States. The twenty-nine pupils show a range of more than 3½ years in chronological age, 104 pounds in weight, 14 inches in height, 62 points in IQ, and 8 years 4 months in mental age. Their achievement, as measured by the Iowa Every-Pupil Tests of Basic Skills, ranges from 4.3 to

9.9 in grade average, . . . from 4.4 to 9.5 in reading, and from 3.5 to 11.4 in spelling (Cutts & Moseley, 1960, pp. 1–2).

Cutts and Moseley argue that ". . . children so carelessly and mistakenly lumped together as average are the forgotten children of American education" (p. 7). To bolster their contention, they cite statements written for them by pupils

. . . on the topic "Last year in school I didn't learn as much as I should have liked because. . . ." Three replies are particularly to the point: "My teacher just gave full directions to the whole class"; "I was never quick to answer"; "I just sat and daydreamed" (Cutts & Moseley, 1960, p. 7).

Other pupils elaborated on the point. Some desired more explanation in arithmetic than the teacher provided. Others complained of favorite curriculum areas that received slapdash treatment in favor of more fundamental subjects. And so on. While we admit the validity of Cutts and Moseley's argument, it should also be recognized that the open stem provided to the children is designed to elicit critical responses. How significant these responses are in the totality of the child's classroom experience is not established.

EDUCATIONAL ADAPTATIONS TO INDIVIDUAL DIFFERENCES

Cronbach (1967) has suggested that discussions of individual differences in education are frequently vague and ambiguous and that the explanation for such ambiguity may lie in the fact that no careful logical or philosophical analysis of the problem has been conducted. Cronbach provides something of a start in that direction by his observation that several alternatives are definable, although they may not be mutually exclusive. These alternatives are presented in Table 10.2.

Of the various alternatives, the one that Cronbach finds psychologically interesting is the last one, which involves matching instructional procedures to pupils. The crux of this problem lies in discovering interactions between methods of instruction and pupil abilities. Interaction is used here in a statistical, not a social, sense. To illustrate, suppose that two methods of teaching multiplication, a drill method and a meaning method, yield comparable results between groups, on the average. But it is discovered that pupils of lower ability achieve better when taught by a drill method rather than by a meaning

TABLE 10.2 PATTERNS OF EDUCATIONAL ADAPTATION TO INDIVIDUAL DIFFERENCES

EDUCATIONAL GOALS	INSTRUCTIONAL TREATMENT	POSSIBLE MODIFICATIONS TO MEET INDIVIDUAL NEEDS
Fixed	Fixed	1a) Alter duration of schooling by segmental selection. 1b) Train to criterion on any skill or topic, hence alter duration of instruction.
Options	Fixed within an option	2) Determine for each student his prospective adult role and provide a curriculum preparing for that role.
Fixed within a course or program	Alternatives provided	3a) Provide remedial adjuncts to fixed "main track" instruction. 3b) Teach different pupils by different methods.

Source: Cronbach (1967, p. 24).

method. There is an interaction between ability in arithmetic and method of instruction. To continue the illustration, Cronbach would urge that less able pupils be instructed in multiplication by drill methods because they will master those facts more completely or in less time than if taught by a meaning method. At the same time, he acknowledges that the school has some responsibility for helping those students learn from more meaningful operations. "We have two coordinate problems: capitalizing on the existing aptitude pattern and modifying that pattern. The school need not deal with both at the same moment, but neither should be neglected" (Cronbach, 1967, p. 36).

Carroll (1967), in a critique of Cronbach's proposals, agrees that psychologists must assume responsibility for constructing viable differential instructional procedures.

> Cronbach is correct, I think, when he says that the school as an institution should be free only to select educational goals, i.e., to identify the criterion of success, whereas it is the task of the psychologist to devise or select instructional methods that interact with pupil differences so that the achievement of all pupils *seeking a given educational goal* will be significantly greater than what it would be if a *single* "best" method were employed (Carroll, 1967, p. 40).

Carroll also raises the fundamental and difficult value question which we alluded to in the introduction to this chapter. What is the proper and moral stance for the schools to adopt in selecting goals? Should the schools strive for the eradication of individual differences, or might there be some merit in the notion of cultivating and valuing differences among students?

Cronbach finds his final alternative in Table 10.2 the most intriguing one because the earlier ones are essentially administrative devices for handling individual differences. Our attention focuses now on some of these administrative patterns, beginning with an assessment of efforts at grouping pupils as a means of dealing with significant individual differences.

Administrative Devices for Coping with Individual Differences

We shall see in the following pages that the educator's answers to the complex problem of individual differences among pupils have characteristically been administrative ones. It is easy to criticize the superficiality of many such adjustments on the grounds that they were and are frequently made without a convincing evidential basis to support them. But the flow of criticism is sometimes stanched when we develop a more comprehensive understanding of the conditions which undergird decisions.

One issue that has appeared repeatedly in American public education is ability grouping. On the surface, solutions to this issue appear simple and straightforward. Since, as we have already seen, children who are differentiated only on the basis of age and grade exhibit large variations with regard to intelligence and achievement, why not stratify pupils on one or the other of those variables? For example, if we have a hundred fifth-grade pupils to distribute among four teachers, why not place the brightest twenty-five in one teacher's room, the dullest twenty-five in another, and so on? Modifications of that sort have been tried periodically over the past fifty years. At times they have been widely adopted; at other times, many fewer schools have retained such ability grouping or teaching procedures. The stark simplicity of such arrangements has a strong appeal, particularly since they appear to promise so happy a solution at so meager an expenditure of intellectual effort. Rafferty, for example, scores those educators who failed to see the simple beauty of the system until Conant pointed the way.

> Once upon a time, and not so very long ago at that, it was the sacred duty of Education's loyal sons to fight to the death against any form of ability grouping which might raise its horrid head.

> Research projects spawned like rabbits, each proving beyond
> a doubt that taking smart kids away from their stupid classmates
> and educating them separately was undemocratic, reactionary,
> and generally pernicious. Besides, it was impossible. Everybody
> knew a few years ago that ability grouping never worked because
> children who were homogeneous in one respect were bound to
> be heterogeneous in all others and so on and on, right down to
> the last standard deviations.
>
> So what happens?
>
> So Conant comes along and recommends homogeneous
> grouping. Suddenly we all find ourselves nodding and saying,
> "Of course. Common sense indicates that gifted kids are going
> to progress faster if the shackles are taken off."
>
> We try the treasonable but reasonable suggestion, and behold!
> it works. Common sense, for a change, triumphs. Conant is right.
>
> But where was all this common sense just five short years ago,
> hmmm? (Rafferty, 1962, p. 46.)

Rafferty is probably correct in this sense, at least: educators have
shown a proneness to follow recommendations of high prestige individuals outside the establishment of professional education, especially when those recommendations are made without equivocation.
Research evidence in direct contradiction to Rafferty's assertion
provides a very mixed picture about the assets and liabilities of
homogeneous grouping. A later discussion reviews some of the
highlights of this body of evidence and attempts to place it in an appropriate and contemporaneous context.

Morgenstern (1966) has provided a brief historical summary of the
various efforts at grouping that have been attempted in this country.
Characteristically, grouping has been aimed at reducing the variability among pupils in either age, ability, or accomplishment—sometimes in all three. As school populations grew, the lack of teachers
and facilities demanded ingenuity on the part of educators. The ingenuity was usually available, although its implementation did not
necessarily result in high quality education. At the opening of the
eighteenth century, for example, Joseph Lancaster in England developed the idea of a monitorial system, sometimes still called the Lan-
casterian system, after its founder. According to this procedure, a
trained teacher who might be responsible for the education of a very
large number of pupils would reach all his pupils through monitors.
Monitors were members of the class, usually among the oldest and
brightest. They would first be taught a lesson by the teacher. Then,

having learned it verbatim, each monitor would retreat to his own group of the pupils, and communicate it to them.

The increasing pressure of more pupils presenting themselves to the schools for instruction led to the development of graded schools to replace the earlier one-room school. Horace Mann, who had observed the success of Prussian graded schools, strongly urged that a similar system be instituted in Massachusetts. By the beginning of the Civil War, the age-graded public school system was well established in the United States. Uniform lessons, texts, and methods of instruction were adopted on a large scale.

By the close of the First World War in 1918, every state then in the Union had adopted a compulsory school attendance law. The aspiration of the American people to offer education through the secondary school to all its young citizens was advancing hard toward reality. But the dream outstripped the accomplishment in some important ways. Academic standards that had perhaps been suitable for a day when schools were more selective by design were being employed to weed out and to discourage the academically less able and less motivated students. For many children, completion of the eighth grade and arrival at the school-leaving age occurred simultaneously, with pupil and school bidding each other adieu, never to meet again by mutual agreement.

That the design for mass public education—glorious in its politico-philosophic conception of the school as the great equalizer—was falling short of its acknowledged goal had been obvious for some years. In 1909, Leonard Ayres had published a book, *Laggards in Our Schools,* in which he demonstrated that, on the average, about one-third of the school population had been retained in grade on at least one occasion. Cronbach's alternative *1a*—Alter duration of schooling by segmental selection—characterizes this situation. Goals and treatments are standardized. Students are differentiated in terms of what they achieve, or how early they leave the school.

Individual difference had reared its head with a vengeance. The American public could not have its dream of education for all the children of all the people *and,* at the same time, insist upon uniform lessons, methods of teaching, and standards of evaluation. Ayres had documented the results that issued from the marriage of the characteristic American vision about the equality of man with the characteristic American stinginess toward the cost of fulfilling its public dreams. It was left for the educators to develop a means for resolving this dilemma.

Many efforts were and have been attempted in this respect. It would be inaccurate to leave uncorrected the impression that school people were oblivious to the ills of single standards before Ayres's report, or that no steps had been taken to allow for individual differences prior to that time. Most of those steps, however, were minor variations upon the central theme of age-grade placement. They provided for quick promotion of more competent students. For example, Supt. William Torrey Harris of St. Louis introduced the quarter system into the administrative structure of that school system in 1869. Pupils who made rapid progress could have adjustments in the curriculum to which they were exposed as frequently as every ten weeks during the school year.

One cannot today review the efforts of men like Harris and many others of a century ago without feeling the nobility of purpose which characterized their pursuits. Faced with all but insuperable obstacles and problems, the public school systems of St. Louis, New York, Chicago, and the other great urban centers did provide education for the children of their cities, as they continue to do today, still confronted with all but insuperable obstacles and problems.

Early in the twentieth century the infant science of differential psychology was born. Spurred by intensive social problems, Binet developed his world-famous test of intelligence, and the testing movement grew rapidly during the First World War. At its end, schoolmen and, to some extent, the general public were conversant with concepts of individual differences, intelligence quotients, and tests designed to measure them.

Among the earliest efforts to institute homogeneous grouping in the schools, if not actually the first, was the Detroit plan, commonly known as the XYZ Plan. Introduced into the Detroit system in 1919 by its superintendent, Dr. Charles Perry, the plan utilized intelligence and achievement test data to stratify pupils into three sets of classes: X, Y, and Z. The top and bottom 20 per cent of students were segregated into X and Z classes, respectively, leaving a large middle group composed of the remaining 60 per cent in the Y classes.

During the 1920s and early 1930s, programs of homogeneous grouping were very common, at least in the larger cities. A 1936 Yearbook of the National Society for the Study of Education was devoted to *The Grouping of Pupils*. Although recognizing the complexity of the issue of grouping and the morass of semantic and definitional confusion surrounding the topic, the chairman of that yearbook committee nonetheless felt confident enough to write, "The contributions of research studies tend to give some evidence that, at least in traditional subject matter, pupils make more development under a system of ability grouping than under other systems of grouping" (Coxe, 1936, p. 309).

There was sufficient professional opinion, if nothing formal in the way of evidence, that the early glow of ability grouping had dimmed and its use diminished by the late 1930s and early 1940s. In the 1950s and 1960s, however, ability grouping was once more very much a topic of interest. Writing in 1959, Ekstrom concluded that investigations of homogeneous grouping conducted in the 1920s were divided among those that gave results favorable to such grouping or showed no differences or no differences unfavorable to grouping, and those that resulted in mixed differences, some favorable to homogeneous grouping and some unfavorable. Of course, no firm generalizations about the advisability of homogeneous grouping are possible when the weight of evidence supporting one alternative is countered by evidence tending to favor another conclusion.

Recent Evidence on Homogeneous Grouping

Borg (1965) recently reported a careful comparison between the results that occurred in two Utah public school districts, one of which employed ability grouping (A district), the other of which used enrichment procedures with classes of heterogeneous ability randomly assigned (R district). The Borg study has several features that recommend it as a means of evaluating the comparative merits of homogeneous and heterogeneous grouping. First, several grades were examined. The study began with groups of fourth, sixth, seventh, eighth, and ninth-grade pupils. Second, the study was longitudinal. Most of the classes were studied for a period of four years. Thus, early but unstable differences, or differences that require long periods of time to develop, could be detected. Third, a variety of pupil variables was measured, not academic achievement alone. Fourth, the results and consequences of grouping for superior, average, and slow pupils are considered independently.

We shall generally follow Borg's outline in presenting the overall findings of the study, considering first the results for elementary schools subdivided by ability levels, and then for junior high school pupils, also stratified according to ability.

Borg concluded that ability grouping is somewhat more desirable than heterogeneous grouping in the intermediate elementary grades for pupils of *superior ability*. These youngsters achieved more academically than their counterparts in the R district. However, most of this difference occurred during the first of the four years for which data were collected. On other measures, scores for superior pupils are higher in the heterogeneous groups. For example, measures of study methods showed that superior pupils in the R classes were better organized and more efficient in procedure. Fewer superior pupils obtained "star" sociometric status (accepted once by their peers) in the A district classes, although they were not rejected or isolated with any greater frequency than pupils in heterogeneous groups. Borg apparently construes that finding to have a salutary effect upon superior pupils, as well as the finding that superior pupils in ability groups have lower self-concepts than those in groups organized heterogeneously.

For pupils of *average ability,* most of the findings favor assignment to heterogeneous classes. They achieve about equally well under either condition, and enjoy higher sociometric status in ability groups. (However, one wonders whether this is a statistical artifact.) In the heterogeneous groups, pupils of average ability had better study habits and more favorable scores on tests of personality and measures of self-concept. They also reported fewer personal problems.

The academic achievement of *slow pupils* is less in ability groups, but their sociometric status is much superior compared with random assignment groups. Self-concepts are slightly lower in the ability groups. Overall, Borg sees ability grouping as a better decision for low ability elementary pupils. He does not comment upon the paradox implied in recommending ability grouping for those in the middle.

Results at the junior high school level are similar, but not identical to those for elementary school pupils. Borg views ability grouping as advantageous for superior pupils and, on balance, sufficiently better for average pupils to recommend it. For pupils of low ability at the junior high school level, achievement and self-concept are better in heterogeneous classes. Other results seem to be inconclusive. Borg concludes that random assignments are slightly superior for junior high school students of limited ability.

One of Borg's closing comments seems particularly germane in light of the inconsistent and inconclusive research history of this topic. Differences certainly do occur, and they are sometimes statistically significant, although the difference is seldom of an impressive magnitude. A teacher or administrator's set of values would seem to be a much more crucial and valid basis for decisions of this order, assuming that the review we have given of Borg's findings is an accurate estimate of the empirical nature of the issue. Borg, in reviewing the results of personality measures made with slow junior high school pupils, reported as follows:

The personality data for slow pupils were characterized by a complete lack of consistent differences favoring either treatment. The lack of significant differences on aggression, depression, and inferiority feelings found in the projective phase of the personality study leads us to question some of the dire consequences that have been predicted by critics of ability grouping (Borg, 1965, p. 92).

Goldberg, Passow, and Justman (1966) studied the effects of ability grouping in the absence of any planned modification either in curriculum or methods of teaching. Five ability levels were designated: A—gifted, IQ 130 and above; B—very bright, IQ 120–129; C—bright, IQ 110–119; D—average, IQ 100–109; and F—low and below average, IQ 99 and lower. The aim was to study each ability level by itself and in combination with one, two, three, or all four of the others. A total of fifteen organizational patterns were constituted. Some eighty-six fifth-grade classes enrolling about three thousand New York City children participated in the study. Classes were tested periodically through the fifth and the sixth grades on achievement; interests; attitudes toward school, toward self, and toward other pupils.

The authors include several timely statements concerning limitations upon their study. They had restricted their selections of participating schools to those in the various boroughs of New York City which enrolled at least four children in the fifth grade with IQs of 130 or higher. A consequence of that limitation is that their sample contains virtually all schools located in white, middle-class areas of the city. Further limitations concern the achievement tests used, some of which had too low a ceiling to reflect properly the achievement of especially the A-level pupils. It is also true that achievement measures were restricted to standardized tests suitable for the middle grades of the elementary school. If the combination of intelligence levels of pupils influenced the breadth and depth of subject areas studied in addition to the common ones, such accomplishments were not reflected in the achievement batteries.

Few differences in academic growth or attitudes emerged in this study as a direct result of the grouping patterns. The authors use this information to suggest that grouping in itself is neutral, and that differences in learning can be expected only as the curriculum and methods of instruction are adapted to capitalize upon the restricted range of ability provided by homogeneous grouping. One wonders if this conclusion was equally evident prior to conducting the study. The authors' summary paragraph is instructive.

At least until such times as procedures for more completely individualized instruction become incorporated into school policy and teacher preparation, schools will continue to rely on various kinds of grouping in their attempt to differentiate instruction. It is, therefore, essential to recognize that no matter how precise the selection of pupils becomes or how varied and flexible the student deployment may be, grouping arrangements, by themselves, serve little purpose. Real differences in academic growth result from what is taught and learned in the classroom. It is, therefore, on the differentiation and appropriate selection of content and method of teaching that the emphasis must be placed. Grouping procedures can then become effective servants of the curriculum (Goldberg, Passow, & Justman, 1966, p. 169).

Atkinson and O'Connor (1963) reported the results of two experiments in which the role of need achievement in relation to ability grouping was examined. "The basic hypothesis investigated was that ability grouping would have differential effects on the motivation and performance of students depending upon the relative strengths of their need to achieve and disposition to be anxious about failure" (p. 109).

One of these studies was conducted with a sample of junior high school pupils who were examined through the high school years. The hypothesis received little support. Atkinson and O'Connor explain the failure, at least in part, as a result of their untenable assumption that the achievement motivation of boys and girls remains stable through the years of secondary school. For boys there is minimal stability; for girls, none at all.

A second study conducted with sixth graders is better controlled. In general, the outcomes of that study tend to confirm the hypothesis. Hypothetically, the more competitive atmosphere of the ability-grouped classes would serve as an incentive to accomplishment for students whose motive to achieve is stronger than their anxiety to avoid failure. Where the motivational component weights are reversed, students should show less interest in the homogeneous class and experience a decrease in academic achievement.

The sixth-grade classes from ten schools in the same district constituted the experimental classes. Ten control groups (classes which used heterogeneous grouping) were selected from two schools, one of which contributed experimental classes the first two years of the study and then abandoned the practice. Atkinson and O'Connor conclude that pupils with high-need achievement learn more in homogeneous rather than heterogeneous classes and that they also achieve better in homogeneous classes than pupils with low achievement motivation. Their reasoning requires close examination.

In the first place, the second conclusion, that pupils with high achievement motivation achieve better in ability-grouped classes than classmates with low achievement motivation, is not supported statistically; that is, the conventional level of significance is not achieved ($p < 10$), and most researchers would conclude that their hypothesis has not been confirmed. Second, the first conclusion rests on the interpretation of changes in achievement test scores from the fifth to the sixth grade.

In Table 10.3 we present the basic comparisons between pupils of varying levels of motivation in homogeneous and heterogeneous

TABLE 10.3 PERCENTAGE OF STUDENTS HIGH, MODERATE, AND LOW IN RESULTANT ACHIEVEMENT MOTIVATION WHO SCORE ABOVE MEDIAN IN READING AND ARITHMETIC ACHIEVEMENT FOR GRADES FIVE AND SIX

ACHIEVEMENT TEST ANXIETY	HOMOGENEOUS CLASSES (% above Median)		HETEROGENEOUS CLASSES (% above Median)	
	Reading		*Reading*	
	6th	*5th*	*6th*	*5th*
High	69	58	69	80
Moderate	41	45	45	61
Low	46	22	30	42
	Arithmetic		*Arithmetic*	
	6th	*5th*	*6th*	*5th*
High	73	44	67	75
Moderate	45	37	42	61
Low	32	25	44	45

Source: Adapted from Atkinson and O'Connor (1963, pp. 94–95, Tables 3.2 and 3.3).

classes. Note that the final achievement levels for sixth grade differ little from each other. Atkinson and O'Connor argue the superiority of ability grouping with respect to achievement motivation on the grounds of relative change in standing between the fifth and sixth grades. Indeed, we do see that, for example, 73 per cent of the "high" pupils in homogeneous classes scored above the median in arithmetic at the end of the sixth grade, whereas only 44 per cent of the same group scored above the median a year earlier. Comparable figures for pupils in heterogeneous classes are 67 per cent and 75 per cent. Thus, although the final statuses are comparable, the homogeneous group has improved and the heterogeneous group has declined. However, the argument in favor of ability grouping seems highly tenuous and not easy to accept, since we would expect similar trends (regressions toward the mean) to occur in the absence of special treatments.

The possibility of an interaction between grouping and motivation of pupils is an intriguing one. Until larger bodies of more convincing evidence accrue, however, it would be prudent to treat the interaction as an interesting hypothesis to explore and not as a firm basis for educational practice. Interest expressed in schoolwork declines for pupils with low achievement motivation who are placed in ability groups.

A recent book on grouping in education is of special interest because of its international scope. Under the sponsorship of UNESCO, Yates (1966) edited a volume of reports based upon the individual and joint thought of a number of educational scholars from various countries. This group of writers argues that aims of education emerge along two dimensions, social and personal. On the social dimension, there are three logically possible sets of relationships between grouping and the teaching-learning process. The school may train pupils to live in society as it now exists, or it may provide them with the pattern of a new society in school with the expectation that the school pattern will transform the society or, finally, the school can teach new patterns of negotiation and interaction since the new generation of students may be expected to produce some kind of new society. The second alternative, that schools will create a new social order, is not a viable one, the authors contend.

> We may, therefore, define our societal aims continuum in the most fundamental language; at one end, the aim is to maintain the status quo and the culture as it now is. At the other end, the aim is to allow the society to change and to create the expectation that social change is the norm rather than the exception (Yates, 1966, pp. 89–90).

The writers propose as a principle of interpretation that the school is, in a sense, a replica of the society into which the child is to be socialized. The kind of social aim toward which the school is working can be inferred from three kinds of observations: (1) heterogeneity or homogeneity of the student population; (2) the extent to which groups of pupils share common facilities; and (3) the degree to which groups mutually carry out functions.

In general, we would expect that the school system oriented

to adaptive changes in society would have: the greatest variety of pupils, the greatest overlap in the use of facilities, and the largest number of functions carried out interdependently. The school whose aim is to maintain the status quo would show the greatest isolation between groups, the least sharing of facilities, and the minimum of contrast among members of different groups (Yates, 1966, p. 94).

An important and easily overlooked qualification is that statements of aims may be quite different from the aims toward which the actual operations of the school seem to lead.

PROMOTION vs. NONPROMOTION: A PERSISTENT PROBLEM

At first glance, what is identified in the above subhead as a persistent problem may appear to be no problem at all. Despite scattered traces of change to a less firmly age-graded structure, the typical organization of elementary and secondary schools is still along grade lines. Even in some districts where the grade label has been replaced by a euphemism, children, teachers, and parents continue to regard the school as an age-graded institution. Given that condition, others follow. A graded school implies a set of standards by which transition from one grade to another is achieved. Knowledge and the curriculum are so structured that the child must have mastered the essentials of grade one before he can be "promoted" to grade two. Thus formulated, the problem does seem to be simple.

When asked, teachers often cite the same reasons to justify both promotion or nonpromotion: the pupil will learn more; his adjustment will be better. Goodlad and Anderson (1959) summarize a large body of research literature that has been accumulated over many years. In general, this literature tends to prove that pupils who "fail," that is, who are retained in grade for a second year, learn less during that year than if they had been allowed to pass to the next grade with their classmates. In some cases, Goodlad and Anderson contend, the child actually makes a poorer showing on tests of academic achievement at the end of the second year than he did at the close of the previous year. However that may be, or for whatever reasons his test performance might be adversely affected by retention, it does appear that a teacher who decides not to promote a pupil on the grounds that his academic achievement will be fostered by repeating is flying in the face of a body of evidence that argues overwhelmingly for the opposite contention.

Some years ago, Cook (1941) was able to show that different promotion policies in elementary schools ultimately influence the levels
of achievement attained throughout the school. He compared nine
pairs of Minnesota schools which differed in the extent to which
seventh graders were "overaged" (the high overaged schools averaged .80 of a year retarded; the low overaged schools .27 of a year)
but which were very much alike in class size, socioeconomic status of
families in the district, and training and experience of the teachers.
Comparisons between the two sets of classes showed that the classes
in schools with the lower ratio of overaged pupils had higher IQs;
superior achievement, except in arithmetic fundamentals; and ranges
of abilities no greater than those who held higher standards for
promotion.

Personal and social adjustment of pupils as it relates to promotion and nonpromotion has also been the subject of educational
research. Goodlad and Anderson's (1959) summarization of that research tends to support the thesis that pupils who are promoted in
spite of failure to attain grade standard are generally better accepted
in the long run by their classmates and by themselves. Interestingly,
pupils who are retained in grade command an early visibility and
acceptance by their classmates, which entirely disappears by the
end of the year. On the other side of the ledger, pupils who are promoted express more fear of failure and engage in more cheating.
They are marginal group members who clearly do not lead problem-
free lives.

> However, neither promotion nor nonpromotion by itself takes
> care of pupils' nonlearning or the teachers' problems of individ-
> ualizing instruction. The increasing spread of attainment as
> pupils advance through the grades is the natural concomitant of
> the increasing spread of the pupils' abilities. Pupils more and
> more achieve above or below grade levels with the result that
> these levels become increasingly burdensome to teachers who
> see the conflict between the grade standards and the realities of
> pupil development. When teachers recognize this conflict, it
> may be best simply to pull the grade barriers away (Goodlad &
> Anderson, 1959, pp. 41–42).

Goodlad and Anderson develop the theme that the graded structure of the elementary school must be changed in order to eliminate
a variety of persistent and difficult problems historically associated
with elementary education. A large body of research findings and

professional opinion has developed in the last decade with respect to ungraded schools, a topic which we shall develop in the closing chapter.

VALUES AND INDIVIDUAL DIFFERENCES

It is easy to identify and empathize with people whom we perceive to be like ourselves, who value the same activities, institutions, and goals that we value. Teachers, however, are inevitably going to encounter pupils whose value systems are strikingly different from their own. Individual differences pertain in values just as they do in the other psychological and physical dimensions that we have mentioned. But whereas an individual's height, race and, to some extent, intellectual ability can be ascertained with ease, the values that he holds are less easy to read, in part because they are so often not formulated verbally. Even then, verbal statements of values often contradict the values one really holds. Hall (1959) relates an experience which makes this point vividly.

While working as a human relations consultant to the government of a large city, Hall was assigned the task of developing with various administrative personnel a means for effecting new nondiscriminatory labor practices. At the first group meeting, all department heads agreed to meet privately with Hall to discuss tactics and strategies. He made an appointment with each man, emphasizing that at least an hour would be required for their conference. All participants agreed; that is, at a verbal level they expressed awareness of an important problem and indicated a willingness to help find a solution. But, Hall reported, his experience was a series of broken or postponed appointments, long waits in outer offices (which in our culture is insulting behavior), and interviews foreshortened from an hour to ten or fifteen minutes. We require very few such experiences with an individual or a class of people before we conclude that they value rather lightly the activity or interaction in which we hope to engage them.

An important question, but one that Hall does not explore in the given situation, concerns the intentions of the several men with whom he had scheduled appointments. That is, did they with malice aforethought, as it were, decide to detain, embarrass, or frustrate their caller? Of course we have no way of knowing in this case, but we can speculate about it in a general way. We would guess that each of these men has more demands placed upon him than he has time to fulfill. His appointment calendar is probably determined in practice by two major sets of forces: those that are decreed by higher authority to be important, and those which he judges to be important. The man who detained Hall for an hour and then reduced the conference to ten minutes may have been sincerely apologetic and embarrassed about his cluttered schedule, but an astute observer would be unlikely to conclude that he valued an opportunity to explore the employment of minority group members.

The general point made by Hall and others is worthy of consideration by teachers. We communicate more to people than simply the words we speak. Tone of voice, inflection, gestures—all tell something to our audience. The significance for teachers lies in the observation that people are typically unaware of what they are communicating in these nonverbal ways, done unwittingly and not by design. The following quotations from Spindler's (1959) little monograph on the teacher as a cultural transmitter perfectly illustrate the more general issue. Spindler's thesis is that teachers, as transmitters of the culture, generate unintended, unanticipated learning consequences which are at odds with, and sometimes defeat, the stated cultural purpose of the transmission.

> The cultural transmitter in this case was a highly respected teacher in a large elementary school, who had certain duties as a counselor. He originated from a respectable immigrant family and had improved his social status during his lifetime by becoming a schoolteacher. The particular situation from which I have extracted certain verbatim records to follow was one of the "rites of passage" that occur now and then throughout the educational life cycle of children. The students in the eighth grade were being prepared for the choice of programs in high school and were making out proposed study lists under his guidance. The class group consisted of thirty-five children, twenty-four of whom were Mexican-Americans. The range of scores on the California Mental Maturity test was 80 to 120, with a median of 102. There was a broadly corresponding variety of reading and academic achievement represented in the group. I will present a few items from the verbal interaction of the teacher-counselor and the students.

> *T:* In arranging your programs for next year, there are certain things that everyone must take, so we'll just put them down. You will all take P.E., English, and Social Studies. *(Teacher writes these down on the board opposite numbers 1, 2, and 3.)* Now you have to decide whether you want to take Algebra

or not. You have to take math all the way through high school if you want to be an engineer. Now, if you've gotten B's and C's all the way through eighth grade, what are your chances of doing well in ninth grade Algebra? *(Students murmur various things.)* That's right! Not so good! What can you do?

S: Try to raise your grade.

T: Yes.

S: Work harder.

T: That's one thing. But what else? . . . Do like I did when I wanted to be a singer but found I couldn't sing. What did I do? Yes . . . that's right. I changed my plans. . . . With respect to language, how many here speak Spanish? *(Six of the Mexican-Americans raised their hands, but all speak some Spanish.)* It will help you if you do. But you have to realize that there is some work to do—homework! It is good to take Spanish if you want to go on to college and need a language. But you can't take Spanish and General Business. They come at the same period. Now, one of the things you have to do is to be neat and orderly. If you aren't good at that it might be hard for you until you learn to do it better.

T: Now here we have Mechanical Drawing. This is exclusively a boy's class. I don't know why some girls couldn't take it if they wanted to. But only boys take it. Now Homemaking is for girls, so you can take that.

T: Now when you come to see me, if I tell you to take General Business instead of Spanish it should be understood that you don't have to take it. You can do as you wish. But it means that I think you will do better in General Business. *(Several more subject choices are covered.)*

T: And here is typing. It looks interesting when you pass the typing room, doesn't it? But do you know there aren't any letters on those keyboards? You have to watch a chart at the front of the room, and if you look at the keyboard, you fail!

Of course, a great deal more went on during this hour of counseling. I have purposefully selected those verbal items that constitute the most clear indications of bias in cultural transmission. And this is always unfair to the cultural transmitter. But I believe the extracted items accurately reveal persistent trends in his counseling of the mixed Mexican-American and Anglo groups in the eighth grade.

After this particular class session, the teacher-counselor said, "This is a passive group. There is no spark in there. The better groups get quite excited about this. Of course, most of the better groups are college-preparatory and perhaps only three or four of these students will go to college." Previous to the session, in his statement of education philosophy, he had commented, "I believe that our job is to make the most of the potential of each child. Of course there is a wide range of ability among our students. A good many of them will never go on to college. And we have to do the best we can to help them on to a satis- factory adjustment."

I propose that he was defeating his own aims in the way he handled this crucial rite of passage, this point of compression in the relation of the child and his culture where choices made affect future development decisively. He opened the gates to valued channels of development and then shut them in the children's faces. And he did not open the gates to any alterna- tive channels. What he transmitted, it seems to me, was that the only worthwhile goal was to go to college so that one could become an engineer or something equivalent, that if the child did not have the necessary qualifications there was no other dignified and worthy choice, and that most of the members of this class group did not have the necessary qualifications.

I would be less concerned if I thought this person were a small, mean individual with explicit prejudices, and if I thought he were not concerned with making the most of the potential of each child. But he is not small and mean. He is a generous, well-intended person, and believes in democratic opportunity. In his counseling he projects his own struggle to improve his status, mirrors the discrepancy in our culture between ideal and real in the definition of opportunity, and inadvertently defeats his own professed aims (Spindler, 1959, pp. 15–20).

Spindler has argued vigorously that the core values of Americans have been undergoing change. He presents data based upon re- sponses obtained from education students which indicate that even among so apparently homogeneous a population there is not one but several sets of values, sets that are sometimes in opposition to each other. One of Spindler's procedures requires college students to write a brief paragraph describing the "ideal American boy." A composite of characteristics, ranked in order of the frequency with which they are mentioned, gives us this picture of the ideal.

He should be *sociable,* like people, and get along well with them; he must be *popular,* be liked by others; he is to be *well-rounded,* he can do many things quite well, but is not an expert at anything in particular; he should be *athletic* (but not a star) and *healthy* (no qualifications); he should be *ambitious* to succeed and have clear goals, but these must be acceptable within limited norms; he must be *considerate of others,* ever sensitive to their feelings about him and about events; he should be a *clean-cut Christian,* moral and respectful of God and parents; he should be *patriotic;* and he should demonstrate *average academic ability,* and *average intellectual capacity* (Spindler, 1963, pp. 134–135).

That is the model of the ideal boy described by about 40 per cent of the students in Spindler's sample. Individuality, creativity, introspective behavior, deviancy are not highly valued; in fact, they are often a source of suspicion. Spindler hypothesizes that American core values are undergoing a rapid change from *traditional* to *emergent,* and that this transition has serious consequences for the educational system. Traditional values stress puritan morality, a work-success ethic, individualism, achievement orientation, and future-time orientation, whereas emergent values are heavily group oriented and center around sociability, a relativistic moral attitude, consideration for others, a hedonistic present-time orientation, and conformity to the group.

Figure 10.5 shows Spindler's hypothesized placement of various groups concerned with the educational enterprise along the continuum from traditional to emergent values. The reader must not interpret these placements too literally, for not all individuals within the same category actually share values as totally as the sketch suggests. Still, the figure probably places groups fairly accurately in relation to one another. For example, school board members tend to be more traditional in their values than others because of their age, the prevailing values they learned when young, and the fact that these values have served them well; they are successful, prestigious, powerful figures in the community, and are among those who have nothing to gain but much to lose as the social structure of the community changes.

To bring the discussion to the level at which it is of direct concern to teachers, Spindler argues that the model-value pattern of students preparing to teach is an essentially traditional one. This assumption is based upon the fact that most college students who choose to enter

FIGURE 10.5 SPINDLER'S PLACEMENT OF SCHOOL-RELEVANT GROUPS ALONG A CONTINUUM OF VALUES FROM TRADITIONAL TO EMERGENT

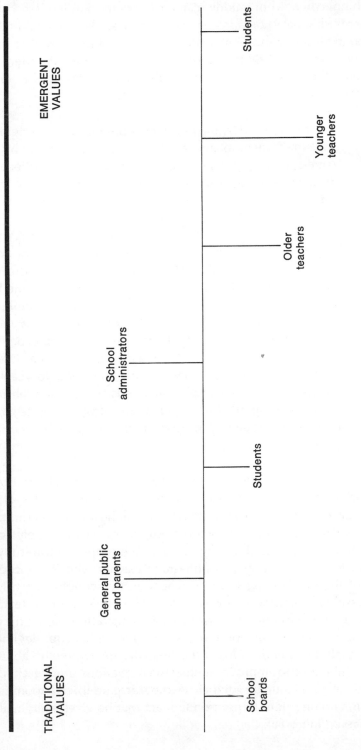

Source: Spindler (1963, p. 139).

teaching come from middle-class or lower middle-class origins, where traditional values are dominant. These students then find themselves in teacher education institutions in which the prevailing values are much closer to the emergent than to the traditional pattern. The student teacher is placed in conflict that may be resolved in one of several ways:

1. The threat posed by the newly encountered value system may drive the student to an even stronger commitment to his own value system, so he becomes a "reaffirmative traditionalist."
2. He may respond to the threat by overcompensating in the degree to which he accepts the new values, thus becoming what Spindler calls a "compensatory emergentist."
3. The "vacillator" accepts parts of both systems, but does not engage in the reflective thought required to reduce or understand the conflicts involved. Consequently, his classroom is characterized by differing modes of communication and leadership, to the consternation of the teacher and his pupils.
4. Finally, there is a reaction which Spindler identifies as an "adjusted" type. The "adjusted" teacher does not experience the threat associated for others with exposure to a different system of values, nor does he feel the need to react defensively or to overcompensate. He is flexible enough to incorporate desirable (to him) elements of various systems, and thoughtful enough to integrate them into a viable, continuous system.

The relevance of these reactions for teachers and, ultimately, for their students is seen from a case study reported by Spindler (1957). This particular teacher was selected because he was a "reaffirmative traditionalist," a type that Spindler supposes to be widely found among teachers throughout the country. The subject of the study is a young man of twenty-five, a fifth-grade teacher who is regarded as one of the outstanding young teachers in the school district. He is professionally ambitious, wishing to do an excellent job of teaching and to move subsequently into school administration. About his educational objectives, this young teacher is quite explicit. Besides knowledge goals, he intends to foster the creativity and expressive ability of each child, and to improve interpersonal relations among children. He strives to encourage each child to participate in classroom interaction, and he prides himself on the fact that he gives every child in his class a "fair break."

Spindler's observations of this teacher tell a story of contradiction between verbal expression of values and his overt behavior. He consistently knew less about the pupils in his class who came from lower social classes than he did about those from the middle classes. When asked to name the best and worst adjusted children, the popular and the socially rejected children, he again assigned favorable values to children more like himself, less favorable ones to the lower class pupils. In addition to his biased reactions to individual class members, the teacher's values were further revealed in the kind of feedback he provided to pupils, as illustrated by the following case of the language lesson:

> In his response to oral reports by the children about what they were reading in their spare time, his gestures, facial expression, bodily postures, comments and silences were all patterned in the framework of the same selective bias. He communicated approval of most of what the children of middle-class origins said, and of what they were reading. He communicated lack of interest, or suppressed distaste for what the children of lower-class origins said, how they said it, and of what they were reading.
>
> . . . He interacted effectively with only a minority segment of his classroom group—that segment which matched his own aspirations and values, derived from his own cultural setting. He opened doors for this selected group to channels of development they were already heading toward, and he sped them on their way. But for the larger number of his students, those who did not match his values and aspirations, he closed doors and left them waiting in the foyer of our culture.
>
> . . . His exercise of the role of cultural transmitter was in contradiction to his own professed aims, and even to his own beliefs about what he actually did in the classroom. He was not giving all children an opportunity to participate; he did not understand their problems; he was not being fair and just to all his students; they were not all getting a "fair break." All these aims and beliefs were contradicted by his highly selective positive interaction with a small segment of his class. He was wearing cultural blinders that limited his perceptions to a single channel. His transmitting apparatus was sending out positive signals only to that segment responding within the frequency of that single channel (Spindler, 1959, pp. 36–38).

REFERENCES

Chapter 10

Atkinson, J. W., & O'Connor, Patricia. Effects of ability grouping in schools related to individual differences in achievement-related motivation. Ann Arbor: University of Michigan, 1963. (Mimeographed)

Ayres, L. *Laggards in our schools.* New York: Russell Sage, 1909.

Borg, W. R. Ability grouping in the public schools: a field study. *Journal of Experimental Education,* 1965, *34,* 1–97.

Carroll, J. B. Instructional methods and individual differences. In R. M. Gagne (Ed.), *Learning and individual differences.* Columbus, Ohio: Merrill, 1967. Pp. 40–44.

Cook, W. W. Some effects of the maintenance of high standards of promotion. *Elementary School Journal,* 1941, *41,* 430–437.

Coxe, W. W. Summary and interpretations. In The group of pupils. *Yearbook of the National Society for the Study of Education,* 1936, 35, Part I. Ch. XVI.

Cronbach, L. How can instruction be adapted to individual differences? In R. M. Gagne (Ed.), *Learning and individual differences.* Columbus, Ohio: Merrill, 1967. Pp. 23–29.

Cutts, Norma E., & Moseley, N. *Providing for individual differences in the elementary school.* Englewood Cliffs, N. J.: Prentice-Hall, 1960.

Goldberg, Miriam L., Passow, A. H., & Justman, J. *The effects of ability grouping.* New York: Teachers College Press, Columbia University, 1966.

Ekstrom, Ruth B. *Experimental studies of homogeneous grouping, a review of the literature.* Princeton, N. J.: Educational Testing Service, 1959.

Goodlad, J. I., & Anderson, R. *The nongraded elementary school.* New York: Harcourt, Brace, 1959.

Hall, E. T. *The silent language*. Garden City, N.Y.: Doubleday, 1959.

Morgenstern, Ann. *Grouping in the elementary school*. New York: Pitman, 1966.

Rafferty, M. *Suffer, little children*. New York: Devin-Adair, 1962.

Spindler, G. D. *The transmission of American culture*. The Burton lecture, 1957. Cambridge: Harvard University Press, 1959.

Spindler, G. D. (Ed.) *Education and culture: anthropological approaches*. New York: Holt, Rinehart & Winston, 1963.

Suppes, P. Modern learning theory and the elementary school curriculum. *American Educational Research Journal*, 1964, *1*, 79–93.

Thomas, R. M., & Thomas, S. M. *Individual differences in the classroom*. New York: McKay, 1965.

Yates, A. (Ed.) *Grouping in education*. New York: Wiley, 1966.

CHAPTER 11

INNOVATION AND
CHANGE IN THE
INSTRUCTIONAL
PROCESS

One of the most obvious facts about American civilization today is the conflict that exists between forces demanding radical change and those which are determined, if not to resist outright, at least to retard the rate at which change can be brought about and to modify its ultimate forms. The causes—for that matter, the crises—are legion: the war in Vietnam, student unrest and revolt, black militancy, the problems of the inner cities, crime, pollution; all of these issues are in the air simultaneously, crying for resolution. How any or all of them can be resolved, or whether they can be resolved, seems very much open to question in the early 1970s. That the form and substance of life for most Americans will be dramatically different by the 1980s from what it was at the beginning of the present decade is one of the few statements that one can make with any assurance.

SOCIAL CHANGE AND THE SCHOOL

Education as a social institution is a reflection of the functioning of the larger society. The problems that beset us on a national basis also plague the enterprise of schooling. How to provide equality of opportunity for all Americans is formulated first as a question of how to provide equality of educational opportunity. The militancy that has become the hallmark of many minority groups in recent years has invaded the teaching profession, which has become one of the latest activist groups. Nonetheless, education has been historically a conservative force in our society, relatively resistant to innovation.

Miles (1964) cites the slow rate of innovation in education (for example, one innovation a year in a sample of New York schools in one study), and he presents a series of factors that would seem to retard the innovation rate of schools. Included among them are the following: ". . . the absence of valid scientific research findings . . . ; the lack of change agents to promote new educational ideas . . . ; and the lack of economic incentive to adopt innovations . . . (since educational products do not have immediate economic payoff, and educational practitioners are paid on the basis of longevity and personal educational attainment rather than on net output, itself very difficult to measure)" (Miles, 1964, pp. 633–634).

It is also possible that certain ideological beliefs in the educational profession serve to block effective innovation by effectively insulating educational practitioners from reality. For example, beliefs that American schools are locally controlled . . . that the school teacher is an independent, autonomous professional . . . and that teaching can never be effectively measured or specified in other than intuitive terms, all appear to serve the function of protective myths (Miles, 1964, p. 634).

Although those statements by Miles were made as recently as the middle 1960s, their validity is dramatically reduced by the events of the intervening years. For example, the issue of local control of schools is hotly contested at this time, and those who favor local control are losing the battle. If the teacher is not an independent, autonomous professional, and the author contends that he is not, he is moving in that direction with a speed and sureness that even a few years ago would have been difficult to believe.

Whether educational researchers will ever be capable of providing the kinds of hard evidence in support of the outcomes of teaching that would be required for certain judgments concerning the efficacy of teachers, of curricula, or of schools is still an unknown. However, today, one hears more and more about "accountability" of schools. By accountability is meant that school administrators are being held responsible by those who supply the economic resources to run the schools for demonstrating the educational products that have been bought with their financial support. We cannot say precisely why this accountability is being pressed so hard at this time; it will be the business of specialists in the economics and politics of education to unravel the total story. However, certain points are clear and unmistakable at this time.

For one thing, government is demanding fuller accounts than in the past as to how money for educational innovations, supplementary programs, etc. has been expended and, more particularly, what benefits have accrued to the educational system as a result of those expenditures. In this connection, it is of consequence that corporations, both profit and nonprofit, are now eligible to receive financial support from the United States Office of Education for purposes of providing training, research, and curriculum development. The day may be near when such corporations, or subsidiaries of them, will directly compete with local public school districts to provide a variety of educational services now provided by the schools themselves. Whether in the long run such competition would be likely to benefit children and the community is of course a matter to be determined, but the pressures stemming from such competition could be predicted to lead to an intensification of efforts to measure teaching, and particularly the outcomes of teaching. If one can judge from the lessons of history as analyzed by Callahan (1962), one would predict that school personnel, especially administrators, will be seeking to find concrete indicators of the efficiency of their schools' operations. One probable form such indicators will assume is an increased frequency of innovations in the schools.

All the evidence that we have strongly suggests that the classroom teacher is not, as Miles (1964) puts it,

> . . . an independent, autonomous professional. . . . Thus it seems likely that local innovative efforts are restricted by the fact that the teacher's role is actually that of a bureaucratic functionary . . . who has little power to *initiate* system-wide change, but—because of the ideology concerning professionalism alluded to above—tends to *resist* innovative demands, like most professionals in bureaucratic organizations (Miles, 1964, p. 634).

However, we are now in a new era of ascendancy and militancy by teachers in which they are making their demands known, and insisting upon those demands being met, with a degree of determination and intensity that has never before been known in the history of American education.

It is the author's contention that the various winds of change that are currently blowing with such force in the society at large, and within education as well, are going to lead to rapid and penetrating changes in the system of education in the years immediately ahead. This book has been devoted to considerations of teachers and pupils in classroom settings, and to the process of teaching itself. To continue that emphasis in this final chapter, we shall concentrate, not upon the total array of prospective changes in education, but on those which most immediately affect the classroom lives of boys and girls and their teachers. Consequently, we shall emphasize in our discussion innovations that tend to change the traditional role of the teacher, and those that have as their central purpose the individualization of instruction. In a number of cases, a single innovation tends to contribute to both of these ends.

We view the attention of the teacher to the learning and development of the individual student as the most central element of the instructional process. It is in those encounters that the teacher may be said most truly to be exercising his prowess as a professional person. At the same time, those changes in education that alter the structure of relationships between teachers and others tend to emphasize this same individualized professional approach to the teaching encounter. Thus, although changes in the roles of teachers and individualization of instruction will be discussed as separate issues, in a larger sense the two are but strands of the same movement toward a recognition of the need for improved means of dealing with the learning problems of individual students.

Curriculum reforms that had their start in the post-Sputnik era of the late 1950s and early 1960s had reached a zenith by the end of the 1960s. Most subjects of the secondary school curriculum and many at the elementary level had been carefully scrutinized by groups of subject matter specialists. The science and mathematics courses were the chief recipients of this attention, but the English and social studies areas were not without their critics and benefactors.

Heightened concern for the "culturally disadvantaged" child led to intensified research and educational programs in his behalf. Recognition of the crucial role of the early childhood years (from birth to age four or possibly five) in the intellectual development of children, and the apparent paucity of perceptual, motor, and cognitive experiences in the daily lives of many children in city slums and remote rural regions, went hand in hand with the development of broad-scale nursery school programs and parent-training programs. Despite its early formalism and lack of articulation with the regular school program, this early childhood education movement may turn out to be among the most significant innovations in education since the establishment of the kindergarten a century ago.

The role of technology in education burgeoned during the decade of the sixties. Although its role had not been clarified by the close of the decade, it was clear that technology would continue to play some role in the study of education and in its practice for the indefinite future. Increasingly the impact of technology in the classroom was being felt, from the advent of the language laboratory and audiovisual equipment to later advances in programmed instruction and computer-assisted instruction.

Finally, changing images of the teaching profession are becoming more evident and crystallized. Unfortunately, these images are not well conceptualized, but they have the merit of confronting some intensely important practical questions about teaching as an occupation that have not been the object of careful thinking until very recently. We will deal with this as the issue of *career development* in teaching, with the consequence that this topic will subsume a number of innovative features in education.

A persistent problem, actually an interlocking set of problems, in education has been the retention of a substantial fraction of trained teachers for an extended period of years; in short, the problem has been to develop career lines that are sufficiently attractive that the brighter, better educated, and generally more competent entrants will remain in *teaching* (as differentiated from administrative or higher educational positions). Many students of education have commented at length upon the existence of this problem and, especially in recent years, several plans for staff differentiation (division of labor) have been formulated. What has less frequently been recognized is that the level of knowledge about the practice of teaching itself has very likely been stunted as a result of the absence in teaching of a role that allows or even compels the practitioner to be reflective, analytical, and systematic in his thought and discussion about the practice of education. As the conceptual bases for differentiating among the roles that teachers can play in the school become better defined, it seems reasonable to assume that the role of the *scholar-teacher* just described will be perceived as a feasible one.

To pursue this issue of staff utilization and teacher role differentiation in more meaningful terms, we must pause now to examine briefly the dimensions of the manpower issue in teaching.

TEACHING: AN OCCUPATION THAT COLLAPSES UPON ITSELF

In the postwar years of the late 1940s and early 1950s, teacher shortages were so acute as to beset almost every public school district in the land. One of the chief reasons for the shortage was the large and growing discrepancy between the number of people eligible to enter teaching and the masses of children reaching school age.

By the 1960s, teacher shortages remained acute, but differentially so. Large cities continued to have vacancies for teachers, especially in schools in the central city, with its dense population and its high crime, disease, and unemployment rates. Teaching jobs that demanded special talent and training, such as classes for emotionally disturbed or mentally retarded children, also often remained available. But in the main, the acute personnel problem in teaching was less one of the supply of teachers than it was of retention. For example, by the late 1950s, approximately one out of every three students graduating from college in the United States was prepared to teach, and about three-fourths of that number actually were entering the occupation. However, in 1957–58, the rate of loss among classroom teachers stood just a shade under 11 per cent. Furthermore, of a sample of beginning teachers polled in 1956–57, *half estimated that within five years, they would leave teaching, either temporarily or permanently* (Mason, Dressel, & Bain, 1959).

Data reported by Charters (1956) suggest that those estimates may exaggerate the length of tenure. His study of 1,000 teacher education graduates from the University of Illinois over a ten-year period revealed that the entire group produced 2,400 man-years of teaching (out of a potential total of 10,000 man-years). *Forty per cent of the sample never taught,* half of the remainder (30 per cent of the total sample) had left teaching by the end of two years, and a full half of the man-years of teaching performed by the original 1,000 trainees was accomplished by 12 per cent of the group. Charters poses the problem of teacher retention as a matter of identifying and training students who are most likely to be long-service teachers. He did not suggest how that might be done, and the problem remains unsolved.

Mason, Dressel, and Bain (1959), in the study previously cited, examined the sex role and career orientation of beginning teachers. Beyond the finding already summarized, a number of interesting results emerged. In the first place, although teaching is commonly thought of as a woman's occupation, it is in fact entered into freely by large numbers of men also. Thirty-six per cent of the nation's beginning teachers in the autumn of 1956 were men.

Beginning teachers, as we have already seen, do not contemplate lifelong careers as classroom teachers. Only 29 per cent of the men and 16 per cent of the women in the Mason sample indicated that it was their intention to remain in the classroom until retirement. On

the other hand, almost three-fifths of the women (58 per cent) anticipate a teaching career interrupted by marriage and child-rearing,
followed by a return to teaching. It would be instructive to learn how
valid that self-prediction is, whether a large proportion of the women
who say they will return to teaching actually do so, and when—at the
point when the youngest child enters nursery school, when all are
teen-agers, or when? We will probably find that two or three fairly
standard patterns exist, and they have implications for the kind of in-
service training the returning teacher needs, and the kind of job to
which she ought to return.

A comparably large fraction of men in the sample (51 per cent) do
not plan to continue as classroom teachers, but they do anticipate
long-term retention in the field of education. Presumably this change
of role may be to a supervisory or administrative post within the
school district, or to a college teaching position, or other education-
related activity.

At any rate we are left with the impression that a very large proportion of beginning teachers will remain in educational occupations as
broadly conceived. Only 19 per cent of the men and 18 per cent of the
women state categorically that they plan to leave the field of education altogether. The reasons that teachers leave the occupation of
teaching are differentially understood. The fact that women outnum-
ber men in teaching, and that the women tend to marry, have children, and thus leave the classroom at least temporarily is obvious.

Problems of Professionalism

Mason and his associates suggest two characteristics of a profession.
First, the profession represents a *dominant* as opposed to a *contingent*
commitment on the part of its practitioners. For example, the commitment to teaching for women is probably contingent: ". . . they
will teach *if* they do not marry, *until* they have children, *when* the
children are all of school age, *if* their husbands' job takes them to a
community that has an attractive teaching vacancy, etc." (Mason,
Dressel, & Bain, 1959, p. 375). Second, the practice of the profession
represents a terminal career point. Thus a lawyer need not become a
judge or enter politics to demonstrate professional progress. The practice of law is a legitimate career goal in itself. However, more than
half the beginning men teachers have already in their first year of
teaching defined success as departure from the classroom. Thus, the
most common career orientations of men and women who enter
teaching, although they are different, militate against the chances

that teaching as it now stands can achieve full professionalization (and thus, presumably, improve its power to hold a larger percentage of the brighter, better educated young teachers whom it attracts).

We have seen some of the reasons for brief teacher tenure. Mason and his associates have emphasized that these reasons tend to be somewhat different for men than for women. Men are more concerned about salary and working conditions than women are. They need some means to experience progress in their occupation if they are to stay in it. On the other hand, schools need to be more creative in developing ways to allow women to continue working without inducing conflict between their work role and their role as wife and mother. It is, of course, considerably easier to state these problems than it is to solve them.

There is some evidence that this problem is critical in the wealthier, high-prestige communities. Kleinert (1968) reports that school administrators in the affluent suburban North Shore school districts of metropolitan Chicago surveyed the salary and working conditions of teachers. Both were rated excellent. In Kleinert's own district, where he was principal of the high school, the beginning salaries of teachers were $6,200 for those with a bachelor's degree, and $6,600 for those with a master's degree. The average maximum salary for teachers with graduate work beyond the M.A. level was $13,400. (These figures were for 1967–68, and compared favorably with those paid in other suburban communities at that time.) Yet an analysis of the turnover rate in his high school revealed that it was markedly higher than the national average.

Over a three-year period, during which the average faculty size was 122, the turnover rate averaged 21 per cent in Kleinert's school. (The national average for the same period was 16 per cent.) After three years, 45 (38 per cent) of the original 122 teachers remained. Kleinert compared certain characteristics of the group of seventy-five "leavers" with those of the forty-five "stayers." On the average, the "leavers" were ten years younger (thirty-two as compared with forty-two), more likely to be single (41 per cent vs. 24 per cent), more likely to be women (57 per cent vs. 42 per cent), and they had less education (40 per cent of the "leavers" had less than a master's degree; 87 per cent of the "stayers" had graduate credits beyond the M.A. degree).

Kleinert's concern is with the 20 per cent of the "leavers" who went elsewhere to teach, and the eleven per cent who left teaching altogether. He believes that two factors account for the large number of teachers who move in and out of "our nation's best school districts" (Kleinert, 1968, p. 299). One is the high cost of living. Even though these teachers are well paid, relative to other teachers, only a third of them live in the community in which they teach. Second, these teachers need greater recognition and challenge than is offered by the conventional teaching job. Kleinert believes that schools and teachers' roles must be reorganized to allow such recognition and challenge to develop. In this way, presumably, school districts will be able to retain in service a greater number of those teachers who now flee to other jobs.

Concept of Staff Differentiation

There is a growing certainty within education that the institution itself must be reorganized and the resources that are allocated to it by the community must be redistributed in ways that markedly heighten the likelihood that entrants will find teaching a sufficiently attractive and rewarding occupation to warrant a lifetime commitment to it. The concept of staff differentiation has emerged during the past decade as one hypothesis bearing upon the solution of the problem. *Staff differentiation* means that members of the teaching corps are assigned different kinds of tasks or given different roles to play, some of which are defined as being more difficult or more demanding in terms of skills, abilities, and special competencies than others. Typically there is a series of roles graduated for difficulty, and also graduated with respect to salary and other perquisites attached to them. In general, the attempt is to broaden the base of responsibilities assigned to older, more experienced, and presumably more competent practitioners, and also to extend the length of the working year for those who are playing the more responsible roles.

Although we cannot delve in great detail about the issues here, the history of the problem deserves at least brief treatment.[1] Historically in the United States, teachers have been viewed largely as interchangeable parts. At least within the same level of education and in the same subject area, official policy has been to treat teachers alike. Teachers with equal years of education and experience are paid equal salaries. A veteran teacher with thirty years of experience who retired on Friday afternoon may be replaced on Monday morning by the

---

[1] The reader is urged to consult Benson (1961) for an excellent and full treatment of the economic considerations involved in single-salary schedules, merit scales, and staff differentiation. Lieberman (1956; 1960) provides detailed accounts of the barriers to professionalization associated with judgments of competence and compensation.

newest of college graduates. Life in the classroom goes on without missing a beat, as it were.

Many efforts have been made to differentiate among teachers for purposes of rewarding those who perform most competently. It obviously becomes very difficult to justify actions of this sort when all role occupants are performing the same tasks. It is not an accident that a major segment of educational research has dealt with problems of teacher competence or teacher effectiveness. If research could reveal the basis upon which teachers are demonstrably different from each other, salary differentiations would become much easier to justify. Despite the fact that a vast body of literature on teacher effectiveness has developed, the answers needed for this purpose have not been forthcoming. Consequently, most efforts at differential reward have been based upon highly public criteria (such as acquisition by the teacher of a graduate degree), and the rewards have been negligible (an increment of $200 for receipt of an advanced degree is typical).

School officials find themselves terribly vulnerable to what Benson (1961) calls the "taxpayer objection," that is, if one fifth-grade teacher is paid $15,000 a year in a district where the average teacher salary is $5,000, all parents want services for their children from teachers of presumably equal superior talents. Or conversely, if parents are well satisfied with the work of a teacher who earns only $5,000, they may challenge the marked discrepancy in salaries. The effect seems to be to keep increments modest in size. In the same way, although there is a willingness to allow increments for continued service, the top salary paid to teachers in most school districts is low compared to the starting salary. Similarly, merit salary schedules have not been notably successful, largely because of the same issues cited here. It is difficult to demonstrate differences among people performing the same services, at least to the extent of justifying vastly different financial rewards for them.

Staff differentiation appears to be one of the more promising innovations on the educational scene at the present time. If such schemes are to be successful, however, they must accomplish three general goals: (1) systems must be designed so that the chief strategy of maintaining instructional contact between pupils and superior teachers is achieved; (2) they must provide legitimate educational functions to be performed, not be merely a contrivance for rewarding teachers whom the school district wishes to retain; and (3) viable procedures must be developed as to how occupants are selected for various differentiated roles.

DIMENSIONS FOR ORDERING EDUCATIONAL ACTIVITIES

The introductory section of this chapter was intended to suggest something of the broad array of innovations and changes—or "reforms," as some prefer to describe them—that have preoccupied educators in recent years. Two of the most fundamental factors involved in planning for and talking about changes in an institution are time and space. How do people spend their time in school? Where do they spend it? What differences ensue, what problems are solved or what goals can be reached by varying our utilization of both these precious commodities?

Space

The self-contained classroom has been such a dominant structural feature of American school buildings for so many generations that few people have questioned or even been aware of the extent to which that given has controlled educational activities. One such obvious control is the size of the class group that can work together. On occasion, architects and educational consultants on school buildings have contrived to construct relatively small rooms as a safeguard against future decisions to enlarge class sizes.

The graded school entered the scene in American education in 1848, embodied in the newly constructed Quincy (Mass.) Grammar School, the first to contain a series of cubical classrooms. At that time, the school was an innovation, based upon recent recommendations for age-graded education proposed by Horace Mann following his observations of the Prussian school system. The pattern spread during the second half of the nineteenth century until it became *the* pattern for building, organizing, and staffing schools.

From that time on in the United States, the instructional process, as practiced by teachers and pupils together, has possessed a strong degree of privacy. The teacher and his pupils work together in the enclosure all period or all day throughout the school year. As long as the administration receives no jarring complaints about what goes on behind that closed door, the teacher enjoys some latitude about the substance of what he teaches, and broad freedom as to his method of instruction. An important hypothesis in contemporary education that the tradition of privacy that has grown up around the practice teaching has played a significant role in maintaining teaching level of a craft instead of helping its rise to a more sophisticated Each person's practice has been largely his own affair, and teachers do talk with each other about problems in teach

talk tends to be highly empirical, usually at the level of specific reme-
dies or techniques. Since teachers have seldom had the opportunity
or the obligation to share responsibility for a common group of students, there is infrequently any need for their discussions with each
other to be analytical.

The distribution of time in elementary and secondary schools may
also be thought of as contributing to the same outcome. The teacher's
time during the normal instructional hours is ordinarily assigned in
contact with pupils. The typical one free period a day allotted to
teachers for planning and conferences is scarcely adequate for either
of those functions, to say nothing of allowing him an opportunity to
reflect upon and analyze the quality of educational experience that
he and his classes have been through.

Time

The existence of the self-contained classroom as the standard ap-
paratus for the conduct of teaching has exerted powerful influence
upon the ways in which we think about teaching. Until recent years,
for example, our tendency has been to think of instruction occurring
between one teacher and a group of students. Although we have historically differentiated the roles of teachers of older children and
adolescents along subject-matter dimensions, even at the senior high
school level the assignment of a single teacher to a group of students
has been the traditionally accepted means for accomplishing instruction within the several curricular areas. All teachers of history are
responsible for meeting four or five groups of students each day, but
the kind of history to be taught may vary somewhat, as may the age
and ability levels of the classes. Also the physical environment in
which instruction occurs has tended to be standardized with few
exceptions, most notably those of physical education and the laboratory sciences.

Gores (1966) writes that when the Quincy Grammar School opened
its doors in 1848, it established a pattern for schools that was to last
for well over a century.

> Its basic unit was a box—a room of more or less fixed size and
> shape. Within the room, one teacher was all things to a set
> number of students, grouped by age rather than by ability, all of
> them learning the same thing at the same time and all taking
> prescribed subjects during prescribed years. The class might be
> larger or smaller, the students might be sub-divided into more
> manageable groups, or they might be shifted from room to room

at regular intervals. The rooms themselves could be arranged in squares, strung out in rows, piled one on top of another, but they remained boxes. And as they multiplied, more solitary boxes accommodated more solitary teachers, each with a set number of charges (Gores, 1966, p. 137).

Formulas developed to control the number of pupils for which elementary and secondary classrooms and schools should be constructed. In a sense, these formulas represented some fundamental aspects of an educational philosophy rendered in brick and steel. As Gores puts it, questions were raised about self-contained classrooms, but they tended to be questions of whether the rooms should be square or rectangular, and how large. Ironically, Gores states, "though we never were sure how large a classroom should be, a kindergarten, it was believed, should always be one and a half times as large" (p. 137).

But today's classroom, small or large, is breaking up. In its place is emerging zones of space, thousands of square feet in area, the equivalent of four or five classrooms, great bodies of mutable, malleable, universal loft space. These great spaces, easily divided in accordance with what the teachers and the children have planned to do together at any particular time, serve the individual in independent study, the seminar group when a teacher and a dozen children discuss important matters together, the standard class, and the larger groups assembled for a common experience—a demonstration, a film, a talk or other contribution by a selected visitor.

This is universal space; schools without walls. It ends the ancient custom of enclosing a teacher and 25 or 35 children in 780 square feet of space from September to June, there to work out in solitude a year's education. The provision of the zone of space indicates that thoughtful schools are reversing the hallowed arrangement of isolated teachers and grouped children. The emerging arrangement ungroups the children and groups the teachers (Gores, 1966, pp. 139–140).

ORGANIZATIONAL SCHEMES THAT DIFFERENTIATE TEACHER ROLES

In the early pages of this chapter we identified staff differentiation or the differentiation of teachers' roles as a promising change on the educational scene. Our principal emphasis in those preliminary remarks was upon the opportunities which role differentiation can extend to teachers to continue in a career of teaching rather than be diverted into another area of education in order to find a continuing challenge, sufficient financial rewards, and other desired outcomes. We paid less attention in that discussion to what now becomes the issue of central focus: the prospects that schemes of role differentiation offer for the improvement of the quality of education that is experienced by children.

Team Teaching

Among the major changes in the roles played by teachers are those generated by team teaching. Unfortunately both for purposes of our discussion and for those of investigators who are attempting to assess the strengths and weaknesses of the movement, many kinds of teaching arrangements have been styled "team teaching." Shaplin (1964) provides a definition of the minimal conditions that must exist before a cooperative venture can appropriately be called team teaching. "Team teaching is a type of instructional organization, involving teaching personnel and the students assigned to them, in which two or more teachers are given responsibility, working together, for all or a significant part of the instruction of the same group of students" (Shaplin, 1964, p. 15).

Shaplin scores the team teaching movement for its failure to examine the accumulated body of theory and data from both sociology and psychology that bear upon the operations of small groups. Concepts such as leadership, organization, social structure, and others have not been analyzed or appealed to by promoters of team teaching.

One way to analyze the effects of team teaching upon those who are most intimately involved with it, namely teachers and pupils, is to examine the claims that are made in behalf of team teaching, to describe team-teaching programs (or at least some of the many variants) in operation, and to review such evidence as exists about the consequences for participants. This is the general approach that we shall use in the balance of this section, keeping in mind that the term *team teaching* is applied to a broad array of sometimes quite different programs, that, therefore, no common set of claims or description of operations can encompass all of them, and that analytical and evaluative studies of team teaching lag behind the action programs themselves. Thus, at this time, our ability to definitely assess the success of team teaching is much more restricted than is our power to present claims or to describe the action components.

Although we cannot unequivocally characterize team teaching, it may be helpful to present some descriptions of how teams may be organized so that the ensuing discussion of objectives and the results of research may be made more meaningful. At the elementary level, let us suppose that a school has 100 pupils and three full-time teachers assigned to the intermediate grades (fourth, fifth, and sixth). In a team situation, these three teachers would collectively share responsibility for the educational experiences of these 100 children, just as in previous years each teacher had assumed more or less complete control over thirty-odd pupils.

To elaborate the theme a bit, let us suppose that one of the teachers is designated the "team leader," and the team is given the half-time services of an instructional aide, a paraprofessional worker who provides clerical services and other noninstructional assistance to team teachers and pupils. If the school is engaged in a working relationship with a teacher education institution, the team might be expanded to include a teacher intern or one or two student teachers. At any rate, it is clear that the team members are confronted with rich opportunities and with severe problems that they have never previously encountered as teachers in self-contained classrooms.

Among the best of the opportunities is the possibility for subject-matter specialization and curriculum development. Thus, one of the teachers who enjoys teaching reading, literature, and other elements of language may take on, as the major burden of her team role, curriculum planning and instruction in language arts for all 100 pupils. (In exchange, this may mean no longer having to contend with the, for her, onerous chores of teaching science, and a reduction in her anxiety and sense of inadequacy.) This same virtue of team teaching, however, harbors a potential pitfall. Those who write about subject-matter specialization in team teaching at the elementary school level seem to assume that, given three or four team members, each can now concentrate upon that curricular area of his choice. This principle can really work, of course, only in those circumstances where each teacher's interests, knowledge, and desire to specialize reside in different fields.

There are, however, other obvious advantages. At times when one teacher wishes to deal with individual children for instructional or counseling purposes, other competent adults are available to work with the group. And, conversely, on those occasions when a teacher has demonstrations to perform or a block of subject matter that is relatively appropriate for all, the team may meet as a whole. In ways such as these, a degree of flexibility in grouping and time allocation is possible that is never available to a single teacher in her self-contained classroom.

At the same time, this programmed flexibility is gained at the sacrifice of whatever spontaneous flexibility is associated with teaching in a more solitary setting. We use the phrase programmed flexibility advisedly, for the team teachers must cooperatively plan the division of labor for the team on a daily or weekly basis, as well as on an extended one. Much of the testing of the team concept occurs in the nature of the team planning. If the planning conferences are to be held before or after normal working hours, the chances seem quite good that sessions will be as infrequent and as superficial as possible. To the extent that time for planning is built into the teachers' regular schedule of work, we may expect it to be more thoughtful and more likely to penetrate beyond such superficial organizational notions as flexible grouping and scheduling.

Team teaching at the secondary level offers many of the same challenges and potential rewards and obstacles as are found in the lower grades. Of course subject-matter specialization is a hallmark of the secondary school and ought not to introduce conflicts of first and second choices of teaching areas with the same frequency and intensity as is true for elementary school staffs. Nonetheless, similar issues will be confronted when secondary teachers of the same curricular area team together.

A different pattern at the secondary school level is cross-discipline teaming in which the age or grade level of pupils, rather than subject matter, is the point of organization. Hudgins and Bridges (1966) have described the purposes and operations of such a team at the junior high school level. All the seventh-grade pupils in a large suburban junior high school were assigned to one of three teams. Each team consisted of four teachers, each of whom in turn represented one of the major branches of study: English, social studies, mathematics, and science. The teams also had the services of a half-time instructional aide. Because of the care with which scheduling had been accomplished in this junior high school, the members of the team had instructional responsibilities for large groups either in the morning or during afternoon school hours. Pupils devoted the other half of their school hours to instruction in art, music, physical education, and independent study. The team teachers had half of each school day for team planning, individual planning, and conferences with individual pupils or small groups of pupils.

Thus, the operations of teams in team teaching may be widely different from each other. At one extreme teachers may share little more than a cooperative scheme for pupil accounting; at the other, teaming may become the overriding element in the planning and teaching activities of the staff. Team members may share responsibilities not only for scheduling and grouping, but for curriculum development and instruction. One would suppose that the demands upon staff would be very different for the two extremes. Strangely, no effort appears to have been made by the proponents of team teaching to order the several degrees of "teamness" that can clearly exist and to make some analysis of the demands that each would seem to make upon those who choose to adopt it; nor have they projected the potential educational benefits to be derived from each form of organization.

Claims made for team teaching. Proponents of innovations are sometimes guilty of making claims on behalf of their ideas or innovations which are unrealistic compared to the contribution that the innovation is designed to make. Excessive claims, of course, tend to make members of the profession and of the community skeptical about any value accruing from the innovation. Advocates of team teaching appear to be cautious in the claims that they are willing to make. Most of these claims center around redefining certain elements of the teacher's role, and only indirectly do they claim that team teaching leads to superior learning outcomes for pupils. The point is also carefully made that team teaching primarily alters organizational characteristics of the teacher's role rather than instructional ones.

Nonetheless, a variety of claims have been put forward. We shall enumerate and comment upon several of them before reviewing a small number of investigations that have been made of various elements of team teaching. Unfortunately claims and research are not well matched at this time. However, we shall try to impose some unity on the rather badly articulated present findings, and also suggest what are some of the more pressing issues in team teaching for research and analysis.

The specific claims that are argued for team teaching can be grouped into two separate categories, one concerning redefinitions of the teachers' role vis-à-vis the institution of the school, and the other having to do with changes in the relationships expected to occur among teachers, or between the teacher and the definition of his role.

Proponents of team teaching frequently identify as a major goal the transfer of certain managerial functions from administrative personnel to the teaching staff, functions that have to do with the grouping and scheduling of pupils and the assignment of teachers to tasks in terms of their interests and talents. The emphasis of those who advocate this rearrangement of responsibility within the school is clearly upon the increased latitude and flexibility for grouping and teacher assignment that is characteristic of team teaching.

At the same time, team-teaching proponents tend to ignore or at least to de-emphasize the fact that specific managerial skills are required both for handling the interpersonal relationships that are involved in such decision making, and for executing the technical elements of schedule building, grouping, and so forth. Teaching experience and skill do not necessarily make teachers versed in performing such managerial roles, not to mention the additional burdens of work and responsibility that are attendant upon the role. We do not say this necessarily to challenge the initial claim but to try to place it in a more realistic perspective. Among other things, to play this and other roles involved in team teaching effectively, teachers must learn what it means to be part of a team, and how to play the part of a team member. A number of the problems that are created by team teaching reside in this issue.

Related to what we have already said, the claim is sometimes advanced that team organizations help to conserve the time of teachers so that they can devote more time directly to teaching activities, and otherwise enhance their productivity. This appears to be an unrealistic claim since, if anything, team arrangements impose additional tasks upon teachers and do not tend to diminish existing ones.

A third claim to be cited under our first category of redefining the teacher's role in relation to the school is that teams tend to make more use of resource and technical materials than do teachers who are not working in teams, and to use such materials more effectively. If one member of a team is given responsibility for supervising and coordinating such things as audiovisual equipment and supplies, it is easy to understand why the predicted increased efficiency should occur. The delegated member is likely to possess both more skill and more interest in such materials and equipment than is true of teachers on the average. If he further perceives that his role on the team is defined to include expertise in these matters, he is more likely to encourage his colleagues to draw upon his skills, and indeed to help them gain the educational benefits that are a natural derivative of many teaching aids, while at the same time exempting other teachers from the onerous chore (to many of them) associated with procuring and manipulating the requisite hardware and media.

Any innovation that meets even the minimal criteria demanded by Shaplin's definition of team teaching will necessarily introduce change into the traditional pattern of interaction between and among teachers. Our earlier analysis of the consequences of self-contained classrooms for the development of a set of concepts that are widely shared among practitioners suggests some of the anticipated outcomes for team teaching ventures. The argument is speculative, even more than hypothetical at this time. As long as teaching occurs in the relatively private context of teacher and pupils only, the external pressures upon the teacher to clarify and reflect upon his practices are relatively weak. The greater the points of tangency between teachers, we can hypothesize, the more intense these pressures will become for one to justify the legitimacy of his professional behavior.

Both the inherent strengths and weaknesses of team organization are crystallized in this issue. If teams are constructed to facilitate communication among colleagues under conditions that allow conflicting points of view and rationales to emerge in a supportive, inquiry-oriented environment, productive tensions may be generated that can ultimately be resolved in favor of improved teaching practice for all parties involved. This is the happy hypothesis and, of course, it is this kind of resolution that is envisioned by advocates of team teaching. But it is equally easy to predict that tensions may not be productive, that views may polarize, and that, in practice, inflexibility may occur with resulting anxiety, discord, and conflict for the adults in the team, and a less than desirable learning experience for the children.

We undoubtedly do not know enough at this time to insure one kind of outcome over the other, and teachers are going to have quite different experiences with team teaching under conditions that may resemble each other closely, at least superficially. We may hypothesize, though, that some variables are extremely relevant in determining the direction of these outcomes.

Two related claims are now pertinent. One is that team teaching extends increased opportunity for teachers to specialize ·in subject matter. We would suppose that such specialization would tend to reduce the points of tangency between practitioners and thus, by reducing both the range and intimacy of shared decision-making, tend to reduce the chances for conflict and tension. At the same time, occasion for mutual problem-solving would not occur frequently and, when it did, would focus on more peripheral issues, such as scheduling and grouping. The demands imposed by these issues are obviously not very productive of new insights into matters of curriculum and teaching, nor in general are they likely to force the production of clarified concepts about teaching and classroom learning. The related claim is that team teaching may foster increased interaction among teachers as subject-matter specialists. The issues here seem to be similar to those we have already reviewed.

Perhaps the relevant variable is that of the centrality of the domain within which teachers must share decision-making with one another. Hypothetically, the more central the issue, the greater the sensitivity toward it. It could, for example, be very rewarding for team teachers to consider the differences between *style*, which is highly central and idiosyncratic, and *skill*, which involves the expertness with which the art of teaching is practiced. Discussions of style are likely to be unproductive, but the reverse could be true for considerations of skill.

Closely related, and a variable of seemingly equal importance with centrality, is that of the selection of team members. It is probably an error to think of this as a single variable. It is much more likely that clusters of variables are involved relevant to the success of selection procedures. Although we presently know relatively little in a systematic way about how individuals should be selected to participate in teams, it is obviously not a trivial issue. One senses, and evidence will surely be forthcoming in support of the intuition, that success or failure of teams will hinge directly upon the ability and willingness of groups of teachers to accept the collegial responsibilities and the altered role explicated for them by cooperative teaching arrangements.

We have tried to make clear that schools have at their disposal a variety of alternative plans for engaging in team teaching, and that a given plan may be more or less desirable, depending upon its centrality (how broad and intimate are the areas of shared decision-making?) and the school's estimate of the ability of staff to work together productively. To state the obvious, a school that assigns teachers to a team operation in which many decisions about curriculum, materials, and teaching methods must be made jointly should have reliable prior information that the teachers involved are able to relate effectively with each other, and can do so without excessive stress being imposed upon any of the participants. In general, a school would seem well advised to begin team efforts that make relatively few central demands upon participants. The junior high school cross-disciplinary team described previously is an example of a preliminary, peripherally oriented venture.

A final and important claim for team teaching remains to be discussed. That is the claim that team teaching offers a vehicle for retaining capable personnel in the ranks of teachers by creating expanding areas of responsibility and extending additional rewards beyond those that have typically been available to classroom teachers. Certainly a strong case can be made for team teaching as such a vehicle. We prefer to view team teaching in this sense as a subcase of efforts at staff role differentiation, to which we shall turn shortly.

Research on team teaching. As is characteristic of educational activities, changes in practice evolve, become accepted, and may even fade from the scene before researchers are in a position to provide reasoned and carefully weighed answers to questions about an educational innovation. Team teaching is scarcely a recent arrival among innovations in education. It has been well over a decade since the first team efforts were introduced into schools. Yet research still tends to be sparse, noncumulative, and directed at those questions which are most easily answered but are seldom the ones really worth asking. Still, some evidential basis for evaluating an innovation is better than none.

Heathers (1964) is quite explicit in demanding that educational innovations should go through a series of stages: (1) design, (2) implementation, (3) evaluation, and (4) dissemination. What happens in practice, however, is that concern for the second and third stages is negligible, and innovations are disseminated directly from the design stage, long before enough is known about their validity to warrant such dissemination.

Pupil achievement. Although the history of research on methods of teaching as a means of influencing pupil achievement is a dismal one, investigators seemingly never tire of asking the question, phrased for the purposes of team teaching as, "Do children learn more under team-teaching arrangements than they do in self-contained classrooms?" When we remember that proponents of team teaching have emphasized the *organizational* characteristics of team teaching as distinct from efforts to alter *pedagogical* arrangements, the question seems rather pointless. We would predict that gross examination of achievement would reveal few meaningful differences between team students and self-contained classroom students. That prediction is confirmed by a variety of empirical studies.

Heathers (1964) describes a project in Jefferson County, Colo., in which fifteen hundred students in seven high schools were taught by three-teacher teams in the areas of mathematics, history, English, science, and typing. Control groups of pupils were constituted, and their achievement for the school year was compared with that of the students in team-teaching programs. No significant differences occurred except for two semesters of English. In one, team teaching produced better results; in the other, conventional teaching seemingly did the superior job. It seems unlikely that these differences are due to differences in the two English courses; probable explanations lie in poor control and in measurement errors. Thus, as has been true of experiments in methods of teaching for many years, no reliably superior results for the innovative method appear.

Heathers also describes some outcomes of the Norwalk (Conn.) Plan at the elementary school level. It included seven three-teacher teams at grades two through six. After three years of operation, using control groups, no consistent differences in achievement appeared. Team teaching seemed to produce good results, especially in the areas of spelling and reading; language arts and arithmetic achievement were fostered under self-contained classroom teaching.

Also at the elementary level, Lambert et al. (1965a) conducted a two-year comparative study of achievement between team and self-contained classroom procedures. After two years, they concluded:

> It is felt that the team organization concept warrants further development and research. This study does not demonstrate that the team structure leads to significantly better achievement, but it does suggest that such improvement might come by continuing development of the team concept, especially if the development is supported by teachers who accept the task of molding a team that is characterized by polished desk-side manners and professional interrelationships among its members (Lambert et al., 1965a, p. 219).

Pupil adjustment. Lambert and his associates (1965b) also compared the adjustment of pupils in teams or classrooms for the same two-year period. No consequential differences were detected. Similarly, pupils in Norwalk, according to Heathers, manifested no harmful personality effects of team teaching; that is, team teaching seemed to affect their general adjustment little, if at all. However, pupils with the team-teaching experience were less anxious about their transfer to the junior high school than were the pupils who came from the traditional self-contained classes of the elementary school. This is a small finding, it is true, but it is consistent with the organizational theme of team teaching and appears to approach the level of impact that we ought more reasonably to expect from educational innovations. In other words, these pupils had experienced some of the altered conditions in their last year of elementary school that typically are not met until the transition to the junior high school, thus rendering that transition relatively anxiety-free for them.

We need not always anticipate that change in educational practice is going to result in changed pupil achievement. Achievement, as we argued earlier, is a major variable in the growth of children. It is influenced by a host of conditions, only one of which is the school. We place great and unrealistic stress upon our treatments when we hold out the expectation that rather trivial variations, such as ways of grouping teachers and pupils, will have direct influence upon achievement. Relationships between variables in education are seldom so simple and straightforward.

Needed research and the future of team teaching. Heathers argues that current research on team teaching not only fails to take account of relevant organizational variables in schools, a point whose significance we have already implied, but that measures of important outcome variables, such as pupil achievement and adjustment, are much too gross to reflect the impact of team teaching. This latter point seems in opposition to our remarks about the Norwalk experience unless Heathers would agree to include data on ease of transition from elementary to secondary school, etc., in the category of refined measures of adjustment.

At this writing the prospects of team teaching as a major organizational arrangement appear to be bright. Teachers and administrators (to say nothing of research workers) need to be clear about the outcomes to be expected from team teaching. We can identify several that are important to education generally and relevant to team teaching.

Team teaching would deserve to be ranked as a major contemporary educational innovation if it could be demonstrated that such an organization does (or can be constructed to) retain competent personnel in teaching positions for periods of years significantly greater than orthodox single teacher-class patterns tend to do. Similarly, one of its chief and more realistic claims is that individual teachers can have opportunities to specialize to an extent. Particularly for the upper grade elementary teacher, this opportunity can represent a real boon. At the fifth- and sixth-grade levels, the substantive demands upon teachers, who must prepare daily across all the common subjects of the curriculum, become onerous. Given the chance to concentrate their preparation and teaching upon one, or perhaps two, closely related fields (the language arts, social studies, or mathematics and science in combination are the most likely specialized areas), these teachers can be expected to become expert in their curriculum field and in the teaching of that field. It would not then be unreasonable, after a period of years, to anticipate that the achievement of pupils would be superior compared to experiences that all but the unusually talented generalist teacher can provide.

Finally, we would hope that team-teaching organizations could demonstrate their efficacy both as training grounds for initiates into teaching and as an arena for the development and testing of new concepts about the professional practice of teaching. We would urge that carefully planned and executed long-term analyses of these issues in team teaching be undertaken by qualified research agencies so that the education profession may have, as soon as possible, a firmer and more broadly founded basis for making decisions about whether to implement the team concept and, if so, under what kinds of circumstances.

As an example of one kind of research on team teaching that begins to provide preliminary answers to one of our questions, we cite the work of Borg (1967). Sixty-four teachers, members of fifteen teams located in six different high schools, were studied to test the hypotheses that more and less effective team teachers differ in personality, in their perceptions of the small-group characteristics of their teams, and in their verbal behavior during planning sessions. A second set of hypotheses concerned the bases upon which teams that are perceived as effective and ineffective by the principal differ from each other.

Each of the fifteen teams tape-recorded three of its planning sessions, and each team member was rated by his team mates. Highly rated team members tended to be more responsible and more active. In team-planning sessions, they talked more often and longer than others, made more suggestions, and both gave more opinions and sought opinions more often than did other members. Highly rated teachers tended also to see the team as more unified and cohesive than their peers. Compared with teams that were rated low in effectiveness by their principals, highly rated teams tended to perceive the team as more central to them and more pleasure giving. These team members showed less tension release, agreed with each other less, and asked less often for orientation from others.

Staff Differentiation

The Temple City (Calif.) school district has announced plans for the adoption of a differentiated staffing plan (Rand & English, 1968) that can serve as an example of this educational phenomenon. The plan was developed cooperatively by teachers and administrators, and it represents an early but definite effort to reach the goals we have previously cited for such programs. The strategy of the Temple City plan is to create several grades of positions that are superordinate to the staff teacher position, the only position in the structure to carry tenure. The three superior roles pay higher and differential salaries in exchange for (1) additional education or training, (2) the assumption of greater professional responsibility, and (3) an extended working year. Figure 11.1 shows the outline of the plan in some detail. The figure requires some comment.

Note that a variety of paraprofessional skills are provided for educational technicians and the academic assistants. The latter might or might not be motivated to continue their studies and move into teaching positions. The program contains two highly noteworthy features. A beginning teacher, let us assume, accepts a staff teacher position. It is much like a teaching position he might accept in countless other districts, at least in certain particulars: full-time teaching, a ten-month teaching year, and a starting salary roughly competitive with that offered by other districts. However, our beginner has open to him the possibility of advancing through a series of roles as he gains experience and maturity. The second feature, of course, is that the pupils in the district do not lose contact with the teacher who is recognized for his talents, and rewarded for them. Even the teaching research associate is scheduled to devote 60 per cent of his time to staff teaching.

Laudable as this scheme is, and as much as we may hope to see comparable staff differentiation programs developed in school districts throughout the nation, it seems evident that this one (and others, too, no doubt) are going to encounter some severe tests and be forced to solve some difficult problems before they work effectively. At Temple City the questions seem to center around personnel selection and the definition of roles. It is easy enough to see promotion from staff teacher to senior teacher on the grounds of successful teaching experience and the completion of a first graduate degree or some equivalent professional training.

But what criteria does one use to select a teaching curriculum associate and, more especially, a teaching research associate? The task of the latter is to translate research into instruction, a rather nebulous and extremely difficult task. There seems to be an assumption built into the program that individuals will be rewarded for outstanding teaching service with a position that involves innovative and research related activities. It is our guess that the skills and abilities involved in

FIGURE 11.1 TEMPLE CITY (CALIF.) UNIFIED SCHOOL DISTRICT: A MODEL OF DIFFERENTIAL STAFFING

				REGULAR SALARY SCHEDULE PLUS FACTORS
NONTENURE (1) Academic Assistant, A.A. or B.A. Degree	TENURE (2) Staff Teacher, B.A. Degree + 1 year	NONTENURE (3) Senior Teacher, M.S., M.A. or equivalent	NONTENURE (4) Teaching Curriculum Associate, M.S., M.A. or equivalent	NONTENURE (5) Teaching Research Associate, Doctorate or equivalent	12 months ($16,000–20,000) (5)
					11 months ($14,000–16,000) (4)
					10–11 months ($11,000–14,000) (3)
					10 months ($6,000–11,000) (2)
					10 months ($4,000–5,000) (1)
some teaching responsibilities	100% teaching responsibilities	80% staff teaching responsibilities	60–80% staff teaching responsibilities	60% staff teaching responsibilities	

Educational Technician

Source: Rand and English (1968, p. 267).

the two tasks (teaching and research) are not highly correlated. Put a little differently, there seems no reason to believe that one can select a research associate on the basis of his teaching credentials any more adequately than one can identify teaching ability by perusing an individual's research productivity. Furthermore, it seems unrealistic to anticipate that people assigned to these roles can perform them effectively and still spend 60 per cent or more of their time teaching. It will be interesting to see whether and how the Temple City plan, as an example, will modify its selection procedures and role definitions in the future.

INNOVATIONS THAT INDIVIDUALIZE INSTRUCTION: IMPACT UPON THE SOCIAL SYSTEM

Our earlier chapter on individual differences stressed the range of perplexing problems for education that are posed by differences among children who must be taught as members of groups. It should be recalled that historically no very good solutions have been developed for problems of individual differences in learning, but that educators continue to regard such problems as of paramount importance. It is not, then, very surprising to learn that one major thrust of innovations growing out of the improved technology of education is toward the treatment of individual differences. This attention is evident in the movements of programmed instruction and computer-assisted instruction.

Rather than attempt to catalogue all the innovations and their variations that are addressed toward individualization of instruction, we shall concentrate upon a single innovation that has recently received wide and growing acceptance at the elementary school level. The program is known as *individually prescribed instruction* (IPI), and although it has been extended to several curricular areas, the first and best known is arithmetic. Our discussion will be restricted to that area.

Individually Prescribed Instruction is a system of instructional materials that was developed at the Learning Research and Development Center of the University of Pittsburgh. It has been, until recently, most extensively used in an experimental sense at the nearby Oakleaf Elementary School in suburban Pittsburgh. The first curriculum developed was in arithmetic and represented an attempt to define all the skills and abilities that children require in elementary mathematics and to scale them so that, in general, a lower skill must be mastered before the next skill can be successfully undertaken.

Work materials for each skill are available and can be acquired by the individual child when he is ready for new practice material. When the child feels that he has mastered a skill, he confers with his teacher. She may then prescribe a new task for him. The IPI system has the characteristic of individualizing the rate at which children are able to work on arithmetic. This is by no means a trivial modification from ordinary provisions for the teaching of arithmetic, but it is limited in scope nonetheless. There are few if any provisions built into the system to allow children to pursue alternative topics in mathematics, or to delve more deeply into some areas than their classmates do. Instead, the program tends to demand minimum uniform mastery by all pupils, with the rate at which topics are mastered left free to vary.

IPI involves not only a curricular modification, but also a change in the organization of the classroom and even, to some extent, of the school itself. For example, arithmetic is no longer taught to the class as a whole. Each child works on problems that are appropriate to his skill at the moment. Thus, in a fourth-grade class, one child may be working on materials designated second-grade level, another may be successfully handling problems that are typically solved by fifth or sixth graders.

In part these variations are possible because teachers are free to move about the classroom, conferring in private with individual pupils. As the developers of IPI point out, the fact that teachers' roles are changed to the extent that they confer with much greater frequency with individual or small groups of pupils does make it possible for additional individualization of instruction to occur as the child and his teacher together probe and explore content related to the study of the moment. We would guess that this is an extension of the procedure that may be, but is not automatically, built into the role of the teacher.

In this connection, Edling (1964) interviewed teachers and students in a secondary school which had adopted programmed instruction. One consequence of such materials, or of individualized instruction more broadly conceived, is captured in the comment of a teacher of high school mathematics who was interviewed by Edling:

> We as teachers do miss the conventional classroom, where we can lead the kids from idea to idea throughout the course. Now, the programmed material does this for us and all we do is help them in their problem areas and through difficult concepts, rather than leading them from idea to idea. Another point is that you're not able to prepare for any one subject at a time. You might have in one period anything from an elementary algebra

problem to a college trig problem, or even a calculus problem. This means you certainly have to know your subject. You couldn't have somebody who is trained, for instance, in home economics, teaching mathematics; it must be a person trained in mathematics. A person who is trained to keep ahead of his children by one jump is doomed to failure. It just can't be done, because the kids move faster than you can anticipate in many instances (Edling, 1964, p. 81).

An unanswered question is whether the average classroom teacher, one who is well prepared in his discipline, can provide thorough teaching, on demand, of any specialized topic within the broad limits of his subject-matter field. If careful preparation of specific lessons is as important for good teaching as we commonly believe it to be, how can the teacher prepare adequately to fulfill his teaching role when each student's "lesson" is different?

A CONCLUDING NOTE

The note on which we will bring to a close this discussion of automation and the individualization of instruction has been sounded by Jackson (1968). He predicts that the changes in teaching that are prophesied by the advocates of "the machines," that is, of programmed instruction, computer-assisted instruction, and other of the new media, will be far less dramatic and pervasive than is commonly anticipated. According to Jackson, this will be so for several reasons, some of which we have mentioned previously.

For example, teachers are accustomed to hearing from experts in education or allied fields about the impact that the latest fad or innovation will have upon the nature of education and the school. Since these fads usually arrive on the educational scene to the accompaniment of loud assertions about how they will change the course of education, and depart unheralded and largely unnoticed, teachers cannot be expected to be overly impressed until or unless some more concrete evidence of their contribution becomes manifest. But it is usually difficult to demonstrate the relative merits of one teaching innovation as against another. That is, unless a new device or material or method for teaching can show such a clear superiority over the results that teachers are already attaining with older, more accustomed procedures, they see little point in supporting the changes.

Two other observations can be made in this connection. The first is that proponents of the newer media, as we have seen, argue that these media deliver degrees of flexibility in instruction that are beyond the capacity of the human teacher to furnish. Thus, in computer-assisted instruction, the machine is built to assess the progress of an individual student after each of his responses, and to present an optimal sequence of stimuli to him, as determined according to some explicit set of theoretical decision statements. There is no doubt that the demands imposed by those calculations upon memory and computation ability, if nothing more, far surpass the capability of the human teacher, but are well within range for the computer. Although the specifics of the claim differ from one kind of medium to another, each can be said to provide a kind of flexibility that the teacher cannot match.

Jackson contends that the introduction of newer media reduces the teacher's administrative flexibility; that is, their use demands longer range and more precise planning by the teacher. In Chapter 9 we illustrated this point with a description of the minor irritations a teacher may encounter in planning to use an instructional film. Jackson's point goes beyond this, however, to include the fact that the teacher's own flexibility as an intelligent human being is minimized by the newer media and is maximized by such implements as their old standbys, the chalkboard and the book. Thus, the teacher, chalk in hand, can outline, sketch, diagram, or provide whatever instruction seems necessary to him on the spur of the moment. There is a wistful quality in the comments made by Edling's mathematics teacher: "We [used to] lead the kids from idea to idea. . . . Now, the programmed material does this for us. . . ."

The second observation is not unlike the first. Newer media, especially those that involve electronic and mechanical devices, have an engineering orientation; efficiency, speed, performance are the kinds of variables emphasized in the media and valued by those who develop and advance them. But, Jackson argues, teachers are not engineers, not by training, and not by inclination. In fact, he contrasts the roles of engineer versus teacher as masculine versus feminine, tough-minded versus tender-minded. Jackson's point is extremely well made that although teachers sometimes use the physicalistic terms of engineers—objectives, criteria, programs—the usage is metaphorical rather than literal.

We might wish to agree with Jackson that the rate and intensity of such changes in teaching will be retarded or even diluted by the "tender-minded" orientation of teachers, but we suspect that, for the first time in well over a century, the form and structure of teaching in this country is undergoing irreversible change. There are many forces that are converging to bring this about, forces that we have sketched in the preceding pages. Certainly the newer media, taken as a whole, constitute one of the strongest of these. But we think the mightiest of all is the demand of teachers themselves to strive toward professional standing.

The only way to achieve the goal of professionalism is by penetrating to the essence of teaching—the basic encounter between a teacher and a child. We think this will happen in circumstances that are physically quite different from the schools that we now know. But teachers will remain teachers, with the same humane interest in the development of children and youth, that they have always had. We believe that the change in the schools will be accompanied by increased knowledge about the nature of teaching and of learning, and that these developments, in combination, will make it possible for tomorrow's teacher to provide the finest education American children have ever had.

REFERENCES

Chapter 11

Benson, C. S. *The economics of public education.* Boston: Houghton Mifflin, 1961.

Borg, W. R. Teacher effectiveness in team teaching. *Journal of Experimental Education,* 1967, *35,* 65–70.

Callahan, R. E. *Education and the cult of efficiency.* Chicago: University of Chicago Press, 1962.

Charters, W. W., Jr. Survival in the profession: a criterion for selecting teacher trainees. *Journal of Teacher Education,* 1956, *7,* 253–255.

Edling, J. V. Programmed instruction in a "continuous progress" school. In *Four case studies of programmed instruction.* New York: Fund for the Advancement of Education, 1964. Pp. 65–96.

Gores, H. B. Schoolhouse in transition. In The changing American school. *Yearbook of the National Society for the Study of Education,* 1966, *65,* Part II. Pp. 135–151.

Heathers, G. Research on team teaching. In J. T. Shaplin & H. F. Olds, Jr. *Team teaching.* New York: Harper & Row, 1964. Pp. 306–375.

Hudgins, B. B., & Bridges, E. M. Cross-disciplinary team teaching in a suburban junior high school. St. Ann, Mo.: Central Midwestern Regional Educational Laboratory, 1966.

Jackson, P. W. *The teacher and the machine.* Pittsburgh: University of Pittsburgh Press, 1968.

Kleinert, J. Teacher turnover in the affluent school district. *The Clearing House,* 1968, *42,* 297–299.

Lambert, P., Goodwin, W. L., Roberts, R., & Wiersma, W. Comparison of pupil achievement in team and self-contained organizations. *Journal of Experimental Education,* 1965a, *33,* 217–224.

Lambert, P., Goodwin, W. L., & Wiersma, W. Comparison of pupil adjustment in team and self-contained organizations. *Journal of Educational Research,* 1965b, *58,* 311–314.

Lieberman, M. *Education as a profession.* Englewood Cliffs, N.J.: Prentice-Hall, 1956.

Lieberman, M. *The future of public education.* Chicago: University of Chicago Press, 1960.

Mason, W. S., Dressel, R. J., & Bain, R. K. Sex role and the career orientations of beginning teachers. *Harvard Educational Review,* 1959, *29,* 370–383.

Miles, M. B. (Ed.) *Innovation in education.* New York: Bureau of Publications, Teachers College, Columbia University, 1964.

Rand, M. J., & English, F. Towards a differentiated teaching staff. *Phi Delta Kappan,* 1968, *49,* 264–268.

Shaplin, J. T., & Olds, H. F., Jr. (Eds.) *Team teaching.* New York: Harper & Row, 1964.

CREDITS AND ACKNOWLEDGMENTS

CHAPTER 2
Pages 40, 41–42: Reprinted from *The Psychology of Meaningful Verbal Learning* by David P. Ausubel. By permission of Grune & Stratton, Inc. Copyright 1963.

CHAPTER 3
Pages 58, 58–59: The brief quotes from Elliot Eisner, "Educational Objectives: Help or Hindrance?" appeared in *School Review,* Vol. 75, copyright 1967 by the University of Chicago.

CHAPTER 5
Pages 88, 89, 92–93: References to and quotations from the work of Ernest Horn are reprinted with the permission of the publisher from E. Horn's *Distribution of Opportunity for Participation Among the Various Pupils in Class-room Recitations* (Contributions to Education No. 67), New York: Teachers College Press, 1914.

CHAPTER 6
Pages 108, 109, 110, 116, 117: Reprinted with the permission of the publisher from Bellack, Kliebard, Hyman, and Smith, *The Language of the Classroom,* New York: Teachers College Press, © 1966.

CHAPTER 8
Pages 159–62, 163–64: Reprinted with the permission of the publisher from Romiett Stevens' *The Question as a Measure of Efficiency in Instruction: A Critical Study of Class-room Practice* (Contributions to Education No. 48), New York: Teachers College Press, 1912.
Pages 164–65: The brief quotes from S. M. Corey, "The Teachers Out Talk the Pupils," appeared in *School Review,* Vol. 48, copyright 1940 by the University of Chicago.

CHAPTER 9
Pages 195–96: From "The Case for and Use of Programmed Texts," by Michael Scriven, in *Programmed Instruction: Bold New Venture,* edited by Allen D. Calvin. Copyright © 1969 by Indiana University. Reprinted by permission of Indiana University Press.

CHAPTER 10
Pages 206, 207, 208, 209: Material from R. M. Thomas and S. M. Thomas, *Individual Differences in the Classroom,* copyright 1965, is used by permission of David McKay Company, Inc.
Pages 221, 222: Excerpts from the monograph, "Effects of Ability Grouping

in Schools Related to Individual Differences in Achievement-Related Motivation," by J. W. Atkinson and Patricia O'Connor are reprinted with the permission of the senior author from the original mimeographed version distributed through the University of Michigan, Ann Arbor. The material has subsequently been published as Chapter 15, "Motivational Implications of Ability Grouping in Schools," by Patricia O'Connor, J. W. Atkinson, and Matina Horner, in *A Theory of Achievement Motivation*, edited by J. W. Atkinson and N. T. Feather. New York: John Wiley & Sons, 1966.

Pages 230, 231: The quotation and figure from "Education in a Transforming American Culture " by George D. Spindler originally appeared in *The Harvard Educational Review*, XXV, 1955, pp. 145–56. © 1955 by the President and Fellows of Harvard College.

INDEX

Printed in U.S.A.